Litigating Fiduciary Duty Claims

JASON R. DOMARK, Editor

AMERICAN BAR ASSOCIATION
Litigation Section

Cover design by ABA Design

Printed in the United States of America.

26 25 5 4 3 2

Library of Congress Cataloging-in-Publication Data

Names: Domark, Jason R., editor. | American Bar Association. Commercial & Business Litigation Committee, sponsoring body.

Title: Litigating fiduciary duty claims / Jason R. Domark, editor.

Description: Chicago, Illinois : American Bar Association, [2022] | Includes index. | Summary: “This book is a practical guide for lawyers who are either beginning a fiduciary litigation practice or who are handling a fiduciary duty case in an unfamiliar area”— Provided by publisher.

Identifiers: LCCN 2022004637 (print) | LCCN 2022004638 (ebook) | ISBN 9781641059978 (paperback) | ISBN 9781641059985 (epub)

Subjects: LCSH: Business enterprises—Law and legislation—United States. | Corporate governance—Law and legislation—United States. | Trusts and trustees—United States. | Liability (Law)—United States.

Classification: LCC KF1355 .L58 2022 (print) | LCC KF1355 (ebook) | DDC 346.73/065—dc23/eng/20220208

LC record available at https://lccn.loc.gov/2022004637

LC ebook record available at https://lccn.loc.gov/2022004638

CONTENTS

PREFACE

This book represents the collaborative effort of the Commercial & Business Litigation Committee of the American Bar Association's Section of Litigation. The Committee focuses on issues facing litigators with broad commercial practices, including substantive areas such as bankruptcy, creditor rights, professional liability, and trade secret law, and procedural matters such as e-discovery, privilege, ADR, and international litigation. The Committee conceived this book as a practical guide for lawyers who are either beginning a fiduciary litigation practice or who are handling a fiduciary duty case in an unfamiliar area. This book is written to provide guidance regardless of which party (plaintiff or defendant) the reader represents. While there are many topics that are not covered in this book, the Committee believes it is a good place to start. We hope you agree.

The opinions expressed in this book are those of the authors alone and are not necessarily the opinions or positions of their firms or their clients. Similarly, authors' statements should not be taken as legal advice, and if a reader is seeking legal advice, the reader should reach out to a lawyer—including any of the authors—directly.

EDITOR'S ACKNOWLEDGMENTS AND DEDICATION

The editor wishes to acknowledge the chapter authors and American Bar Association editors, without whose hard work and dedication this book would not exist.

A special acknowledgment goes to Aaron Krauss, who encouraged us all to write the book, contributed a chapter, offered editing advice and guidance, and promised that the editor could now tell people he "wrote the book on fiduciary litigation."

This book is dedicated to Charles Kline and Jaime Bianchi, who taught me not only how to litigate a fiduciary duty case, they taught me how to be a lawyer. This book is also dedicated to my wife and kids, who tolerated a lot of late night editing during COVID-19.

—Jason R. Domark

ABOUT THE AUTHORS

Chapter 1

Jason R. Domark is a commercial litigator who practices in Cozen O'Connor's Miami office. Jason focuses his practice on complex commercial litigation, with an emphasis on fiduciary litigation, international litigation, and real estate–related litigation. Jason frequently litigates fiduciary duty issues for corporations, partnerships, trusts, professionals, and other entities and individuals. Jason has also created and managed litigation strategies for multinational corporations and individuals in disputes around the world. Jason serves on the board of directors for the Estate Planning Council of Greater Miami and for the Everglades Law Center. Jason also maintains an active pro bono practice, having worked on matters for Lawyers without Borders, Lawyers Serving Warriors, the United Nations, and others. Jason received his bachelor's degree, with honors, from the University of Miami, and earned his law degree, magna cum laude, from the University of Miami School of Law, where he participated in the *University of Miami Law Review*. Jason can be reached at (305) 358-2996 or jdomark@cozen.com.

Ashley Gómez-Rodón is a commercial litigator who practices in Cozen O'Connor's Miami office. She focuses her practice on business litigation. Ashley received her law degree, magna cum laude, from the University of Miami School of Law, which she attended on a full-tuition scholarship. While studying for her law degree, Ashley served as an executive editor for the *University of Miami Law Review* and participated in the Federal Appellate Clinic, Children and Youth Law Clinic, and Miami's STREET Law program. While in law school, she was a summer associate for Cozen O'Connor and a judicial intern for the Honorable Darrin P. Gayles, U.S. District Court for the Southern District of Florida. Ashley received her undergraduate degree from the University of Florida, which she attended on a full-tuition Bright Futures scholarship. Prior to practicing law, Ashley served as a corps member for Teach for America and taught high school mathematics at North Miami Senior High School.

Chapter 2

Eric C. Milby is a shareholder and commercial litigator at Lundy, Beldecos & Milby, handling primarily "business divorce" cases involving contract and fiduciary duty disputes between the owners of closely held corporations, limited liability companies, partnerships, and other businesses. In addition, he helps clients resolve disputes involving construction projects, commercial contracts, and real estate matters. Eric is a vice chair of the Business Divorce subcommittee of the ABA Business Law Section's Business and Corporate Litigation Committee and a former chair of the Philadelphia Bar Association's Business Law Section and its Business Litigation Committee. Eric holds a degree in business administration from Old Dominion University, and a JD, cum laude, from Widener University School of Law. He is a graduate of the National Trial Advocacy Institute at the University of Virginia. Eric lives in Merion, Pennsylvania, with his wife, three daughters, and a golden retriever who can often be found at his office.

Chapter 3

Lawrence D. Rosenberg is a partner at Jones Day in its Washington, DC office. For 25 years, Larry has tried cases and argued appeals throughout the country, and has been lead counsel in numerous matters in the U.S. Supreme Court. He has considerable experience in regulatory, statutory, and constitutional litigation; intellectual property; antitrust, international litigation; labor and employment; products liability; fiduciary duty; and securities litigation. Larry has litigated cases involving the U.S. Departments of Agriculture, Defense, Education, Energy, HHS, Homeland Security, Interior, Justice, State, and Transportation, as well as the EPA, EEOC, FAA, FCC, FDA, FDIC, Federal Reserve, FERC, FTC, and USPS. He also has been counsel in more than 20 appeals in the Federal Circuit. He is very active in the American Bar Association Section of Litigation, directing its publications division, and having served on its governing Council and chaired its trial and appellate practice committees and its Book Board. He directs the West Virginia University College of Law Supreme Court Clinic and is an author of *A Practitioner's Guide to Appellate Advocacy, The Trial Lawyer's Guide to Success and Happiness* and the forthcoming *Winning Bench Trials.* Larry recently argued in and won a 9–0 decision from the U.S. Supreme Court in *Dawson v. Steager*, which held that states cannot give income tax benefits to state employees without extending them to similarly situated federal employees. He also served as lead counsel in *Dubroff v. Wren Holdings* and *In re Nine Systems Corp. Shareholder Litigation* in the Delaware Court of Chancery, in which the court ruled after trial in favor of more than 40 shareholders of a startup hi-tech company on a breach of fiduciary duty claim against self-interested directors; these cases established significant precedents for breaches of the duty of loyalty by corporate directors and liability under the entire fairness test. Before joining Jones Day, Larry served as a trial attorney in the Attorney General's Honor Program in the U.S. Department of Justice. He clerked for Judge Jane Roth, of the Third Circuit Court of Appeals. He received his law degree, magna cum laude, from the University of Pennsylvania, where he was a member of the Order of the Coif, an editor of the Law Review, a world and national finalist in the Jessup International Moot Court Competition, and a finalist in the Keedy Cup Moot Court Competition. He received his undergraduate degree from Cornell University where he was a dean's scholar and an American Forensics Association national champion in extemporaneous speaking.

Chapter 4

Richard F. Munzinger is a civil trial lawyer and a partner at Shartsis Friese LLP in San Francisco, California. During his 20 years of practice, he has tried numerous "business divorces" and other disputes between co-owners of companies of all forms and fiduciary duty cases, including claims against officers, directors, majority shareholders, and advisers. In addition to his litigation practice, Mr. Munzinger also advises and negotiates on behalf of CEOs and other executives, shareholders, and directors in connection with internal corporate governance. Mr. Munzinger received his law degree from Stanford Law School and received his undergraduate degree, magna cum laude, from the University of Notre Dame, where he was a member of Phi Beta Kappa.

Sanjeet S. Ganjam is a business litigator and practices with Shartsis Friese LLP in San Francisco, California. He represents clients in a range of business disputes, specializing in fiduciary disputes among owners and managers of closely held companies. He has tried several fiduciary disputes in court and in arbitration. Mr. Ganjam received his law degree, cum laude, from University of Michigan Law School and received his undergraduate degree, with honors, from the University of California, Davis.

Chapter 5

Dale Schian is a shareholder at Gallagher & Kennedy and practices bankruptcy and creditors' rights law. He represents businesses and individuals in commercial creditor and debtor matters, emphasizing out-of-court workouts, restructurings, and Chapter 11 reorganizations. Over the years, Dale has represented clients in a wide variety of businesses, including manufacturing, retail, high-tech, agribusiness, commercial real estate, multifamily housing, and real estate development. His experience in complex financial litigation provides a solid foundation for his services in alternative dispute resolution, both as an advocate and as a neutral, and as a leader in the emerging practice area of settlement advocacy. Dale is a Super Lawyers and Best Lawyers in America honoree, a member of Arizona's Finest Lawyers, and listed in Corporate Counsel's Top Lawyers in Bankruptcy Debtor-Creditor Rights Law.

Kortney Otten is an attorney at Gallagher & Kennedy and practices commercial bankruptcy and bankruptcy litigation, business and cannabis law, including contracts, transactions, and settlement resolution. She is also a mediator and settlement advocate. Kortney completed a clerkship for Chief Judge Daniel P. Collins at the U.S. Bankruptcy Court for the District of Arizona. She also externed for Judge Eddward P. Ballinger Jr. at the Bankruptcy Court while in law school. Prior to going into law, Kortney was a business owner of multiple franchised restaurants and an owner of companies involved in real estate interests and the manufacturing of nutraceuticals. She has more than 20 years of vast business experience. She is licensed in Arizona and Colorado, and is a member of the State Bar of Arizona's Bankruptcy, ADR, and Business Law sections.

Dominick (Dom) San Angelo is an attorney at Gallagher & Kennedy and practices in the areas of business law and transactions, focusing primarily on mergers and acquisitions, securities, and corporate governance matters for clients across a broad spectrum of industries. In addition to his legal practice, Dom is an adjunct professor of business at the Colangelo College of Business Grand Canyon University. He serves on the board of directors of the Scottsdale Area Chamber of Commerce and is the chairperson of its Scottsdale Rising Young Professionals division. Dom is committed to philanthropy and pro bono service and has volunteered with a number of local and national nonprofits, including serving as a pro bono lawyer for the Society of St. Vincent de Paul in the greater Phoenix area. Dom holds a JD/MA in philosophy from Duke University and a BA/BSBA from the University of Arizona.

Chapter 6

Stephen L. Brodsky is a litigation and corporate partner with Kaufman Dolowich & Voluck, LLP and is resident in the firm's New York City and Long Island offices. Stephen represents companies, owners, and executives in their commercial disputes and advises them in connection with their business dealings. Over his 20-year career, he has litigated high dollar matters in courts throughout the country through trial and appeal. In addition to his practice, Stephen regularly publishes and speaks on legal and business topics. He also serves in several leadership roles with both the American Bar Association and New York State Bar Association. He is currently one of 19 attorneys appointed across New York state to serve on the NYSBA COVID-19 Task Force. Stephen is also committed to giving back. He is a board member of and counsel to a New York nonprofit and very active in a national research and advocacy organization. Stephen received his JD from Columbia Law School, where he was a Harlan Fiske Stone Scholar and member of the *Journal of Law and Social Problems*, and his BA in philosophy from the University of Pennsylvania, where he graduated summa cum laude and Phi Beta Kappa.

Chapter 7

Robert Charles Ward is a partner at Shartsis Friese LLP in San Francisco, where his practice is largely oriented toward the real estate and investment management industries. His real estate work includes landlord-tenant disputes, disputes over purchase and sale contracts, partnership dissolutions, broker disputes, construction disputes, secured transactions, and breach of fiduciary duty and corporate governance claims. In the investment management area, he handles partnership disputes, investor claims, employment claims, and other problems arising for investment management companies. Robert also handles several types of disputes faced by growing businesses, such as conflicts among partners or shareholders, trade secret disputes, wrongful termination claims, and disputes arising out of mergers and acquisitions. Another facet of his practice is a focus on "business divorces"—helping clients unwind themselves from companies or investments. Robert's clients include real estate investment and management companies, developers, lawyers, investment management companies, manufacturers and distributors, municipalities, and financial institutions.

Suzanne (Suzy) Spaulding Orza is an associate at Shartsis Friese LLP in San Francisco. She represents clients in disputes relating to the ownership, management, and control of businesses, in consumer litigation, and in trust and estate litigation matters. Suzy also maintains an active pro bono practice working on matters for Kids in Need of Defense (KIND). She received her JD from UC Hastings College of the Law in 2016 and her BA from UC Berkeley in 2013.

Chapter 8

Sonia E. O'Donnell has experience both in government and private practice in litigation and appellate. She graduated from the University of Florida College of Journalism and Law School. Upon graduation she clerked in the Federal Court of Appeals for the Fifth Circuit. She was an Assistant U.S. Attorney in the Southern District of Florida for 16 years where she tried criminal and civil cases and worked on hundreds of appeals while supervising one of the largest appellate divisions in the country. She became the Executive Assistant U.S. Attorney with administrative and substantive supervision of the Southern District. At the USAO, Mrs. O'Donnell was involved in high-profile prosecutions at the trial and appellate levels on issues including constitutional challenges to criminal statutes, international jurisdiction, public and judicial corruption, narcotics and fraud prosecutions, as well as civil defense of government officials and agencies. After leaving government, she spent more than two decades in law firms before opening the O'Donnell Law Firm in 2017. In private practice she has handled federal and state appeals; environmental, commercial, and Indian law litigation; and has represented financial institutions and businesses in class action defense. Mrs. O'Donnell is lead counsel in the state court guardianship case of Mrs. Henry Ford II in Palm Beach and the will and trust case that followed. Her firm recently reversed two criminal convictions, a bank fraud case where the defendant had been sentenced to 40 years, and a case involving U.S. jurisdiction on the high seas. She has served as co-chair of the Appellate Committee of the ABA Litigation Section, the ABA Book Board, and as chair of the Appellate Committee of the International Association of Defense Counsel, as well as a number of community boards and committees.

Robert A. O'Donnell graduated from Harvard College with a joint major in literature and philosophy, and thereafter from Harvard Law School. Robert has an MBA from the University of Miami's Herbert

Business School and studied at the University of Virginia as a Presidential Scholar with the Department of Spanish, Italian, and Portuguese. He clerked in the federal courts in the Southern District of Florida. He founded Elenkos Consulting and is a professor of law and economics at Miami Regional University. He is currently finishing a book on China as a fellow at the University of Miami. At the O'Donnell firm, Mr. O'Donnell specializes in appeals and in international and constitutional law. He was significantly involved in all the major litigation in the guardianship case of Mrs. Henry Ford II and is now involved in the trust and will litigation. He was also involved in the firm's recent reversal of an alleged $300,000 fraud conviction. He has been involved in criminal appeals as defense counsel. Mr. O'Donnell has extensive experience working with young companies through private placements and other initial capitalizations.

Donald E. Christopher, a former office managing shareholder of the Orlando, Florida, office of Baker, Donelson, Bearman, Caldwell & Berkowitz, PC, now practices as senior counsel with the firm. He has handled a broad array of matters, including estate planning, probate, guardianship, and trust litigation. After two years' service as law clerk for Chief Judge George C. Young of the U.S. District Court for the Middle District of Florida, Mr. Christopher became an Assistant U.S. Attorney in Orlando. During his time in the U.S. Attorney's office, he tried scores of cases, including the largest known theft of currency from the U.S. Bureau of Engraving and Printing in Washington, DC; injuries resulting from a Halon explosion at the Kennedy Space Center; extradition of an American bail bondsman to Canada to face kidnapping charges; fraud and embezzlement by senior management at several banks; and numerous income tax evasion cases. He also successfully defended all appeals from his verdicts and convictions. In private practice during the ensuing decades after leaving the government, Mr. Christopher has tried dozens more cases before both judges and juries, including trust and probate matters. Besides handling litigation, Mr. Christopher has incorporated businesses, overseen mergers of companies, drafted and negotiated a wide variety of business contracts, and represented both purchasers and sellers of commercial real estate. Admitted to the Virginia, DC, and Florida bars, over the years, Mr. Christopher has been chair of the Orange County Bar Association's Corporate and Business Law Committee and served on its Arbitration Committee, Professionalism Committee, and its Judicial Relations Committee. As a member of the Florida Bar, he served six years each on its Rules of Judicial Administration Committee and its Civil Procedure Rules Committee, including a year as vice chair and the next year as chair of the latter. He has authored several chapters in the *Florida Civil Practice before Trial* and the *Business Litigation in Florida* books published by the Florida Bar. A graduate of Harvard College, Mr. Christopher went to the University of Virginia School of Law.

Chapter 9

Siobhan Briley is litigation partner at Pugh Hagan Prahm PLC, where she uses her extensive litigation experience to achieve favorable results in and out of court. Her practice encompasses business, commercial, and corporate litigation, both for-profit and nonprofit; land use, boundary, and other real property disputes; probate litigation, including will contests; tax controversies, both civil and criminal; contract disputes; family law disputes; and landlord-tenant disputes. She has also represented businesses and individuals in bankruptcy proceedings, civil and criminal health care cases, and civil and criminal tax litigation. Siobhan received her JD from the Georgetown University Law Center, magna cum laude, where she was elected to the Order of the Coif. After law school, Siobhan clerked for then-Chief Judge Mary M. Schroeder on the Ninth Circuit Court of Appeals. She received her bachelor and master of fine arts degrees from the University of Oregon. Siobhan serves on committees of the Iowa State Bar Association and the ABA, as well as the boards of two nonprofit organizations.

Chapter 10

Alicia Hickok is a partner in Faegre Drinker's Philadelphia office. She co-leads the appellate team and focuses her practice on appeals in both state and federal courts, including ten of the federal Courts of Appeals and the U.S. Supreme Court. She has a wealth of pretrial experience as well, particularly including matters involving commonwealth or local government or agency actions and corporate governance. She is active in the American Bar Association, and currently serves as the co-chair of the Book Publishing Board of the Litigation Section. In addition to her work at Faegre Drinker, Alicia is an adjunct professor of appellate advocacy at the University of Pennsylvania Law School. Prior to joining Faegre Drinker, she clerked for Judge Marjorie O. Rendell on the Third Circuit Court of Appeals. She received her law degree (cum laude) from the University of Pennsylvania, and her undergraduate degree (cum laude) from Texas Christian University.

Chapter 11

Mitchell Edwards is a commercial litigator in Hinckley Allen's Providence office. For more than 20 years, he has represented companies and individuals in complex business disputes, including fiduciary litigation, shareholder and partnership disputes, real estate litigation, and product liability claims. Mr. Edwards has litigated or arbitrated disputes in at least 15 states. He serves as co-chair of the ABA Banking and Lender Liability Subcommittee of the ABA's Litigation Section. Prior to entering private practice, he clerked for the Honorable Robert W. Lovegreen, Magistrate Judge in the U.S. District Court for the District of Rhode Island. Mr. Edwards received his law degree from Cornell Law School, where he served as managing editor of the *Cornell International Law Journal*. He received his undergraduate degree, summa cum laude, from Binghamton University, where he was a member of Phi Beta Kappa.

Katherine (Kat) B. Savage is a commercial litigator in Hinckley Allen's Providence office. Her practice focuses on litigating all manner of contract disputes, ranging from employment law issues to intellectual property disputes to problems associated with regulatory compliance. Prior to entering private practice, Ms. Savage clerked with the Honorable William P. Robinson III on the Rhode Island Supreme Court and the Honorable Chief Judge William E. Smith in the U.S. District Court for the District of Rhode Island. Ms. Savage received her law degree, magna cum laude, from Roger Williams University School of Law, where she served on law review and the moot court board. She received her bachelor of arts and bachelor of music degrees, cum laude, from Lawrence University in Appleton, Wisconsin. When she's not practicing law, Ms. Savage enjoys baking desserts with her favorite sous chefs—her husband and her two-year-old son.

Chapter 12

Aaron Krauss is a commercial litigator who practices in Cozen O'Connor's Philadelphia office. Aaron can be reached at (215) 665-4181 or akrauss @cozen.com. He has spent the last 30 years representing companies (or officers or directors of companies) in disputes with other companies who they used to like, but now don't. In his spare time, when he hasn't been chasing his children around, serving on nonprofit boards, or practicing law, Aaron has served in multiple leadership positions within the ABA, most recently as the chair of the Litigation Section's Health Law

Litigation Committee and as a member of the Litigation Section's book publishing board. This chapter should not be construed as giving legal advice. If you would like to receive legal advice, call Aaron Krauss. The views expressed in this chapter are the views of Aaron Krauss alone, and are not necessarily the views of Cozen O'Connor.

Chapter 13

Sherilyn Pastor is a partner at McCarter and English, where she chairs its Insurance Recovery, Litigation & Counseling Practice. She is a formidable advocate for corporate policyholders who leverage her decades of experience litigating complex coverage matters throughout the country and abroad. Her well-established track record of success has engendered the trust of an impressive roster of corporate policyholder clients for whom she has recovered well over a billion dollars in coverage through negotiation, arbitration, litigation, and trial verdicts. Sheri has litigated many of the industry's most significant and high-stakes coverage disputes, achieving wins that not only resulted in substantial awards but also set precedent, leading to significant advances for corporate policyholder litigants. Sheri is the president of the American College of Coverage Counsel (ACCC). She also is the past chair (Policyholder Side) of the ABA Litigation Section's Insurance Coverage Litigation Committee (ICLC), having served as vice chair from 2009 to 2012 and as co-chair of various ICLC subcommittees since 2002. She was a member of the New Jersey Supreme Court's Professional Responsibility Rules Committee for over a decade and a member of the New Jersey Supreme Court's Working Group on Ethical Issues Involving Metadata in Electronic Documents. She also serves as an editorial consultant to *Law360: Insurance* and was on the editorial boards of the *Insurance Coverage Law Bulletin* and a consultant on the *New Appleman Insurance Law Practice Guide*. Prior to joining McCarter and English, she clerked for Judge David Landau of the New Jersey Superior Court's Appellate Division. She received her law degree (magna cum laude) and her undergraduate degree (cum laude) from Seaton Hall.

Chapter 14

Lori A. Goldman is the general counsel, executive vice president, and corporate secretary of Bryn Mawr Trust, a full-service bank and financial services institution headquartered in the greater Philadelphia area.

Ms. Goldman has been advising clients in M&A, securities, and corporate governance matters for more than 15 years. She is a graduate of Cornell Law School and Boston University, where she graduated summa cum laude, and is a member of Phi Beta Kappa. While in college, Ms. Goldman interned at the United Nations Library for Women's Issues and spent a year of study in France (Grenoble and Paris). Ms. Goldman also completed Cornell Law School's summer program at the Sorbonne in Paris. Ms. Goldman began her career as an associate in the Corporate Department of Kaye Scholer, LLP in New York (now Arnold Porter Kaye Scholer LLP), and later transitioned to Stradley Ronon Stevens & Young, LLP in Philadelphia. Most recently, Ms. Goldman completed the Stonier Graduate School of Banking program at the University of Pennsylvania's Wharton School. She has also previously been designated as a certified community bank compliance officer. As internal counsel, Ms. Goldman has valuable insight into fiduciary and corporate governance matters, and how they play out within the confines of a highly regulated institution.

Chapter 1
What Is, and What Triggers, a Fiduciary Duty?

By Jason R. Domark and Ashley Gómez-Rodón

Betty Beneficiary arrived at your office, sat down in the conference room, and after the coffee was poured and the niceties done, she regaled you with the facts of her case. Her stepbrother, Fred Fiduciary, had helped her invest the money their father left to her after he passed. That made sense to Betty. Not only was her stepbrother much older, he worked in finance. He understood these things and she trusted him. Betty admitted that she hadn't really been paying much attention to where her money was invested, or what it was invested in. She was busy working on graduating from medical school, and Fred seemed to know what he was doing. He had a successful career, a beautiful penthouse apartment, and a nice car. But now graduation was near, and Betty wanted to someday invest in her own practice. She therefore asked Fred how much money she had, and where it was invested. At first Fred avoided her calls and provided evasive answers. He finally explained that all of Betty's funds were invested in Fred's "side hustle," a start-up entity exploring artificial intelligence. Fred explained that the funds, together with his own inheritance, were being used to pay the start-up's operating costs, including compensation to executives. Fred promised Betty that his start-up would be the next "unicorn" and that, following his planned IPO, her investment would be worth exponentially more. All Betty had to do was be patient. But when Betty pressed further, Fred claimed he was unable to provide Betty with the entity's financial statements, or any other accounting for how Betty's funds were invested or utilized. Betty was concerned. What was the status of her investment? What type of investment was it? Was she a partner? A shareholder? Could she get her money out? Would she ever see a return? As Betty told her story, your "Spidey sense" undoubtedly went off. This was not just another breach of contract action or tort claim. Fred Fiduciary had so much more knowledge, so much more experience, than Betty. Betty had placed her trust in Fred and had relied on him. It sounded like Fred might owe fiduciary duties to Betty.

I. What Is a Fiduciary Duty?

Fiduciary duties arise when a beneficiary justifiably puts their trust in another person (i.e., the fiduciary) and relies upon that person's skill and judgment, and where the other person knowingly accepts the relationship of trust and confidence. As discussed in more detail later, this can occur where the other person has a responsibility to protect the beneficiary's interests or to offer advice for the beneficiary's benefit. A key indicator that a fiduciary duty exists is where the beneficiary's relationship with the other person suggests a dependence.

If you can prove that your client was the beneficiary of a fiduciary relationship, then an array of duties can be imposed to your client's benefit. These duties are specific to a fiduciary and grounded in the idea that a fiduciary must deliberately put the beneficiary's interests before their own. Also, in many cases, these duties cannot be delegated to another person. These duties are generally described as duties of care, loyalty, and good faith.

A. Duty of Care

One of the main tenets of any fiduciary relationship is the fiduciary's duty of care toward the beneficiary. Depending on the transaction, this duty can take on various forms, many of which are discussed in later chapters. Generally, the duty of care means that the fiduciary must act with the same care, skill, and diligence that an ordinarily prudent person would use under similar circumstances. However, if a fiduciary is possessed of specialized skills or knowledge, the fiduciary may be held to an even higher standard and will have to have used those skills appropriately.

At times, the duty of care is described as "the duty to act on an informed basis."[1] This means fiduciaries must exercise reasonable diligence in discovering facts that are likely to affect the beneficiary's interests or actions and be proactive in the entire decision-making process.

1. *In re* USDigital, Inc., 443 B.R. 22, 41 (Bankr. D. Del. 2011).

Although a fiduciary must be informed, a fiduciary is not required to be clairvoyant. Courts judge a fiduciary's actions based upon the information available at the time of the action, rather than from the vantage point of hindsight.[2] As a result, the duty of care requires prudence, not prescience.

As an example, and as discussed in Chapter 8, if Fred Fiduciary was acting as a trustee of a trust, the duty of care would require him to, among other things, prudently manage trust assets. This means Fred would have to be fully informed and proceed cautiously when deciding where, how, and when to invest trust assets. And if Fred possesses special skills or knowledge—for example, if he is an investment adviser—he will be held to a higher standard than a layperson.

As discussed in Chapters 2 and 3, if Fred Fiduciary is a corporate officer or director, he may enjoy a wider range of latitude in exercising his fiduciary duty of care. To abide by his or her duty of care, a director must be diligent in managing the corporation's affairs and must exercise an unbiased judgment in pursuit of corporate interests. But, for example, under section 102(b)(7) of the Delaware General Corporate Law, an exculpation clause may shield corporate directors from liability for a breach of the duty of care. If a company has limited the potential liability of its directors under section 102(b)(7) or another similar state law (and most companies have), a corporate director can only breach a fiduciary duty of care by being grossly negligent.[3]

B. Duty of Loyalty

The duty of loyalty can be characterized as the fiduciary's responsibility to act for another's benefit, even at the expense of the fiduciary's own interests. This duty prevents fiduciaries from engaging in transactions involving self-dealing or conflicting interests. Indeed, fiduciaries must act in the best interests of the beneficiary and not put any personal interests ahead of the beneficiary's interests.

In some instances, a fiduciary may avoid liability by disclosing potential conflicts of interest.[4] To avoid liability, disclosures of potential conflicts must be specific so that the client has full knowledge of all the facts. Boilerplate disclosures may not hold up as a defense to a claim of breach of the duty of loyalty.

---

2. Hugler v. Byrnes, 247 F. Supp. 3d 223, 232 (N.D.N.Y. 2017).

3. *See USDigital*, 443 B.R. at 43; Cargill, Inc. v. JWH Special Circumstance LLC, 959 A.2d 1096, 1112–13 (Del. Ch. 2008).

4. Werner v. Miller Tech. Mgmt., L.P., 831 A.2d 318, 334 (Del. Ch. 2003).

As discussed in Chapter 8, if Fred Fiduciary is acting as a trustee for Betty Beneficiary, a court is likely to heavily scrutinize his duty of loyalty. Because of the duty of loyalty, Fred cannot personally profit from his position as a trustee and he has an affirmative obligation to fully disclose to Betty all facts relevant to any transaction involving trust assets. In essence, this duty forbids Fred from engaging in self-dealing. If Fred does engage in self-dealing, Betty may pursue a claim for breach even without any evidence of fraud.

The duty of loyalty is also heavily litigated in the context of corporate directors. Thus, as discussed further in Chapters 2 and 3, if Fred Fiduciary is acting in such a role, the duty of loyalty generally mandates that he put the best interests of the company's shareholders over any personal interests not held by the shareholders generally.

C. Duty of Good Faith

The duty to act in good faith is "qualitatively different from, and more culpable than, the conduct giving rise to a violation of the fiduciary duty of care."[5] Generally, the duty of good faith is characterized as the fiduciary's responsibility to conduct business in an honest, appropriate manner and without violating the law. Fiduciaries must act on an informed basis and in a good faith belief that their decisions will serve the best interests of their client. Because of the overlap, the duty of good faith is described at times as a subsidiary of the duties of loyalty and care.

In corporate law, the Delaware Supreme Court recognizes three nonexclusive, distinct ways a director may breach his or her duty to act in good faith.[6] First, a director may intentionally act for a reason other than advancing the best interests of the company. Second, a director may intentionally violate the law. Third, a director may intentionally fail to act upon a known duty, demonstrating a conscious disregard for his fiduciary duties.[7]

Thus, for example, if Fred Fiduciary intentionally ignores a corporate transaction that favors another director rather than the shareholders of a corporation, then he may have violated his fiduciary duty to act in good faith.

---

5. *In re* W.J. Bradley Mortgage Capital, LLC, 598 B.R. 150, 163 (Bankr. D. Del. 2019).
6. *In re* Walt Disney Co. Derivative Litigation, 906 A.2d 27, 67 (Del. 2006).
7. *Id.*

D. Other Duties

Depending on the type of fiduciary relationship, other duties may arise, including duties to disclose, to prefer (or give preference to), and to account.

1. Duty to Disclose

In corporate governance, courts discuss an additional duty of corporate directors—a duty to disclose. This duty arises where directors request discretionary action from stockholders, and, in essence, requires that directors disclose fully and fairly all material facts within their control regarding the request.[8] When an alleged omission or misrepresentation is material, directors breach their fiduciary duty of disclosure.

2. Duty of Preference

Another duty that arises in the context of trusts and corporate governance is the duty of preference.[9] Similar to the duty of good faith, this duty is sometimes characterized as a subset of a fiduciary's duty of loyalty. For trusts, this duty generally requires the trustee to give priority to the best interests of all the beneficiaries and not administer the trust in a way where one beneficiary receives preference over another. For corporate governance, this duty may be breached when a director causes a corporation to sell off assets to satisfy a liquidation preference of its preferred stockholders.

For example, consider the scenario of Fred Fiduciary as trustee of a trust where Betty Beneficiary holds a future interest. Fred, as trustee, opts for an investment of trust assets on property that will depreciate in value in the long term, but yield a large return in the short run. Although this investment may benefit the current beneficiaries, Betty, as a future beneficiary, could argue Fred failed to preserve the trust property for her future interest. Thus, Fred may have violated his duty of preference by not remaining impartial to all the beneficiaries of the trust.

---

8. Dohmen v. Goodman, 2020 WL 3428213, at *4 (Del. June 23, 2020).
9. Oakland Raiders v. Nat'l Football League, 32 Cal. Rptr. 3d 266, 273 (Ct. App. 2005).

3. Duty to Account

A duty to account arises in the context of trusts and estates.[10] As a fiduciary, a trustee has a duty to account to the trust's beneficiaries. This means the trustee is obligated to keep records of all transactions affecting the assets of the trust and disclose them to the beneficiaries. Failure to do so may be grounds for a breach of this duty.

Similarly, executors of an estate have a duty to inform the beneficiaries of all the assets the executor controlled for distribution. Not all of a decedent's assets go through an executor; for example, a life insurance policy with a designated beneficiary usually will be paid directly to the named beneficiary without probate. This duty is important not only for the beneficiaries but to minimize liability for the executor. Without an accounting of what assets the executor controlled, a dispute may ensue over an asset that never even went through probate.

A duty to account also arises in partnerships and can be a valuable litigation tool if a dispute arises between partners. For example, consider the scenario where Betty Beneficiary provides the funding for a partnership and Fred Fiduciary runs the day-to-day business. At some point, Betty Beneficiary becomes dissatisfied with the lack of returns from the partnership and her inability to obtain information related to the partnership assets. During the course of litigation, Fred attempts to thwart Betty's discovery efforts to retrieve this information. In response, Betty can show a duty to accounting is owed among the partners. Once that duty is established, the burden shifts to Fred to then show that he used the partnership funds properly.

II. What Triggers a Fiduciary Duty?

A. Generally

Unsurprisingly, a fiduciary relationship triggers fiduciary duties. Not so clear-cut is what triggers a fiduciary relationship.

In our example, Fred and Betty likely have a fiduciary relationship if Betty has rested trust in Fred and relied upon Fred's skill and judgment, and if Fred knowingly accepted that relationship. A fiduciary relationship connotes a dependence that induces trust and confidence. These relationships typically develop where a party is sworn to protect

---

10. Libbey-Owens-Ford Co. v. Blue Cross & Blue Shield Mut. of Ohio, 982 F.2d 1031, 1036 (6th Cir. 1993), on *reh'g en banc* (Feb. 23, 1993).

the interests of another. A fiduciary is generally a person entrusted with the power to manage and control the property of another.

Certain relationships are nearly always considered fiduciary in nature. Most, if not all, jurisdictions recognize that trustees have fiduciary duties when managing a trust.[11] Delaware courts also recognize the following relationships as special enough to be considered fiduciary: general partners, administrators or executors, attorney-client, guardians, and in some circumstances joint venturers or principals and their agents.[12]

Even normal business dealings can give rise to a fiduciary relationship. For example, contracts between parties can create a fiduciary relationship where one party acts as an agent for another. Contracts, however, can also diminish certain fiduciary duties. For example, general partners typically owe fiduciary duties to their limited partners. But the parties can enter into a contract that limits the general partner's fiduciary duties.[13]

Courts are hesitant to disrupt commercial relationships and do not extend the high standards of fiduciary duties to commercial transactions lightly.[14] In part, this is to prevent courts from interfering with behaviors permissible in a business world for those acting at arm's length, which actions might be forbidden to those engaged in a fiduciary relationship.[15]

B. Examples of Fiduciary Relationships

1. Corporate Officers and Directors

As discussed in Chapters 2 and 3, corporate officers and directors owe fiduciary duties of care and loyalty to a corporation and its shareholders in regard to the management and operation of the corporation.[16] Such duties require directors and officers to act in good faith, offer their best judgment, and promote the best interests of the company. As previously mentioned, fiduciary duties generally preclude corporate officers and directors from engaging in self-dealing, especially at the

11. *See, e.g.*, Zastrow v. Journal Commc'ns, Inc., 718 N.W.2d 51, 58 (Wis. 2006).

12. Bird's Constr. v. Milton Equestrian Ctr., 2001 WL 1528956, at *4 (Del. Ch. Nov. 16, 2001).

13. See Cont'l Ins. Co. v. Rutledge & Co., Inc., 750 A.2d 1219, 1235 (Del. Ch. 2000) (upholding the contractual terms that diminished a general partner's fiduciary duty of care owed to the limited partners).

14. Wal-Mart Stores, Inc. v. AIG Life Ins. Co., 901 A.2d 106, 114 (Del. 2006).

15. Meinhard v. Salmon, 164 N.E. 545, 547 (N.Y. 1928).

16. Gantler v. Stephens, 965 A.2d 695, 709 (Del. 2009).

expense of the corporation. However, such duties do not require corporate officers and directors to be infallible or avoid reasonable risks. Additionally, as set forth in Chapter 12, if a corporation becomes insolvent, the corporation's creditors can sue for breach of fiduciary duty.

2. Majority Shareholders

As discussed in Chapter 4, majority shareholders may also owe fiduciary duties to minority shareholders in certain circumstances.[17] For example, in a closely held corporation, majority shareholders owe minority shareholders a fiduciary duty of good faith and loyalty.[18] Courts recognize this duty to protect minority shareholders from a majority shareholder engaging in self-interested transactions, such as borrowing corporate funds.

3. Members and Managers of Limited Liability Companies

As discussed in Chapter 5, fiduciary duties also arise in limited liability companies. For limited liability companies, members and managers may owe a fiduciary duty to the company, depending on whether the company is member managed and on the scope of the member's responsibilities in management. In some jurisdictions, members may broaden or eliminate these fiduciary duties in the company's operating agreement. Again, such modifications are upheld in order to minimize judicial interference in everyday business transactions.

4. Investment Advisers

As discussed in Chapter 6, investment advisers registered either with the SEC or a state securities regulator have fiduciary duties of care and loyalty to their clients. For those advisers not registered with either the SEC or a state securities regulator, a fiduciary relationship may still arise, especially in the context of discretionary accounts. This is because an adviser of a discretionary account has the ability to select and invest without seeking prior approval. In contrast, advisers of nondiscretionary accounts merely execute the investment decisions of the customer, and so are generally not fiduciaries. The more the client entrusts an

---

17. *E.g.*, Sinclair Oil Corp. v. Levien, 280 A.2d 717, 723 (Del. 1971).
18. Wilkes v. Springside Nursing Home, Inc., 370 Mass. 842, 353 N.E.2d 657 (1976).

adviser with the ability to "move money," the more likely the adviser is to be a fiduciary.[19]

5. Partnerships

As discussed in Chapter 7, a partnership is a fiduciary relationship. Partners owe each other and the partnership a duty of care and loyalty.[20] Even where relationships are strained, partners are not typically relieved from their fiduciary duties. However, state law may allow a modification or enhancement of these duties through the partnership agreement. Delaware law in particular permits a limited partnership to eliminate certain fiduciary duties through the partnership agreement.[21]

6. Trusts and Estates

As discussed in Chapters 8 and 9, fiduciary duties also arise in probate administration. An executor of an estate owes a fiduciary duty to the estate and its beneficiaries. This means that the executor must carry out the terms of the will and seek the estate's best interests.[22] Similarly, trustees also have a fiduciary duty to the beneficiaries of the trust. An executor or trustee can be liable if, among other things, they use assets for risky investments, fail to make timely distributions or payments to the beneficiaries, or enter into transactions that constitute self-dealing.

7. Banks and Other Financial Institutions

As discussed in Chapter 11, a bank or other financial institution might, depending on the service provided, have a fiduciary duty to its customers. For standard deposit account customers, banks typically do not owe a fiduciary duty. Similarly, the ordinary debtor-creditor relationship generally does not trigger a fiduciary relationship because the customer is not seeking financial advice from the bank when opening an account or credit line. Some states have allowed a "limited fiduciary

---

19. *See* Independent Order of Foresters v. Donald, Lufkin & Jenrette, Inc., 157 F.3d 933, 940–41 (2d Cir.1998); Patsos v. First Albany Corp., 741 N.E.2d 841, 850 (Mass. 2001).

20. Gotham Partners, L.P. v. Hallwood Realty Partners, L.P., 817 A.2d 160, 170 (Del. 2002).

21. Del. Code Ann. tit. 6, § 17-1101(d).

22. *See, e.g.*, Greene v. First Nat'l Bank of Chicago, 516 N.E.2d 311, 315 (Ill. App. Ct. 1987).

duty," whereby banks must abide by a heightened duty of care if it provides "expanded" or "nontraditional" services. For example, Florida recognizes certain scenarios where a bank enters a fiduciary relationship in an otherwise arms-length transaction.[23] These situations emerge where a bank acts beyond its role as a lender and offers financial advice or orchestrates purchase agreements. If a bank assumes the role of a financial adviser, then the bank owes fiduciary duties of care and loyalty, requiring the bank to disclose material facts relevant to each transaction.

8. Miscellaneous

a. Parent Companies and Subsidiaries

Fiduciary duties may also arise between parent companies and their subsidiaries. A wholly owned subsidiary generally owes a fiduciary duty to its parent corporation. Because of the obligations to the parent, wholly owned subsidiary directors must act in the best interests of the parent and its shareholders, even if it means allowing the subsidiary to drop in value. Likewise, a parent company may assume fiduciary duties through ownership of a subsidiary's majority shares and exercise of control over the subsidiary's operations. Courts consider such a relationship as akin to a controlling shareholder, who would owe fiduciary duties to the company and minority shareholders.

b. Employment Relationships

In certain cases, an employee can owe fiduciary duties to his or her employer. Courts typically find that an employee is a fiduciary in cases in which the employee acts as an agent for his or her employer. For example, a breach of the duty of loyalty may be found based on an employee's disclosure of confidential information to a competitor or based on an employee's theft.[24] Some employees even have a heightened duty of loyalty to their employers. This heightened duty arises where an employee is in a position of trust and confidence, such as a high-level executive.

---

23. See First Nat'l Bank & Trust Co. of the Treasurer Coast v. Pack, 789 So. 2d 411, 414 (Fla. 4th DCA 2001); Maxwell v. First United Bank, 782 So. 2d 931, 934 (Fla. 4th DCA 2001).

24. Zastrow v. Journal Commc'ns, Inc., 718 N.W.2d 51, 60 (Wis. 2006).

c. Real Estate Agents and Brokers

Real estate agents and brokers generally owe fiduciary duties to their clients.[25] Real estate agents and brokers must be honest and candid and disclose all material information that they possess or obtain regarding a transaction. This becomes a challenge when a broker takes on the task of acting as a dual agent of the seller and buyer—now the broker owes fiduciary duties on both sides and may be liable on either end if the deal turns sour. For real estate agents in particular, compliance with fiduciary duties can be a condition precedent to collecting their commissions on sales.

d. Attorneys

Attorneys also owe fiduciary duties to their clients. Specifically, all attorneys owe a fiduciary duty of care and loyalty to their clients and must not engage in transactions that could lead to self-dealing or conflicting interests. Indeed, attorneys must not place their own interests ahead of their clients' interests, at any cost. In some scenarios, an attorney's breach of fiduciary duty may be considered legal malpractice. Some jurisdictions do not recognize a separate action for legal malpractice and for breach of fiduciary duty.[26] Legal malpractice cases typically stem from the attorney's performance of his or her duties in the representation. But a breach of fiduciary duty claim can differ from a legal malpractice claim, even when based on an attorney's conduct. For example, consider the scenario where a lawyer engages in a sexual relationship with his or her client. If the lawyer still represents the client adequately, then a legal malpractice claim may not be available. However, those same facts may be considered a breach of the lawyer's fiduciary duty of loyalty and avoidance of self-interest. Another difference in some jurisdictions for these claims is the relief available to the affected client; in a legal malpractice claim, a client may have to prove damages as a result of the attorney's actions. However, in a breach of fiduciary claim, even if the affected client cannot show actual damages, the client may be able to seek disgorgement of the attorney's profit derived from his or her representation.[27]

---

25. Precision Glass Tinting, Inc. v. Long, 293 A.D.2d 594, 595, 740 (N.Y. App. Div. 2002).

26. *See, e.g.*, Majumdar v. Lurie, 653 N.E.2d 915, 921 (Ill. App. Ct. 1995).

27. *See, e.g.*, Parkinson v. Bevis, 448 P.3d 1027, 1033 (Idaho 2019).

e. Architects and Contractors

Fiduciary duties have even emerged in the construction context. Some jurisdictions have found a fiduciary relationship to exist between a client and an architect.[28] One court rationalized that an architect is expected to furnish plans and supervise construction, which leads to a relationship of "trust and confidence."[29] Courts have likewise recognized that a contractor might owe fiduciary or similar duties to property owners in certain circumstances.[30]

III. Breach of Fiduciary Duty Claims and Defenses

A. Claim Elements

Generally speaking, a breach of fiduciary duty plaintiff such as Betty Beneficiary must prove the following elements to succeed on a breach of fiduciary duty claim: (1) a fiduciary duty existed between her and Fred Fiduciary, (2) Fred Fiduciary breached that duty, and (3) the breach is the proximate cause of her damages.[31]

Additionally, many jurisdictions allow claims against third parties who facilitated a breach of fiduciary duty. These claims are typically referred to as aiding and abetting a breach of fiduciary duty. To establish such a claim, a plaintiff such as Betty Beneficiary must prove "(1) the existence of a fiduciary relationship, (2) the fiduciary breached its duty, (3) a defendant, who is not a fiduciary, knowingly participated in [the] breach, and (4) damages to the plaintiff resulted from the concerted action of the fiduciary and the non-fiduciary."[32] The first

28. *See, e.g.*, Palmer v. Brown, 127 Cal. App. 2d 44, 59 (Cal. Ct. App. 1954) ("An architect owes to his client a fiduciary duty of loyalty and good faith") (citation omitted); RCDI Constr. v. Spaceplan/Architecture, Planning & Interiors, P.A., 2001 WL 1013241, at *5 (W.D.N.C. Jan. 25, 2001) ("The same would appear to apply to architects, inasmuch as a fiduciary duty is imposed between architect and client, and procedures are in place for leveling professional grievances."), *aff'd*, 29 F. App'x 120 (4th Cir. 2002); Canton Lutheran Church v. Sovik, Mathre, Sathrum & Quanbeck, 507 F. Supp. 873, 878 (D.S.D. 1981) ("Thus, it follows that an architect-employer relationship under South Dakota law is a fiduciary relationship[.]").

29. *Canton Lutheran Church*, 507 F. Supp. at 878.

30. *See, e.g.*, Goes v. Vogler, 937 N.W.2d 190, 196–97 (Neb. 2020).

31. *See, e.g.*, Gracey v. Eaker, 837 So. 2d 348, 353 (Fla. 2002).

32. Gotham Partners, L.P. v. Hallwood Realty Partners, L.P., 817 A.2d 160, 172 (Del. 2002) (quoting Fitzgerald v. Cantor, 1999 WL 182573, at *1 (Del. Ch. Mar. 25, 1999)).

element—the existence of a fiduciary relationship—remains the lynchpin because "Delaware law does not recognize the concept of aiding and abetting a breach of contract."[33] Even where a fiduciary relationship does exist, some jurisdictions reject this ancillary cause of action altogether.[34]

B. Common Defenses

In response to a breach of fiduciary duty claim, a defendant such as Fred Fiduciary usually responds with one or more of the following defenses.

1. No Existence of a Fiduciary Relationship

Unless the relationship is considered fiduciary by its very nature, Fred would likely argue that a fiduciary relationship between him and Betty never existed. Fred would compare his dealings with Betty to a normal arms-length business relationship, where he did not have a duty to protect Betty's interests.

2. No Breach of Fiduciary Duty

Assuming Betty can show a fiduciary relationship existed, Fred would also argue that his action did not constitute a breach. This defense is case-specific. For example, as an investment adviser, Fred could justify a poor investment decision based on the information available to Fred at the time.

3. Statute of Limitations

Even if Betty can prove all the elements of her claim, Fred could still argue that the statute of limitations has run. The statute of limitations varies by jurisdiction, so Betty's attorney must understand what law applies and must determine the applicable time period. Betty's attorney should also carefully investigate whether a "discovery rule" tolled the running of the statute of limitations because of Betty's reliance on Fred.

33. Feeley v. NHAOCG, LLC, 62 A.3d 649, 658 (Del. Ch. 2012).
34. *See* Cohen v. Dulay, 94 N.E.3d 1167 (Ohio App. Ct. 2017).

4. Full Disclosure

If Betty's claim stems from self-dealing or a conflict of interest, Fred could argue that he fully disclosed all material facts to Betty. In some cases, full disclosure is a complete defense against liability for a breach of fiduciary duty.

5. Reliance on Experts

Another defense Fred may raise against Betty's claim is that he relied on experts, who were selected with reasonable care and in good faith. This defense is relevant in situations where Fred relied on work completed by a skilled professional, such as an accountant or lawyer, in the scope of his fiduciary duties.

IV. Conclusion

A fiduciary relationship can arise in many situations. Once that relationship arises, the fiduciary may owe multiple different duties to the beneficiary. Fiduciaries must be cognizant of those duties and careful not to breach them. And when breached, such claims can be a valuable tool for litigants.

Chapter 2
Derivative Claims

By Eric C. Milby

I. Introduction

When the phone rang at 4 p.m. on a Friday afternoon, Lisa Lawyer was packing up her stuff and heading out early for a game of tennis with her husband before dinner. It was Sarah, her best friend since college, and Lisa was delighted to get the call because they had not spoken in months. Lisa's delight over hearing from Sarah quickly turned to a dreaded realization that she was not going to make that tennis match. Sarah breathlessly explained that her husband Sam Shareholder had just been fired from his job, indeed *his* company, that he had started with two college friends 22 years ago. Sarah was a wreck. She explained that the whole idea for this company was Sam's and he invited his two best friends Olivia Officer and Dave Director to join the company with him. In fact, the company name, SOD, Inc., is an amalgam of Sam, Olivia, and Dave's initials. The three of them each own one-third of the shares in the company but, make no mistake about it, it was Sam that made this company successful. Sam was on the line. He interjected that Olivia had obtained their first client and that one of Dave's clients was their biggest client over the years, although he, Sam, was the Director of Sales and he and the three salespeople that worked for him were responsible for the vast majority of total sales. Anyway, the problem, Sarah explained, was that Olivia Officer and Dave Director had become romantically involved after college and were now married. They were ganging up on Sam and just wanted to squeeze him out of the company.

Although the shareholders all took equal salaries, Olivia and Dave were resentful that they had agreed, 20 years ago, to let Sam have 5 percent of the sales annually as a bonus incentive on top of his compensation. The company reported very little profit because in addition to Sam's bonus, the three owners increased their base salaries as the company revenues grew. Each of them was taking a salary of over $400,000, and Sam was receiving a bonus of more than $200,000 per year in recent years. Sarah and Sam figured that Olivia and Dave would promote Sam's best salesperson, who is earning a base salary of $70,000 per year plus a 5 percent commission, but only on the first year of sales from any new client that she generated, and name her the new Director of Sales. Sam and Sarah wondered whether Sam's $400,000+ salary and $200,000+ annual commissions would go back into the company and be distributed in equal thirds as a distribution of profits to the shareholders. That would cut Sam's earnings from $600,000 to $200,000 and Olivia and Dave would each take another $200,000. Worse, they suspected that Olivia and Dave would increase their salaries again, eliminate the distributable "profits," and thus wipe out Sam's earnings altogether.

Sam had very little insight into what Dave and Olivia were thinking because they had stopped having meetings and it was as if all decisions were being made around the dinner table at Olivia and Dave's house when Sam was not present. To make matters worse, Olivia was the chief financial officer and Sam had no real insight into how company funds were being spent. Sam had started asking questions after he had heard that Olivia and Dave had bought the building where their offices were located and had caused the company to pay them a substantially above-market rent. Sam had also heard that Dave, who was in charge of operations, had recently acquired the small trucking company that made all of the company deliveries. That might explain why the shipping and handling costs had increased.

Lisa Lawyer, processing all this information, asked the appropriate question: "Do you have a shareholder's agreement?" Sheepishly, Sam Shareholder confessed that when they started this business, they had all been such good friends that they never thought that they would need a written agreement. Without a written agreement, Lisa would have to be guided by the default provisions of Delaware General Corporation Law.

II. Derivative Claims

A. What Is a Derivative Claim?

The derivative form of action permits an individual shareholder to bring "suit to enforce a corporate cause of action against officers, directors, and third parties."[1] Devised as a suit in equity, the purpose of the derivative action was to place in the hands of the individual shareholder a means to protect the interests of the corporation from the misfeasance and malfeasance of "faithless directors and managers."[2]

The U.S. Supreme Court in 1881 recognized the existence of a derivative action in the United States.[3] There, the Court explained that for a shareholder to bring an action in the name of the corporation, there must exist a foundation for the suit, which could mean action or threatened actions by the board of directors that are "beyond the authority conferred on them by their charter," or "such a fraudulent transaction completed or contemplated by the acting managers that would result in serious injury to the corporation or to the interest of the other Shareholders," or where "the majority shareholders themselves are oppressively and illegally pursuing a course in the name of the corporation" that violates the rights of other shareholders.[4] However, the Court explained that in addition to having a foundation for the lawsuit, the shareholder seeking to bring an action in the name of the corporation must exhaust other remedies to obtain redress directly from the corporation, and, as such, "he must make an earnest, not a simulated effort, with the managing body of the corporation, to induce remedial action on their part, and this must be made apparent to the Court."[5] Finally, the Court explained that such earnest efforts to obtain redress from the corporation itself, prior to a lawsuit, must be demonstrated to the Court and stated with particularity.[6] That early pronouncement of the nature of and requirements for a derivative suit, the demand requirements, and the pleading of such demands with particularity, essentially survives today in the common law, statutes, and rules of all states and federal courts.

When pleading breach of fiduciary duty in a corporate governance, or a "business divorce" type claim, an important early task is determining whether each of the claims are derivative or direct. This is not always an easy task. A derivative claim is a claim that is brought in the name of the corporation because the corporation is the proper plaintiff

1. Kamen v. Kemper Fin. Services, Inc., 111 S. Ct. 1711, 1716, 500 U.S. 90, 95 (1991) (quoting Ross v. Bernhard, 396 U.S. 531, 534, 90 S. Ct. 733, 736, 24 L. Ed. 2d 729 (1970)).

2. *Id.* (quoting Cohen v. Beneficial Loan Corp., 337 U.S. 541, 548, 69 S. Ct. 1221, 1226, 93 L. Ed. 1528 (1949)).

3. Hawes v. City of Oakland, 104 U.S. 450 (1881).

4. *Id.* at 460.

5. *Id.* at 461.

6. *Id.*

and entitled to the recovery. In other words, Lisa Lawyer has to decide whether the lawsuit should be:

(1) *Sam Shareholder v. Olivia Officer and David Director* (direct) or
(2) *SOD, Inc. v. Olivia Officer and David Director* (derivative) or
(3) both *Sam Shareholder, individually and on behalf of SOD, Inc. v. Olivia Officer and David Director* (direct and derivative).

So, it was important for Lisa to figure out which claims were derivative, and which were direct. If she did not plead them properly, she risked having the claims dismissed.

B. Direct versus Derivative Claims

Lisa Lawyer was concerned about what law would apply to Sam Shareholder's claims. She knew that SOD was a Delaware corporation, but she also knew that beyond its corporate existence, it functioned almost entirely out of its offices one state north in the city of Philadelphia, Pennsylvania. To be safe, she decided to brush up on both states' law. Lisa Lawyer quickly found a seemingly simple sounding test in the state of Delaware. The two-prong test merely asked (1) who suffered the alleged harm, the corporation or the shareholder bringing the action, and (2) who would receive the benefit of any recovery in the litigation, the corporation, or the shareholder?[7] The *Tooley* court explained that if either question was answered in favor of the corporation, the claim is derivative. In other words, if it were the corporation that suffered the alleged harm or if the corporation would receive the benefit of any recovery, then the claim was derivative.[8] Common examples of a derivative claim would include mismanagement that depresses the stock value,[9] misappropriation of corporate opportunities, excess compensation, misappropriation of corporate funds, minority oppression, waste, violations of the duty of oversight, and other breaches of fiduciary duties that the directors and officers owed to the corporation and the shareholders. Direct claims, on the other hand, would arise whenever a shareholder had suffered an injury that was independent of any alleged

---

7. Tooley v. Donaldson, Lufkin, & Jenrette, Inc. 845 A.2d 1031, 1033 (Del. 2004).
8. *Id.* at 1039.
9. Kramer v. W. Pac. Industries, Inc., 546 A.2d 348, 353 (Del. 1988).

injury to the corporation.[10] Specifically, the proponent of a direct claim must be able to "prevail without showing an injury to the company."[11]

Lisa Lawyer knew that she had an important analysis on her hands. Some of the claims seemed easy to classify. If Olivia and Dave had bought the building where SOD was located, without inviting Sam to participate in that opportunity, and if Dave had bought the trucking company that handles SOD's deliveries without offering Sam the opportunity to participate, those would make for good usurpation of opportunity claims that would belong to the corporation and would have to be filed derivatively. Further, if Olivia and Dave are charging SOD excessive rent for the use of the building they had purchased, or if Dave was overcharging for the trucking, that would be a waste or misappropriation of corporate funds claim that would also belong to the corporation and have to be filed derivatively.

On the other hand, the termination of Dave's employment appears to be a wrong that is unique to him. After all, he was the only one who was fired and the only one who has lost his salary. If he were to prevail, the lost salary would be paid to him and not to the corporation. So, it seems like a clear-cut direct claim at first. However, if Olivia and Dave increased their own salaries with the money saved from Sam's salary, that excessive compensation could be the subject of a derivative claim. Fortunately, courts have recognized hybrid, or dual-natured claims for those occasions when a director's or officer's wrongful actions result in both harm to the corporation and a unique injury to a shareholder. Lisa Lawyer believes she should bring both claims but decides first to take a deeper dive by reviewing Chapter 3 on dual direct and derivative claims against a control group. But first, she decides that, before bringing any derivative claims, she better check the rules and statutes to make sure that she satisfies all the prerequisites.

III. Pre-Suit Considerations

There are several matters that a prospective plaintiff must consider before filing suit; prerequisites that must be satisfied and pleading requirements that must be met. One should consider whether to demand information to investigate or confirm the validity of the claim before making demands on the board or filing a lawsuit. If the decision to file has been made, a plaintiff must satisfy several conditions. For example,

10. 845 A.2d at 1039.
11. *Id.*

a plaintiff must be able to adequately represent all parties who are similarly situated, and a plaintiff must be a shareholder at the time of the filing and must remain a shareholder throughout the lawsuit.

A. Books and Records Requests

After talking with Sam Shareholder, Lisa is convinced that nothing short of litigation will convince Olivia and Dave to budge from their positions. Lisa must gauge how to proceed. Lisa's first challenge is that she is working with limited information. Dave has nothing more than his own K-1s to prove his ownership and share of the profits and his W-2s to prove his salary history. He does not have adequate financial information sufficient to help Lisa, or a forensic accountant hired by her, determine whether Sam is correct that Olivia and Dave are mismanaging the company. Sam believes that Olivia and Dave will not share any financial information unless compelled to do so. Fortunately for Lisa, she has tools available to her—a Books and Records request. A Books and Records request is a statutory right of a shareholder or director to, for a proper purpose, inspect the Books and Records of the company. Enforcement of that right is often available in a summary action. In Delaware, these Books and Records actions are often called a "220 Action" referring to section 220 of the General Corporation Law of the State of Delaware.[12] Lisa knew that many of the claims that Sam was contemplating would have to be filed derivatively, in the company name, and that meant demanding that the company file the suit before Sam can file in the company name. If she failed to describe the demand with reasonable particularity, she could risk losing some of the claims.[13] The information available on a Books and Records inspection is usually far narrower than the information traditionally available in discovery.[14] However, refusal by David and Olivia to provide information would be a strong indication that they had something to hide.

B. Prerequisites

Every court has some level of prerequisites or pleading requirements that must be established to maintain a derivative action. Rule 23.1(b)

---

12. DEL. CODE ANN. tit. 8 § 220.

13. *See, e.g.*, Allison on Behalf of General Motors Corp. v. General Motors Corp., 604 F. Supp. 1106, 1117 (D. Del. 1985); Stoner v. Walsh, 772 F. Supp. 790, 797 (S.D.N.Y. 1991).

14. Thomas & Betts Corp. v. Leviton Mfg. Co., Inc., 681 A.2d 1026, 1035 (Del. 1996) ("The plaintiff bears the burden of proving that each category of books and records is essential to accomplishment of the stockholder's articulated purpose for the inspection.").

of the Federal Rules of Civil Procedure expresses some of those prerequisites as pleading requirements. That rule states:

> The complaint must be verified and must: (1) allege that the plaintiff was a shareholder or member at the time of the transaction complained of, or that the plaintiff's share or membership later devolved on it by operation of law; (2) allege that the action is not a collusive one to confer jurisdiction that the court would otherwise lack; and (3) state with particularity: (A) any effort by the plaintiff to obtain the desired action from the directors or comparable authority and, if necessary, from the shareholders or members; and (B) the reasons for not obtaining the action or not making the effort.[15]

Many courts require the plaintiff to demonstrate that they are an adequate representative of the similarly situated shareholders.

1. Adequate Representation

In many states, the proponent of a derivative claim must establish to the court that it represents the interests of all similarly situated shareholders. In other words, the court must be satisfied that a plaintiff in the derivative action is qualified to serve as a fiduciary for other shareholders whose recovery is dependent upon the plaintiff's adequate and fair prosecution of the claims. In federal court actions, this rule is expressed in Federal Rule of Civil Procedure 23.1, which articulates the heightened pleading requirements in federal court derivative actions. That rule requires a plaintiff to, among other things, "allege that the plaintiff was a shareholder or member at the time of the transaction complained of, or that the plaintiff's share or membership later devolved on it by operation of law."[16] Factors that a court may consider when determining whether a plaintiff can fairly and adequately represent the similarly situated shareholders include (1) if economic antagonisms exist between the representative and the class;[17] (2) outside entanglements that render it more likely that the representative may disregard the interest of the others;[18] (3) the plaintiff's familiarity with the

---

15. FED. R. CIV. P. 23.1.

16. *Id.* 23.1(b)(1). *See also* DEL. CT. CH. R. 23.1(a) ("the complaint shall allege that the plaintiff was a shareholder or member at the time of the transaction of which the plaintiff complains or that the plaintiff's share or membership thereafter devolved on the plaintiff by operation of law").

17. Baffa v. Donaldson Lukin & Jenrette Secs. Corp., 222 F.3d 52, 60 (2d Cir. 2000).

18. G.A. Enters., Inc. v. Leisure Living Cmty., Inc., 517 F.2d 24, 27 (1st Cir. 1975).

litigation;[19] (4) other litigation pending between the plaintiff and the defendant;[20] (5) plaintiff's vindictiveness against the defendants;[21] and (6) the degree of support that the plaintiff is receiving from the shareholders that she/he proports to represent.[22] The adequate representation requirement can serve as a significant impediment for representative plaintiffs who merely seek to force a buyout of their own interest because their goal does nothing to further the interest of the similarly situated shareholders. For Sam Shareholder, as with many closely held companies, this initial qualification is perhaps less of a concern because he is the only shareholder not in control of the management. In fact, much of his complaint is that Dave and Olivia appear to be managing the corporation to his exclusion. There are no other minority shareholders that are similarly situated to Dave.

2. Standing to Maintain a Derivative Lawsuit

As with any lawsuit, a plaintiff with a derivative lawsuit must have standing to bring the suit. Standing in a derivative suit, however, has a unique set of rules. Specifically, the plaintiff in a derivative action must be a shareholder at the time the plaintiff files the lawsuit and must remain a shareholder throughout the pendency of the action.[23] Plaintiff must also have been a shareholder at the time of the actions complained of in the lawsuit. In other words, it is not enough for a plaintiff to be a shareholder of a corporation, the plaintiff must be a shareholder who suffered an injury. If a plaintiff loses or sells their interest in the corporation during the pendency of the lawsuit, they will lose their standing.[24] Not all states recognize the contemporaneous ownership rule. But where they do, this can give rise to some interesting litigation strategies. For example, Dave and Olivia could form another corporation, cause that corporation to make an offer for SOD, Inc., and use their two-third majority to approve the sale of SOD, Inc. to their new company. This strategy is often referred to as a "freeze-out merger" or a "cash-out merger."[25] This might be an effective strategy

19. Davis v. Comed, Inc., 619 F.2d 588, 593–94 (6th Cir. 1980).
20. Palmer v. U.S. Sav. Bank of America, 553 A.2d 781, 786 (N.H. 1989).
21. Kayes v. Pacific Lumber Co., 51 F.3d 1449, 1464 (9th Cir. 1995).
22. Larson v. Dumke, 900 F.2d 1363, 1367 (9th Cir. 1990).
23. Fed. R. Civ. P. 23.1, Kramer v. W. Pac. Industries, Inc., 546 A.2d 348, 354–55 (Del. 1988).
24. *Id.*
25. Alpert v. 28 Williams St. Corp., 473 N.E.2d 19, 26 (N.Y. 1984), Weinberger v. UOP, Inc., 457 A.2d 701, 703 (Del. 1983).

with a Delaware corporation. If Pennsylvania law were to apply, it could arguably be a more difficult strategy to employ because Pennsylvania recognizes minority oppression—a cause of action for breach of fiduciary duty whenever a corporate action has had as its goal the elimination of a shareholder's rights.[26] But several cases in Pennsylvania have held that, like in Delaware, the exclusive remedy for a cash-out merger, absent fraud or fundamental unfairness, is an appraisal proceeding.[27] Delaware, however, does not recognize minority oppression as a cause of action and Dave's remedy for a cash out merger would be only an appraisal proceeding to determine the fair value of his buyout price.[28]

C. Demand

1. Pre-Litigation Demand

A prospective plaintiff in a derivative action must make demand on the corporation's board of directors that the board take action to remedy the complaints. In other words, a shareholder must ask the corporation to redress its wrongs before asking the court to intervene. The demand requirement derives from the fundamental concept that it is the board of directors that manages a corporation and has the right to sue or be sued in its name. There are important public policies underpinning the demand requirement. "First, by requiring exhaustion of intracorporate remedies, the demand requirement invokes a species of alternative dispute resolution procedure which might avoid litigation altogether."[29] Second, if the board determines that the litigation is in the best interest of the corporation, the authority of the board to manage the corporate affairs, that is, to control the litigation, is preserved.[30] Third, if the board wrongfully refuses to pursue resolution or resolve the matter, the stockholder retains the right to control the litigation.[31] These policies are:

26. Barter v. Diodoardo, 771 A.2d 835, 839–40, 2001 Pa. Super. 105, ¶ 19 (Pa. Super.) (stating "it is a violation of the majority shareholders' fiduciary duty to minority shareholders to freeze out the minority for the sole purpose of continuing the business for the benefit of the majority") (citing *In re* Jones & Laughlin Steel Corp., 488 Pa. 524, 530–31, 412 A.2d 1099, 1102–03 (1980)).

27. Mitchell Partners, L.P. v. Irex Corp., 53 A.3d 39, 45, 617 Pa. 423, 434 (Pa. 2012).

28. Weinberger v. UOP, Inc., 457 A.2d 701, 703 (Del. 1983).

29. Brehm v. Eisner, 746 A.2d 244, 255 (Del. 2000) (quoting Grimes v. Donald, 673 A.2d 1207, 1216–17 (Del. 1996) (overruled on other grounds)).

30. *Id.*

31. *Id.*

> designed to create a balanced environment which will: (1) on the one hand, deter costly, baseless suits by creating a screening mechanism to eliminate claims where there is only a suspicion expressed solely in conclusory terms; and (2) on the other hand, permit suit by a stockholder who is able to articulate particularized facts showing that there is a reasonable doubt either that (a) a majority of the board is independent for purposes of responding to the demand, or (b) the underlying transaction is protected by the business judgment rule.[32]

Thus, for a shareholder to seek redress on behalf of the corporation, it must first establish that the corporation itself refused to remedy a wrong. As the Supreme Court stated in *Hawes*:

> before the shareholder is permitted in his own name to institute and conduct a litigation which usually belongs to the corporation, he should show to the satisfaction of the court that he has exhausted all the means within his reach to obtain, within the corporation itself, the redress of his grievances, or action in conformity to his wishes.[33]

In conformity with *Hawes*, all states now require a shareholder to make some form of demand before filing a derivative claim. A proper pre-suit demand typically consists of a written demand to the board of directors articulating the complaint and requesting that the board remedy the complaint through some form of corrective action or that the board file a lawsuit seeking a remedy. The demand requirement reinforces the concept that it is the board of directors that has the authority to manage the corporation and gives the board the opportunity to take corrective action if it determines that the complaints asserted in the demand have merit. In most states, the demand is a common law requirement, having been adopted by the judiciary in keeping with *Hawes*. In many states, and in the federal court, the plaintiff is required to plead, with particularity, the efforts to obtain action by the corporation as part of heightened pleading requirements for a derivative action. For example, Federal Rule of Civil Procedure 23.1 requires a plaintiff to plead that the plaintiff was a shareholder at the time of the transaction or that its status devolved upon the plaintiff by operation of law, that the action is not collusive to confer jurisdiction the court would

---

32. *Id.*
33. *Hawes*, 104 U.S. at 460–61.

otherwise not have, and that the plaintiff made demand or state the reasons it failed to do so.[34]

Consequently, a plaintiff's complaint will not have been plead with sufficient particularity if the plaintiff has failed to plead the making and service of a demand. In other states, like Pennsylvania, the statute specifically requires the making of a demand as a prerequisite to a derivative claim.[35] However, even in federal court pleading, the requirement of a demand is a matter of the substantive law of the state of incorporation. Thus, it is the state law that determines whether a demand is required and, if so, whether the demand was adequate.

The form and adequacy of the demand is rarely defined by rule or statute. Rather, the demand is usually considered sufficient if the board of directors has had a fair opportunity to consider the shareholder's claims in advance of the litigation. It has been stated that a demand "must fairly and adequately apprise the Directors of the potential cause of action so that they, in the first instance, can discharge their duty of authorizing actions that in their considered opinion . . . are in the best interests of the corporation."[36] Some of the details that courts have stated should be in a demand include the identity of the complaining shareholder,[37] the identity of the alleged wrongdoers or prospective defendants,[38] a factual description of the alleged wrongdoing,[39] a description of the resulting harm caused to the corporation,[40] and what relief is requested by the complaining shareholder.[41]

2. The Futility Doctrine

Lisa was especially concerned about the requirement of making demand. Because SOD was a Delaware company, she knew that the requirement of making demand on the board of directors might be excused for "futility" where the making of demand would be futile.

To establish futility in states like Delaware, a litigant must "overcome the powerful presumptions of the business judgment rule."[42] A shareholder must establish that, by alleging particularized facts that

34. Fed. R. Civ. P. 23.1.
35. 15 Pa. Cons. Stat. Ann. § 1781(a)(1).
36. Stoner v. Walsh, 772 F. Supp. 790, 796 (S.D.N.Y. 1991).
37. Smachlo v. Birkelo, 576 F. Supp. 1439, 1444 (D. Del. 1983).
38. Lewis v. Sporck, 646 F. Supp. 574, 578 (N.D. Cal. 1986).
39. Simmonds v. Credit Suisse Sec. (USA) LLC, 638 F.3d 1072 (9th Cir. 2010).
40. Seidel v. Allegis Corp., 702 F. Supp. 1409, 1412 (N.D. Ill. 1989).
41. *Id.*
42. Rails v. Blasband, 634 A.2d 927, 933 (Del. 1993).

there is a reasonable doubt as to "whether the directors are disinterested and independent or whether the challenged transaction was otherwise the product of a valid exercise of business judgment."[43] Specifically, the test for futility is a two-part test: "whether, under the particularized facts alleged, a reasonable doubt is created that . . . the directors are disinterested and independent" or "whether the pleading creates a reasonable doubt that 'the challenged transaction was otherwise the product of a valid exercise of business judgment.'"[44] Demand will be excused if either prong is satisfied.[45] It is important to appreciate the mandate that futility must be plead with particularized facts or a case may be dismissed. The "futility" allegations "must comply with stringent requirements of factual particularity that differ substantially from the permissive notice pleadings governed solely by Chancery Rule 8(a). Rule 23.1 is not satisfied by conclusory statements or mere notice pleading."[46]

However, in some states like Pennsylvania and Texas, there is no futility exception to the demand requirement and failure to make demand can cause the complaint to be dismissed.[47] In Pennsylvania, the demand will not be excused for futility but "only if the plaintiff makes a specific showing that immediate and irreparable harm to the business corporation would otherwise result."[48]

3. The Delaware Dilemma

Lisa Lawyer was right to be concerned. After all, SOD is a Delaware corporation and Delaware has adopted a troubling line of cases that sets a procedural trap for parties seeking redress on behalf of the corporation. Like many states, Delaware recognizes the futility doctrine where a stockholder may sue in the name of the corporation "without prior demand upon the directors to sue, when it is apparent that a demand would be futile, that the officers are under an influence that sterilizes discretion and could not be proper persons to conduct the

---

43. *Id.*

44. Brehm v. Eisner, 746 A.2d 244, 256 (Del. Super. 2000) (quoting Aronson v. Lewis, 473 A.2d 805, 814 (Del. Super. 1984)).

45. *Id.*

46. *Id.* at 254.

47. Cuker v. Mikalauskas, 692 A.2d 1042, 1049, 547 Pa. 600, 613 (Pa. 1997) (adopting §§ 7.02–7.10, and § 7.13 of the ALI Principles of Corporate Governance); Equitec-Cole Roesler LLC v. McClanahan, 251 F. Supp. 2d 1347, 1351 (S.D. Tex. 2003).

48. 15 Pa. Cons. Stat. Ann. § 1781(b).

litigation."[49] Delaware has a heightened pleading standard that provides that only particularized and well-supported allegations will excuse demand.[50] With the heightened pleading standard and risk that the court would not excuse the demand, one might ordinarily conclude that the safer approach is to make demand. Indeed, the demand serves the public policies of exhausting of intra-corporate remedies and possibly avoiding litigation, respecting the board's prerogative to pursue litigation it deems in the best interest of the corporation, and enabling the stockholder to retain control of the litigation only where the corporation wrongfully refuses.[51]

A dilemma arises in Delaware, because the making of demand creates a presumption of independence on the part of the board.[52] A demand is treated as a concession that the directors are independent and disinterested. This presumption, while consistent with the policy of judicial noninterference with the management of a corporation, is at odds with the public policy of exhausting intra-corporate remedies with the aim of avoiding costly lawsuits.[53]

4. Board Response to Demand

a. Remedy the Wrongs

Upon receipt of a demand, the board of directors has a variety of options available to it. First and most obviously, it can take action to remedy the alleged wrongs. In Sam Shareholder's case, this could mean

---

49. McKee v. Rogers 156 A. 191, 193 (Del. Ch. 1931).

50. Del. Ct. Ch. R. 23.1(a) ("The complaint shall also allege with particularity the efforts, if any, made by the plaintiff to obtain the action the plaintiff desires from the directors or comparable authority and the reasons for the plaintiff's failure to obtain the action or for not making the effort."); *see also* Aronson v. Lewis, 473 A.2d 805, 812 (Del. 1984) (reversed on other grounds).

51. Brehm v. Eisner, 746 A.2d at 255 (Del. 2000) (quoting Grimes v. Donald, 673 A.2d at 1216–17). *See also* 473 A.2d at 809 ("Rule 23.1 is a rule of substantive right designed to give a corporation the opportunity to rectify an alleged wrong without litigation, and to control any litigation which does arise.").

52. Charal Inv. Co., Inc. v. Rockefeller, 1995 WL 684869, at *2 (Del. Ch. 1995) ("If a shareholder makes a demand on the board, rather than pleading that demand is excused, the law presumes that the shareholder concedes the board's ability to make an independent decision on the matter."), Thorpe v. CERBCO, Inc., 611 A.2d 5, 10, 17 Del. J. Corp. L. 1284, 1294–95 (Del. Ch. 1991) (citations omitted) ("But, under the Delaware case law, once a shareholder makes such a demand upon the board to prevent or remedy an alleged breach of duty, the shareholder is deemed to have made an important concession: that the board is able to function on the question.").

53. Brehm v. Eisner, 746 A.2d 244, 255 (Del. 2000).

restoring his employment, restoring his salary with backpay, resuming shareholder meetings and director meetings, providing Sam with company information, and offering him ownership in the real estate and trucking companies. Sam deemed this unlikely.

b. Issue a Response Denying the Allegations of Wrongdoing

Alternatively, the board could issue a response deeming the complaints without merit. This would give the corporation the benefit of claiming that their decision was appropriate under the Business Judgment Rule. This is where the Delaware dilemma comes into play. When the demand is issued, the board is cloaked with a presumption that they are capable of making an independent decision on the matter and the decision is then protected by the Business Judgment Rule.[54] The prospective plaintiff now must rebut the presumption that its demand created and show that the decision not to remedy the complaint or pursue litigation was wrongful.

c. Appoint a Special Litigation Committee

The board can also appoint a "special litigation committee" to investigate the claims, recommend a course of action, and even control the litigation. The appointment of committees and delegation of board duties is a power commonplace in most corporate statutes.[55] Many states have specifically codified the rules related to a special litigation committee.[56] When presented with a pre-suit derivative demand, the board has the right to appoint a committee to investigate or resolve the claims asserted in the demand. The appointment of a special litigation committee can severely truncate the derivative plaintiff's ability to control the litigation. A truly independent special litigation committee can be a powerful tool for the board in responding to, resolving, or terminating derivative claims. One could be forgiven for thinking that a

54. *Charal Inv. Co., Inc.*, 1995 WL 684869, at *2, *Thorpe*, 611 A.2d at 10.

55. *See, e.g.*, Del. Code Ann. tit. 8 § 141.

56. *See, e.g.*, 15 Pa. Cons. Stat. Ann. § 1783 ("If a business corporation or the board of directors receives a demand to bring an action to enforce a right of the corporation, or if a derivative action is commenced before demand has been made on the corporation or the board, the board may appoint a special litigation committee to investigate the claims asserted in the demand or action and to determine on behalf of the corporation or recommend to the board whether pursuing any of the claims asserted is in the best interests of the corporation."); *see also* Fla. Stat. § 605.0804, Ind. Stat. § 23-1-32-4, N.D. Stat. § 10-32.1-37 N.J. Stat. 42:2C-71, Tenn. Stat. § 61-3-905.

special litigation committee is a "use-it-or-lose-it" tool upon receiving the demand. Such is not the case. Courts have permitted the board to convene a special litigation committee well into the litigation and permitted the committee to take over control of the litigation. A derivative plaintiff may be precluded from voluntarily dismissing the case when a special litigation committee has been appointed even after the case was instituted and seeks to a judgment in the board's favor.[57] In the *Oracle Corp. Derivative Litigation*, the company formed a special litigation committee just days before the answer was filed.[58] The plaintiff then moved to dismiss the case and the Chancery Court denied the motion, finding that a dismissal at the behest of the derivative plaintiff would undermine the discretion of the special litigation committee's "statutory authority to manage the corporation's affairs, i.e., its right to control litigation brought on behalf of the corporation."[59] Conversely, "Board members, owing a well-established fiduciary duty to the corporation, will not be allowed to cause a derivative suit to be dismissed when it would be a breach of their fiduciary duty."[60] However, the limitations on a corporation's ability to control or dismiss litigation when the board has appointed a special litigation committee are narrow. The special litigation committee has broad powers. The Delaware Supreme Court has held:

> [w]e do not think that the interest taint of the board majority is *per se* a legal bar to the delegation of the board's power to an independent committee composed of disinterested board members. The committee can properly act for the corporation to move to dismiss derivative litigation that is believed to be detrimental to the corporation's best interest.[61]

Thus the special litigation committee is a powerful tool in the defense of derivative claims.

IV. Settlement of a Derivative Action

One major drawback of the derivative lawsuit is the lack of autonomy that a plaintiff has in settling the lawsuit. Court approval is usually

57. *In re* Oracle Corp. Derivative Litig., 808 A.2d 1206, 1214 (Del. Ch. 2002).
58. *Id.*
59. *Id.* at 1212.
60. Zapata Corp. v. Maldonado, 430 A.2d 779, 783 (Del. 1981).
61. *Id.* at 786.

required for the settlement of a derivative action.[62] In Delaware, the Chancery Court Rules provide:

> The action shall not be dismissed or compromised without the approval of the Court, and notice by mail, publication or otherwise of the proposed dismissal or compromise shall be given to shareholders or members in such manner as the Court directs; except that if the dismissal is to be without prejudice or with prejudice to the plaintiff only, then such dismissal shall be ordered without notice thereof if there is a showing that no compensation in any form has passed directly or indirectly from any of the defendants to the plaintiff or plaintiff's attorney and that no promise to give any such compensation has been made.[63]

Similarly, the Federal Rules of Civil Procedure provide: "A derivative action may be settled, voluntarily dismissed, or compromised only with the court's approval. Notice of a proposed settlement, voluntary dismissal, or compromise must be given to shareholders or members in the manner that the court orders."[64] States without an express rule have judicially declared that a derivative action requires court approval for settlement.

Typically, a derivative plaintiff is seeking a remedy for his/herself such as a forced buyout or a dissolution of the corporation. However, if the derivative plaintiff is representing a group of similarly situated shareholders, which is usually the case except in companies with only a few shareholders, the resolution must serve the interests of all. Consequently, a settlement is more complicated. For example, a buyout is often not an appropriate remedy. Some states, including Delaware, are very reluctant to award a buyout or a dissolution as a remedy in a derivative action.[65] Other states have approved dissolutions or buyouts in the context of a derivative action.[66] In companies with fewer shareholders, however, a derivative suit may often be a means to force a buyout or dissolution.

In the event of a monetary settlement, the settlement of a derivative lawsuit is always paid to the corporation.[67] Payment of monetary remedy

62. Fed. R. Civ. P. 23.1(c), Del. Ct. Ch. R. 23.1(c); N.Y. Bus. Corp. L. § 626(d).

63. Del. Ct. Ch. R. 23.1(c).

64. Fed. R. Civ. P. 23.1 (c).

65. *In re* Arrow Inv. Advisors, LLC, 2009 WL 1101682, at *5 (Del. Ch. 2009).

66. *See, e.g.*, Cortes v. 3A North Park Ave. Rest Corp., 998 N.Y.S.2d 797, 820 (N.Y. Sup. Ct. 2014).

67. *Tooley*, 845 A.2d at 1036.

to the corporation does not always result in a direct benefit to the complaining shareholder. Reimbursement by a director or officer to the corporation does not require the corporation to then make a distribution of the proceeds. This is a considerable deterrent to a prospective plaintiff in a derivative action who will be required to fund the cost of the litigation with no guarantee of a recovery or return on the investment of time and money in a litigation.

As mentioned earlier, litigants are required to notify the other shareholders of the prospective settlement before presenting same to court so that the nonparty shareholders will have an opportunity to object or be heard.[68] To satisfy due process, the notice "must be sufficiently informative and give sufficient opportunity for response."[69] The notice requirements, however, are often less rigorous than those required for the settlement of a class action lawsuit.[70]

Approval of a derivative settlement requires the court to determine that the proposed settlement is both procedurally and substantially fair. "A court reviewing a proposed settlement must pay close attention to the negotiating process, to ensure that the settlement resulted from arms-length negotiations and that the Plaintiff's counsel have possessed the experience and ability and have engaged in the discovery necessary to effective representation of the class' interest."[71] The court must scrutinize the proposed settlement to determine that it is fair, reasonable, and adequate.[72]

V. Conclusion

After a lengthy discussion with Sam, Lisa decides she has enough information to assert prima facie fiduciary duty and contract claims against Olivia and Dave that will survive a motion to dismiss. She decides to send a statutory demand for information but will forego filing a summary action to enforce the information request if Olivia and Dave refuse to comply in order to avoid the delay and expense of a separate action. She is confident she can get to the bottom of the office and

68. Fed. R. Civ. P. 23.1 (c), Bell Atlantic Corp. v. Bolger, 2 F.3d 1304, 1317 (3d Cir. 1993), Maher v. Zapata Corp., 714 F.2d 436, 450 (5th Cir. 1983).

69. Kyriazi v. W. Elec. Co., 647 F.2d 388, 395 (3d Cir. 1981).

70. *In re* UnitedHealth Group Inc. Shareholder Derivative Litig., 591 F. Supp. 2d 1023, 1030 (D. Minn. 2008).

71. D'Amato v. Deutsche Bank, 236 F.3d 78, 85 (2d Cir. 2001) (quoting Weinberger v. Kendrick, 698 F.2d 61, 74 (2d Cir. 1982)).

72. *In re* Caremark Intern. Inc. Derivative Litig., 698 A.2d 959, 966 (Del. Ch. 1996).

trucking company ownership as well as any additional claims that Sam does not even know about in the discovery phase of a substantive action. Lisa has also decided that she is not going to make demand because it would be futile, and she is confident that she will be able to articulate particularized facts that will show that Olivia and Dave could not be independent or objective in the face of a demand to sue themselves. Although Lisa would have liked to make a demand to explore whether Olivia and Dave would recant their aggression toward Sam and enter into a dialogue that might help avoid costly litigation, she is not willing to concede a presumption that Olivia and Dave could independently and objectively assess the claims against themselves. So, Lisa will schedule Sam to come into her office to go through the "particularized" facts in great detail, as that will be necessary to sustain the claimed futility of a demand. If Olivia and Dave refuse to comply with the information request, that will be another fact that will support the claim of futility as well as the substantive claims. For a deeper understanding of which of Sam's claims are direct and which are derivative and what are dual-natured claims, Lisa decides to read on to Chapter 3. Lisa is getting the distinct feeling that she will be missing a lot of tennis in the near future!

Chapter 3

Dual Direct and Derivative Claims

By Lawrence D. Rosenberg

You might think, after reading Chapter 2, that Lisa Lawyer has to choose whether to assert direct or derivative claims against Dave Director based on his breach of fiduciary duty to Sam Shareholder. Under certain circumstances, however, it may be possible for Lisa Lawyer to raise both direct and derivative claims from the same conduct or transaction. Not only can asserting both direct and derivative claims increase the chances for Lisa Lawyer to recover for her client, asserting both direct and derivative claims can allow Lisa Lawyer to bypass certain procedural requirements of derivative claims that savvy defense counsel often use to derail cases prior to trial. However, it is important to note that the Delaware Supreme Court recently and significantly changed the law applicable to such claims in certain contexts.[1]

I. Direct versus Derivative Claims

As Chapter 2 explained, under the seminal *Tooley* case, a claim is direct if Sam Shareholder (rather than the corporation) "suffered the harm" complained of and Sam Shareholder (rather than the corporation) would "benefit" from the "remedy."[2] As a result, shareholders "'with a

1. Brookfield Asset Mgmt., inc. v. Rosson, 261 A.3d 1251 (Del. Sept. 20, 2021), *overruling* Gentile v. Rosette, 906 A.2d 91 (Del. 2006).

2. *See, e.g.*, Tooley v. Donaldson, Lufkin & Jenrette, 845 A.2d 1031, 1033 (Del. 2004). *See also In re* Terraform Power, Inc., 2020 WL 6375859, at *8 (Del. Ch. Oct. 30, 2020) ("In Tooley v. Donaldson, Lufkin & Jenrette, Inc., the Delaware Supreme Court held that the determination of whether a stockholder's claim is direct or derivative 'must turn solely on the following questions: (1) who suffered the alleged harm (the corporation or the suing

direct personal interest in a cause of action' . . . can bring actions directly."[3] The touchstone of a direct (rather than a derivative) claim is that a direct claim involves "harm unique to the stockholders."[4] For a direct claim, a stockholder must therefore demonstrate that "she can prevail without showing an injury to the corporation."[5] The requirement that the shareholder sustain a "direct injury" that is "independent of any alleged injury to the corporation" does not, however, require that there be absolutely no harm to the corporation as a whole.[6] Instead, all that is necessary is that the damage to Sam Shareholder be different from Sam Shareholder's pro rata share of any damage to the company as a whole. A shareholder therefore has a direct harm if he suffered "some individualized harm not suffered by all of the stockholders at large."[7] Disadvantaged shareholders are injured directly, for example, when they are denied "the right to a pro rata share of the common property,"[8] and when controlling shareholders opt to "pay dividends only to themselves."[9]

A derivative claim, in contrast, is "founded on a right of action existing in the corporation" and is one "in which the corporation itself is the appropriate plaintiff."[10] As a result, if "each . . . shareholder was affected in a proportional measure,"[11] the claim is derivative. Where all of a corporation's stockholders are harmed and would recover pro rata in proportion with their ownership of the corporation's stock solely because they are stockholders, then the claim is derivative. More precisely, when not all of the shareholders are harmed in the same way, pro rata, the harm is direct, but when they are all harmed pro rata, the harm is likely derivative but might not be.[12] So, for example,

---

stockholders, individually); and (2) who would receive the benefit of any recovery or other remedy (the corporation or the stockholders, individually)?'") (footnotes omitted), *rev'd on other grounds by Rosson*, 261 A.3d 1251; Citigroup, Inc. v. AHW Inv. P'ship, 140 A.3d 1125, 1126–27 (Del. 2016) (examining whether the claim "belong[s] to the stockholder").

3. Starr Int'l Co. v. United States, 856 F.3d 953, 966 (Fed. Cir. 2017) (quoting Franchise Tax Bd. of Calif. v. Alcan Aluminum Ltd., 493 U.S. 331, 336 (1990)).

4. *In re* Nine Sys. Corp. Shareholders Litig., No. CIV.A. 3940-VCN, 2014 WL 4383127, at *22 (Del. Ch. Sept. 4, 2014).

5. *Terraform*, 2020 WL 6375859, at *9.

6. *Tooley*, 845 A.2d at 1039.

7. Feldman v. Cutaia, 951 A.2d 727, 733 (Del. 2008).

8. S. Pac. Co. v. Bogert, 250 U.S. 483, 487 (1919).

9. 12B Fletcher Cyclopedia of the Law of Corps. § 5922.

10. Daily Income Fund, Inc. v. Fox, 464 U.S. 523, 528 (1984) (internal quotation marks omitted).

11. *Starr*, 856 F.3d at 964 n.16.

12. *See Tooley*, 845 A.2d at 1037 (stating that, although "an injury to the corporation tends to diminish each share of stock equally," a "direct, individual claim of stockholders

a claim alleging corporate overpayments to controlling shareholders usually gives rise to derivative claims,[13] because the shareholder's damage is "merely" the unavoidable result of the reduction in the value of the entire corporate entity. Similarly, a claim that the corporation's funds were wrongfully depleted as a result of an overpayment for shares,[14] or that there was a loss of profits through a diminution in the value of their stock or through foregone dividends,[15] constitutes a derivative claim.

II. What Is a Control Group?

Until recently, a key consideration for bringing both direct and derivative claims has been whether the so-called "dual-nature" doctrine of Gentile v. Rossette[16] was implicated. Under that doctrine, overpayment for a corporate asset could give rise to *both* direct and derivative claims, if a controller or "control group" gained or "expropriated" equity at the expense of the equity of minority shareholders; in other words, if new money came into the corporation from the "control group," and that group unfairly increased its own equity stake in the company at the expense of the minority shareholders, that could give rise to both a derivative claim for diluting the value of the company's stock and a direct claim for the expropriation of the minority shareholders' equity.[17] But who, exactly, is a member of the control group? Obviously, the majority shareholder (or a number of shareholders, acting in concert, who collectively own the majority of a company's shares) is a member of (or is) the control group. For example, multiple shareholders can constitute a control group if they "work[] together to use their board control and status as significant stockholders to cause [the company] to engage in" self-dealing transactions in which the company treats the minority shareholders unfairly.[18] With that being said, "'control' does not necessarily require the self-dealing party to be a pre-existing

---

that does not depend on harm to the corporation can also fall on all stockholders equally, without the claim thereby becoming" derivative).

13. *See, e.g., Terraform*, 2020 WL 6375859, at *9.

14. *See* Protas v. Cavanagh, 2012 WL 1580969, at *6 (Del. Ch. May 4, 2012).

15. *See* Hometown Fin., Inc. v. U.S., 56 Fed. Cl. 477, 486 (2003).

16. 906 A.2d 91 (Del. 2006).

17. *Gentile*, 906 A.2d at 99–101.

18. *See, e.g.*, Carsanaro v. Bloodhound Techs., Inc., 65 A.3d 618, 658–59 (Del. Ch. 2013); *see also* Patel v. Duncan, 2021 WL 4482157, at *10–*11 (Del Ch. Oct. 4, 2021).

majority stockholder."[19] Instead, a control group could arise (or be created) when a number of shareholders decide to act together.

> Delaware case law has recognized that a number of shareholders, each of whom individually cannot exert control over the corporation (either through majority ownership or significant voting power coupled with formidable managerial power), can collectively form a control group where those shareholders are connected in some legally significant way—e.g., by contract, common ownership, agreement, or some other arrangement—to work together toward a shared goal.[20]

A control group could therefore be shown by "some arrangement among the Entity Defendants to act as a control group,"[21] an agreement "to work together to bring about" the Self-Dealing Transactions,[22] "an agreement or that the Defendants were tied together in some legally significant way,"[23] or a "common undertaking among the Entity Defendants."[24] Similarly, two significant shareholders, neither holding a majority, can constitute a control group if they appointed at least some (but not the majority) of the corporation's directors, and control the board's decisions through their business relationships.[25] This is because such shareholders would be "in a controlling position [and they could have] exploited that control for their own benefit."[26] Because control

19. *Starr*, 856 F.3d at 969.

20. Dubroff v. Wren Holdings, LLC, 2009 WL 1478697, at *3 (Del. Ch. May 22, 2009); *Nine Sys.*, 2014 WL 4383127, at *24 ("A group of stockholders, none of whom individually qualifies as a controlling stockholder, may collectively be considered a control group that is analogous, for standard of review purposes, to a controlling stockholder") (quoting Frank v. Elgamal, No. CIV.A 6120-VCN, 2014 WL 957550, at *18 (Del. Ch. Mar. 10, 2014)).

21. *Dubroff*, 2009 WL 1478697, at *3; *Elgamal*, 2014 WL 957550, at *19 (finding defendants "may have been united in interest through the arrangement contemplated by" a letter and thus could have constituted a control group).

22. *Dubroff*, 2009 WL 1478697, at *4; Silverberg v. Padda, No. CV 2017-0250-KSJM, 2019 WL 4566909, at *6 (Del. Ch. Sept. 19, 2019) ("The law does not require a formal written agreement, but there must be some indication of an actual agreement.") (quotation omitted).

23. *Dubroff*, 2009 WL 1478697, at *4; Nine Sys., 2014 WL 4383127, at *24 ("plaintiff must prove that the group of stockholders was connected in some legally significant way") (quotation omitted).

24. *Dubroff*, 2009 WL 1478697, at *5 n.36; *see In re* Hansen Med., Inc. S'holders Litig., No. CV 12316-VCMR, 2018 WL 3025525, at *7 (Del. Ch. June 18, 2018).

25. Williamson v. Cox Commc'ns, Inc., 2006 WL 1586375 (Del. Ch. June 5, 2006).

26. *Williamson*, 2006 WL 1586375, at *6. With that being said, not every entity that can appoint a board member is part of the control group. *See, e.g.*, Zimmerman v. Crothall, 62 A.3d 676, 700 (Del. Ch. 2013) (finding that the alleged controlling shareholders

can be shown "with regard to the particular transaction that is being challenged,"[27] it is possible for a group of shareholders (or shareholders and board members) to constitute a control group for some purposes, but not for others.

Although there are a large number of combinations or fact patterns that could lead a court to conclude that a control group exists, "Delaware law has consistently held that a party has control only if it acts as a fiduciary, such as a majority stockholder or insider director or actually exercises direction over the business and affairs of the corporation."[28] This contrasts with an "outside third part[y] with leverage," neither having a fiduciary duty nor actually exercising direction over the company's conduct.[29] Simply put, leverage does not equal control unless it is both sufficient to, and is in fact used to, direct corporate action.

III. Do Alterations in a Company's Capital Structure Give Rise to Direct or Derivative Claims?

Changes to the capital structure of a company that harm certain current shareholders and benefit others (whether or not those benefited are current shareholders) are direct, rather than derivative, claims. This is because, by definition, such changes (which may not even harm the corporation) do not harm all shareholders pro rata. Pro rata harm to shareholders is a necessary prerequisite for a claim to be derivative.[30] Additionally, although the reallocation of voting power among

held two of the board's five seats, and that no evidence showed that they "acted together" or "were connected in some legally significant way"); Dawson v. Pittco Capital Partners, 2012 WL 1564805 (Del. Ch. Apr. 30, 2012) (finding that only two of the six alleged control group members stood on both sides of the complained-of merger; defendants sought an independent valuation; defendants notified the plaintiffs in advance of the merger and provided an opportunity to vote on it); Feldman v. Cutaia, 956 A.2d 644, 657–58 (Del. Ch. 2007), *aff'd*, 951 A.2d 727 (Del. 2008) (finding no facts providing any reasonable inference that defendants acted in concert, and finding that all stockholders received the same prior knowledge of an opportunity to participate in the relevant transactions, and that a "great number" of them did); Emerson Radio Corp. v. Int'l Jensen Inc., 1996 WL 483086, at *2, *17 (Del. Ch. Aug. 20, 1996) (finding that the two allegedly controlling shareholders each held one seat on the board; they merely voted against a proposal by the plaintiff).

27. *Williamson*, 2006 WL 1586375, at *4.

28. *Starr*, 856 F.3d at 969.

29. *Id.*

30. El Paso Pipeline GP Co. v. Brinckerhoff, 152 A.3d 1248, 1261 (Del. 2016).

shareholders does not harm the corporation, it does harm the (now disadvantaged) shareholders. This is true even if the harmed shareholders were already in the minority.[31]

More than 60 years ago, in a portion of a dissent with which the majority did not disagree (nor has the Supreme Court since), Justice Frankfurter stated that "[I]f a corporation rearranges the relationship of different classes of security holders to the detriment of one class, a stockholder in the disadvantaged class may proceed against the corporation as a defendant to protect his own legal interest."[32] Courts have consistently followed Justice Frankfurter's lead since that time.[33] As a result, if the conduct of the controlling shareholders imposes distinct harms on the minority stockholders, the minority stockholders can maintain a direct action.[34]

The rearrangement of a company's capital structure contrasts with situations in which a company issues new shares. This is because newly issued equity necessarily results in an equal dilution of the economic value and voting power of the corporation's outstanding shares, which is a defining feature of a derivative claim.[35] "[A]ny dilution in value of the corporation's stock is merely the unavoidable result . . . of the reduction in the value of the entire corporate entity, of which each share of equity represents an equal fraction."[36] As a result, it is unequal dilution, rather than just dilution, that gives rise to a direct claim.

---

31. *See Gentile*, 906 A.2d 91 at 101–02 (holding that a reduction in voting power does not need to be material, and does not have to drop the shareholder from majority to minority, to be actionable). The *Gentile* court reached this holding because "A rule that focuses on the degree or extent of the expropriation, and requires that the expropriation attain a certain level before the minority stockholders may seek a judicial remedy directly, denigrates the gravity of the fiduciary breach and condones overreaching by fiduciaries." *Gentile*, 906 A.2d at 102.

32. Swanson v. Traer, 354 U.S. 91, 99 (1957) (Frankfurter, J., dissenting).

33. *See, e.g.*, Strougo v. Bassini, 282 F.3d 162, 175 (2d Cir. 2002); Jones v. H.F. Ahmanson & Co., 460 P.2d 464, 466–72 (Cal. 1969); Deephaven Risk Arb. Trading Ltd. v. UnitedGlobalCom, Inc., 2005 WL 1713067, at *8 & n.41 (Del. Ch. July 13, 2005); Acker v. Transurgical, Inc., 2004 WL 1230945, at *1 (Del. Ch. Apr. 22, 2004); Fletcher, supra note 8, § 5908 (reciting among examples of direct claims shareholder challenges to "recapitalization, redemption, or similar transactions unfairly affect[ing] minority shareholders").

34. *See* Alleghany Corp. v. Breswick & Co., 353 U.S. 151, 158 (1957). *See also* Pittsburgh & W.V. Ry. Co. v. U.S., 281 U.S. 479, 487 (1930) (explaining that cases of "reorganization . . . deal with the interests of investors" and thus are proper subjects for direct suits).

35. *See Starr*, 856 F.3d at 967 (quoting *Gentile*, 906 A.2d at 100).

36. *Id.*

IV. Under Current Law, When Can Lisa Lawyer Bring Both Direct and Derivative Claims?

Despite the number of cases deciding whether a particular claim is direct or derivative, "courts have long recognized that the same set of facts can give rise both to a direct claim and a derivative claim."[37] As the American Law Institute has put it, "a direct action is not precluded simply because the facts also give rise to a derivative action."[38] Instead, "the same set of facts can give rise both to a direct claim and a derivative claim."[39] Thus, so long as Sam Shareholder suffered direct injuries, he can maintain direct claims without regard to whether the company was also harmed.

A. Under the *Gentile* dual nature doctrine, if a controlling shareholder or group harmed the corporation but, in so doing, also harmed some shareholders for the benefit of the others, the harmed shareholders had a direct claim, even though a claim on behalf of the harmed corporation also exists.[40] More specifically, a claim was both direct and derivative under the *Gentile* doctirne if "(1) the stockholder having majority or effective control causes the corporation to issue 'excessive' shares of its stock in exchange for assets of the controlling stockholder that have a lesser value" (that is, a member of the control group harms the company), and "(2) the exchange causes an increase in the percentage of the outstanding shares owned by the controlling stockholder, and a corresponding decrease in the share percentage owned by the [minority] shareholders" (that is, the member of the control group ensures that the harm to the company does not fall on all shareholders pro rata).[41]

---

37. Grimes v. Donald, 673 A.2d 1207, 1212 (Del. 1996). *See also* Pareto v. FDIC, 139 F.3d 696, 699 (9th Cir. 1998) (observing that "an action may lie both derivatively and individually based on the same conduct"); U.S. Cellular Inv. Co. v. Sw. Bell Mobile Sys., Inc., 124 F.3d 218 (10th Cir. 1997) (table) (noting that "the same set of facts may result in direct and derivative claims"); Borak v. J.I. Case Co., 317 F.2d 838, 844–45 (7th Cir. 1963), *aff'd*, 377 U.S. 426, 431 (1964).

38. American Law Institute: Principles of Corporate Governance § 7.01(c), cmt. F.

39. *Grimes*, 673 A.2d at 1212. *See also* Branzan Alternative Inv. Fund, LLLP v. Bank of New York Mellon Tr., 2015 WL 5693562, at *3 (D. Colo. Sept. 29, 2015) (explaining that under Delaware law "one set of facts may give rise to two separate harms and thus two separate claims, one derivative and the other direct").

40. *See, e.g.*, *Gatz*, 925 A.2d at 1278.

41. *Starr*, 856 F.3d at 968 (quoting *Gentile*, 906 A.2d at 100); *see also Gatz*, 925 A.2d at 1278.

In *Gentile*[42] the Delaware Supreme Court used the dual nature doctrine to hold that "[t]here is . . . at least one transactional paradigm—a species of corporate overpayment claim—that Delaware case law recognizes as being both derivative and direct in character."[43] *Carsanaro*[44] clarified that this type of corporate overpayment claim could be brought in two scenarios. The first was when a control group exists: "Standing will exist if a controlling stockholder stood on both sides of the transaction."[45] The second was in the absence of a disinterested and independent majority of the board: "Standing will also exist if the board that effectuated the transaction lacked a disinterested and independent majority."[46] "[T]he Delaware Supreme Court's decisions preserve stockholder standing to pursue individual challenges to self-interested stock issuances when the facts alleged support an actionable claim for breach of the duty of loyalty."[47]

The *Carsanaro* court observed that the Supreme Court's decisions "do not support" the limitation of "*Gentile*'s expropriation principle" to cases involving a majority stockholder.[48] Instead, *Carsanaro* held that "the core insight of dual injury" can apply to certain "non- controller issuances in which insiders participate."[49] In those cases, the "expropriation principle operates"—because "defendant fiduciaries (i) had the ability to use the levers of corporate opportunity to benefit themselves and (ii) took advantage of the opportunity"—even though plaintiffs may not be able to prove a control group.[50]

B. However, an erosion of the dual-nature doctrine of *Gentile* was suggested by the Delaware Supreme Court's decision in *El Paso Pipeline GP Co. v. Brinckerhoff*.[51] The court in *El Paso Pipeline* held, based on a limited-partnership agreement, that a limited partner's claim of overpayment against the general partner was not direct but rather belonged to the partnership. Initially, then, the case turned (in relevant part) on whether and how to apply *Tooley* and extend the rule of *Gentile*, developed as background law for corporations, "in the limited-partnership context"—in which (1) conflicts of interest between the

42. 906 A.2d 91.

43. *Id.* at 99–100; *see also Terraform*, 2020 WL 6375859, at *1.

44. 65 A.3d 618 (Del. Ch. 2013). *See also Terraform*, 2020 WL 6375859, at *14 (discussing *Carsanaro*'s attempts to reconcile case law, and whether it has been abrogated).

45. *Carsanaro*, 65 A.3d at 658.

46. *Id.*

47. *Id.*

48. *Id.* (citations omitted).

49. *Id.*

50. *Id.* at 658–59.

51. 152 A.3d 1248 (Del. 2016).

general partner and limited partners are inherent; (2) any duties owed to the limited partners are purely contractual, not common-law fiduciary duties such as the duties that corporate directors, officers, and controllers bear; and (3) that contract (the partnership agreement) determines both how to address the inherent conflicts of interest and who has a given cause of action.[52]

More to the point, the limited partner only alleged loss to the partnership, and, thus, any harm he suffered was just "in the form of the proportionally reduced value of his units."[53] The Delaware Supreme Court emphasized this, drawing on the general rule in the corporate context: "Where all of a corporation's stockholders are harmed and would recover *pro rata* in proportion with their ownership of the corporation's stock solely because they are stockholders, then the claim is derivative."[54] Indeed, the case had gone to trial, and the limited partner "presented evidence of harm *only* as to the Partnership, not to the individual unitholders."[55]

Another facet of *El Paso Pipeline* that bears mentioning is its discussion of loss of control and voting power as possible elements of a direct or dual nature claim. There, the limited partner did not allege "that the Partnership's overpayment increased the General Partner's or the Parent's control at the expense of the limited partners."[56] In "declin[ing] to further expand [the dual-nature claim doctrine] in the limited partner-ship context," the court emphasized that "there was no plausible argument that the transaction had the effect of increasing the voting power or control of the general partner at the expense of the unaffiliated unit-holders. From the start, the derivative plaintiff has sought only mone-tary relief for the limited partnership."[57]

In the context of an overpayment claim that did not even include an allegation (much less proof) of harm to the limited partner distinct from harm to the partnership, it made sense to highlight the absence of loss of control as well. Similarly, in the context of a claim by a common stockholder, if there were a loss of voting power, that would be a simple way to show a harm that the stockholder suffered independently

---

52. *Id.* at 1251; *see id.* at 1260 ("[C]ases involving limited partnerships often present unique facts relating to the provisions and structure of the limited partnership agreement and how it defines the rights and responsibilities of the limited partners.").

53. *El Paso Pipeline*, 152 A.3d at 1261.

54. *Id.*

55. 152 A.3d at 1261; *see also id.* at 1265 ("Brinckerhoff never presented evidence at trial of specific harm suffered by the limited partners, as the Court of Chancery stated.").

56. *Id.* at 1264.

57. *Id.* at 1251.

of any harm to the corporation (and that did not harm every shareholder proportionally). Reallocation of voting power among shareholders does not harm the corporation, whereas, as discussed earlier, reallocation of economic value among shareholders might be accompanied by (even if not depending on) harm to the corporation, presenting a less clear picture. But an indicator is not a requirement; it can be sufficient without being necessary.

Indeed, the Delaware Supreme Court in *Gentile* had expressly and unanimously rejected the Chancery Court's holding in that case that a reduction in voting power needs to be "material," meaning dropping from majority to minority.[58] It explained: "A rule that focuses on the degree or extent of the expropriation, and requires that the expropriation attain a certain level before the minority stockholders may seek a judicial remedy directly, denigrates the gravity of the fiduciary breach and condones overreaching by fiduciaries."[59] Yet, reducing voting power that already is in the minority means reducing voting power that is *useless* for controlling the company (particularly when, as in *Gentile* itself, a majority shareholder exists).[60] So loss of "control" could not be the real question. Rather, a loss of (even noncontrolling) voting power is a marginal piece of the plaintiff's overall discriminatory, and thus direct, eco-nomic injury. The cases' evidentiary observations—describing all that happens when a common shareholder suffers expropriation—do not establish a requirement for a court to acknowledge a direct or dual-nature claim. Indeed, if voting power were essential, holders of preferred stock without voting rights could not bring a dual-nature claim. But Delaware law permitted such claims.[61]

C. Notably, however, the erosion of the *Gentile* doctrine that *El Paso Pipeline* signaled became complete in September 2021, when the Delaware Supreme Court expressly overruled *Gentile* in *Brookfield Asset Management Inc v. Rosson*.[62] There, the Court strongly reaffirmed the test for direct and derivative claims set forth in *Tooley*: "Under the *Tooley* test, the determination of whether a stockholder's claim is direct or derivative 'must turn *solely* on the following questions: (1) who

58. 906 A.2d at 101–02.

59. *Id.* at 102.

60. *Id.* at 95.

61. *See* MCG Capital Corp. v. Maginn, 2010 WL 1782271, at *13 (Del. Ch. May 5, 2010) (applying the same dual-nature test to preferred stock with no voting rights); see also Oliveira v. Sugarman, 152 A.3d 728, 747–79 (Md. 2017) (recognizing that, under Delaware law, a direct claim exists "when minority shareholders have suffered a substantial decrease in the value of their stock due to share dilution" for the benefit of a majority shareholder).

62. 261 A.2d 1251.

suffered the alleged harm (the corporation or the stockholders, individually); and (2) who would receive the benefit of any recovery or other remedy (the corporation or the stockholders, individually?'"[63]

Rosson involved claims that the corporation had paid an insufficient price for a large amount of stock sold to the majority shareholder.[64]After minority shareholders brought suit, raising both direct and derivative claims, affiliates of the majority shareholder executed a merger though which they acquired all outstanding shares of stock not already held by the majority shareholder.[65]Accordingly, the derivative claims were extinguished, as the former minority shareholders no longer owned stock in the corporation.[66] The Court of Chancery held that the minority shareholders stated a direct, dual-nature claim of expropriation of their equity interests under *Gentile*.[67]

But the Delaware Supreme Court reversed. It first explained that the question of standing to sue is "properly viewed as a threshold issue 'to ensure that the litigation before the tribunal is a "case or controversy" that is appropriate for the exercise of the court's judicial powers.'"[68] The Court then reasoned that "Dilution is a typical result of a corporation's raising funds through the issuance of new shares. As the Court in *Gentile* recognized, normally such equal 'injury' to the shares resulting from a corporate overpayment is not equated to a specific, individual harm to stockholders. Here, the economic and voting power dilution that allegedly harmed the stockholders flowed indirectly to them in proportion to, and via, their shares in [the corporation], and thus any remedy should flow to them the same way, derivatively via the corporation."[69] The Court reasoned that *Gentile* was effectively a carve-out from *Tooley* that improperly focused on the identity of the "wrongdoer."[70] "The focus on the alleged wrongdoer deviates from *Tooley's* determination which turns solely on the two central inquiries of who suffered the harm and who would receive the benefit of any recovery."[71]

The Court in *Rosson* also reasoned that the *Gentile* doctrine wasn't really necessary, as most claims that were direct under that doctrine could be brought as direct claims under other doctrines of Delaware

63. *Id.* at 1263 (quoting *Tooley*, 845 A.2d at 1033).
64. *Rosson*, 261 A.2d at 1259.
65. *Id.* at 1260.
66. *Id.*
67. *Id.* at 260–61.
68. *Id.* at 1262 (quoting *El Paso Pipeline*, 152 A.3d at 1256 (quoting Dover Historical Soc'y v. City of Dover Planning Comm'n, 838 A.2d 1103, 1110 (Del. 2003)).
69. *Id.* at 1266.
70. *Id.* at 1274.
71. *Id.* at 1274.

law. The Court noted that the *Revlon* doctrine "already accords a direct claim to stockholders when a transaction shifts control of a company for a diversified investor base to a single controlling stockholder."[72] The Court also noted that "'equity holders confronted by a merger in which derivative claims will pass to the buyer have the right to challenge the merger itself as a breach of the duties they are owed.'"[73]

D. So where does this leave the dual-nature doctrine? It still exists, although in a somewhat different form. While the *Gentile* model of dual-nature corporate overpayment claim no longer automatically gives rise to direct claims, they may still exist depending on the circumstances.

First, if shareholders have a claim of harm that is independent of a harm to the corporation, then they should have direct claims under *Tooley*. As noted above, a rearrangement of the capital structure of the corporation, which simply increases the equity of one class of stock at the expense of another class is a classic case of harm to stockholders independent of harm to the corporation.[74] And other unique harms such as transferring stockholders' rights to receive dividends and/or liquidation preferences should also give rise to direct claims under *Tooley*.[75] These harms should be able to give rise to direct claims under *Tooley*, even if the corporation is also harmed by the conduct at issue. Take, for instance, a transaction where corporate assets are sold to a controlling shareholder for an unfairly low price, and in the same transaction the minority shareholders' rights to receive dividends are extinguished. There may exist a derivative claim (or potentially direct claims if there is a merger) to challenge the sale of assets at an unfairly low price, but also direct claims for extinguishing the minority shareholders' rights to receive dividends.

Second, direct claims may also exist if there is a transaction in which a control group dilutes the equity of the minority shareholders and *no new money or assets are added to the corporation*. After all, *Gentile* dealt with *corporate overpayment* claims where new money or assets were added. *Rosson* makes clear that its holding pertains to such claims: "The gravamen of Plaintiffs' Complaint is that the Private Placement alleged harmed the Company by issuing shares to Brookfield for an unfairly low price and harmed stockholders indirectly

---

72. *Id.* at 1276 & n.133 (quoting *El Paso Pipeline*, 152 A.3d at 1266 (Strine, C.J., concurring), referring to Revlon, Inc. v. MacAndrews & Forbes Hldgs., Inc., 506 A.2d 173, 182 (Del. 1986)).

73. *Id.* at 1276 (quoting *El Paso Pipeline*, 152 A.2d at 1252 (citing *Parnes v. Bally Entm't Corp.*, 722 A.2d 1243, 1245 (Del. 1999).

74. *See supra* Part III.

75. *See supra* Part I.

through economic and voting power dilution proportional to their shareholdings."[76] If there is no new money or assets, then there is no dilution proportional to shareholdings, only a transfer of equity from minority shareholders to the control group. That should still give rise to direct claims under *Rosson* and *Tooley*.

Third, of course there are also the *Revlon* and merger claims that the Court in *Rosson* highlighted. If a transaction involves the creation of a controlling shareholder, the now-minority shareholders have the ability to bring a direct claim under *Revlon*. And if a merger will extinguish derivative claims for dilution of equity, the minority shareholders can bring direct claims to challenge the merger. These remedies may be unsatisfying in certain contexts, however. Take, for example, a case in which a control group substantially diluted the minority shareholders' equity with the infusion of a small amount of new money, but did not tell the minority shareholders, and then purported to sell the corporation for a huge profit a few years later, but a profit shared only by the control group .[77] The minority shareholders could presumably bring direct claims to challenge the sale for unfair dealing by the control group. But what if the sale is a great deal for the corporation? A lawsuit to stop the sale might very well eliminate the corporation's best opportunity. In such a circumstance such a direct claim might be ill-advised, but *Rosson* seems to eliminate the alternative of simply bringing a direct claim against the control group. Perhaps future developments will provide an alternative way to proceed in such circumstances.

V. The Benefits of Bringing Both Direct and Derivative Claims

One benefit of a direct claim where there is a control group has been to shift the burden to defendants to prove that the transactions were "entirely fair."[78] "Entire fairness is Delaware's most onerous standard."[79] Indeed, the "entire fairness review invokes a standard so exacting that it ordinarily, but not invariably, results in a finding of liability."[80] In addition to imposing a high standard on defendants, it is the defendants

76. *Rosson*, 261 A.3d at 1268.

77. *See, e.g., In re Nine Sys. Corp.*, 2014 WL 4383127.

78. *Carsanaro*, 65 A.3d at 658–61.

79. Reis v. Hazelett Strip-Casting Corp., 28 A.3d 442, 459 (Del. Ch. 2011).

80. Solomon v. Armstrong, 747 A.2d 1098, 1113 n.39 (Del. Ch. 1999) (citing Nixon v. Blackwell, 626 A.2d 1366, 1376 (Del. 1993)).

who carry the burden to prove entire fairness.[81] Indeed, "[t]o demonstrate entire fairness, the board must present evidence of the cumulative manner by which it discharged all of its fiduciary duties."[82]

"The concept of fairness has two basic aspects: fair dealing and fair price."[83] However, these are not stand-alone inquiries because "the test for fairness is not a bifurcated one as between fair dealing and price."[84] Rather, process and price are viewed in tandem because "process can infect price."[85] On its own, a finding that the price is within the range of fairness "does not satisfy" the entire fairness standard.[86]

Bringing a direct claim also allows a plaintiff to side-step the demand requirement inherent in bringing derivative claims.[87] Although plaintiffs often attempt to sidestep the demand requirement by arguing futility,[88] futility is easier to allege than to prove. And if Lisa Lawyer has the ability to sidestep the demand requirement by invoking the dual nature doctrine, she can defeat the (inevitable) motion to dismiss for failure to make a demand before the motion is even made.

In addition to making a demand (or providing that it would have been futile to make a demand), a derivative plaintiff must own shares

81. *See, e.g.*, Kahn v. Tremont Corp., 694 A.2d 422, 428 (Del. 1997).

82. Emerald Partners v. Berlin, 787 A.2d 85, 97 (Del. 2001).

83. Weinberger v. UOP, Inc., 457 A.2d 701, 711 (Del. 1983).

84. *Id.* at 711.

85. *Reis*, 28 A.3d at 467. *See also Reis*, 28 A.3d at 465 ("Having failed to implement a fair process, the defendants did not serendipitously arrive at a fair price."); *Gentile*, 2010 WL 2171613, at *9 ("From a tainted process, one should not be surprised if a tainted price emerges.").

86. *See Tremont*, 694 A.2d at 432.

87. *See, e.g.*, N.Y. Bus. Corp. L. § 626(c); Del. Ch. Ct. R. 23.1(a).

88. *See, e.g.*, Aronson v. Lewis, 473 A.2d 805, 814 (Del. 1984) (plaintiffs in derivative actions must allege particularized facts which create a "reasonable doubt" that "(1) the directors are disinterested and independent and (2) the challenged transaction was otherwise the product of a valid exercise of business judgment. Hence, the Court of Chancery must make two inquiries, one into the independence and disinterestedness of the directors and the other into the substantive nature of the challenged transaction and the board's approval thereof."); Marx v. Akers, 88 N.Y.2d 189, 200–01 (N.Y. 1996) ("(1) Demand is excused because of futility when a complaint alleges with particularity that a majority of the board of directors is interested in the challenged transaction. Director interest may either be self-interest in the transaction at issue, or a loss of independence because a director with no direct interest in a transaction is 'controlled' by a self-interested director. (2) Demand is excused because of futility when a complaint alleges with particularity that the board of directors did not fully inform themselves about the challenged transaction to the extent reasonably appropriate under the circumstances. The long-standing rule is that a director does not exempt himself from liability by failing to do more than passively rubber-stamp the decisions of the active managers. (3) Demand is excused because of futility when a complaint alleges with particularity that the challenged transaction was so egregious on its face that it could not have been the product of sound business judgment of the directors.").

in the company at the time the wrong occurred and the suit was filed, and must be an appropriate representative for all shareholders.[89] If Sam Shareholder sold his shares (even if motivated by extreme financial need, including the need to pay Lisa Lawyer's bills) it will be fatal to his case as a derivative plaintiff.[90] Even if Sam Shareholder retained his shares until Lisa Lawyer filed suit on his behalf, if he subsequently sold them (again, even if it was to pay Lisa Lawyer's bills), the defendants will almost certainly claim that Sam Shareholder is not an appropriate derivative plaintiff. Even worse (from Lisa Lawyer's perspective), some other lawyer, with some other plaintiff, could claim that they are more appropriate. Even if they shamelessly copied Lisa Lawyer's complaint.

Finally, a derivative suit cannot be settled without court approval.[91] Although most settlements are approved, Lisa Lawyer should not overlook the possibility that some other shareholder would file an objection (including to Lisa Lawyer's fees), or that the court itself might raise objections (especially if the gain to the shareholders is small, either in absolute terms or in proportion to Lisa Lawyer's fees, or if the settlement involves any type of "coupons"[92]). Bringing a direct claim allows a plaintiff to bypass these requirements, and to settle on any terms Lisa Lawyer can negotiate.

VI. The Limits of Bringing Both Direct and Derivative Claims

As excited as Lisa Lawyer may be to bring both a direct and a derivative claim based on the same facts and the same wrongdoing,[93] she should bear in mind that, although "Delaware law dictates that the scope of recovery for a breach of the duty of loyalty is not to be determined narrowly,"[94] she can only recover once.[95] She cannot recover twice for the same injury, even if that one injury leads to both direct

89. *See, e.g.*, Del. Ch. Ct. R. 23.1(b).

90. *See, e.g.*, Del. G.C.L. § 327; Del. Ch. Ct. R. 23.1(a); N.Y. Bus. Corp. L. § 626(b).

91. *See, e.g.*, Del. Ch. Ct. R. 23.1(c).

92. *See, e.g.*, 28 U.S.C. § 1712.

93. Lisa Lawyer's excitement should be tempered by the fact that "Post-*Gentile*, Delaware courts have struggled to define the boundaries of dual-natured claims" (citations omitted). *Terraform*, 2020 WL 6375859, at *13.

94. Thorpe v. CERBCO, Inc., 676 A.2d 436, 445 (Del. 1996).

95. *See, e.g.*, McPadden v. Sidhu, 964 A.2d 1262, 1276 (Del. Ch. 2008) (prohibiting duplicative recovery when both restitution for unjust enrichment and damages for breach of fiduciary duty are sought).

and derivative claims. Lisa Lawyer can, however, choose whether she wishes to seek a "forward looking" remedy (such as requiring the defendants to disgorge any ill gotten profit),[96] or a "backward looking" remedy, such as rescissory damages.[97] Naturally, she should select the one that will yield the greatest recovery for Sam Shareholder. And which will make her look the best, and her fees the most reasonable. Of course.

96. *See, e.g.*, Gesoff v. IIC Indus., Inc., 902 A.2d 1130, 1154 (Del. Ch. 2006).

97. *See, e.g.*, Int'l Telecharge, Inc. v. Bomarko, Inc., 766 A.2d 437, 440 (Del. 2000); Strassburger v. Earley, 752 A.2d 557, 580 (Del. Ch. 2000).

Chapter 4

Claims Against a Majority Shareholder

By Richard F. Munzinger and Sanjeet S. Ganjam

I. Introduction

Shareholders of privately owned corporations often find themselves involved in disputes with officers, directors, or other shareholders regarding the operation of the business.[1] Minority shareholders are disadvantaged in such disputes because they usually have no direct role in or input into corporate management, and they often have no means of forcing a sale of their shares. For example, a majority shareholder may retaliate against a minority shareholder by refusing to share business information with him, exclude him from critical business decisions, or take an action that may appear superficially proper but is intended to and will deprive him of his fair share of the profits or the corporation's value. Since minority shareholders often have no governance rights allowing them to stop such actions, and often cannot exit the corporation, litigation is usually the only resort to protect their rights.

In this chapter, we discuss litigation strategies for minority shareholders, as well as some of the unique practical and legal challenges they face. The most effective strategies require careful planning from the outset of the dispute and usually involve asserting distinct statutory, contractual, and equitable rights. Failure to assert the right claims, at the right time, and in the right sequence could prejudice the minority shareholder's claims.

1. Public corporations involve special considerations, which are not addressed in this chapter.

This chapter focuses on Delaware law, which has the most developed body of law as to corporate disputes and is the most cited jurisdiction in such cases. Many, if not most, other states share basic principles, have similar statutory or common law, and will look to Delaware law for guidance. However, there are differences in the law between states, so it is important to consider the statutes and case law from any potentially applicable jurisdictions. These differences are in some aspects idiosyncratic, but in other aspects reflect deeper divisions. To illustrate, we will show certain ways in which California law materially differs from Delaware law.

II. Hypothetical

We will use a single hypothetical to guide our discussion in this chapter:

> Sam is a minority shareholder (45 percent) and one of two directors in Pied Piper, Inc., which he cofounded with Dave, the majority shareholder (55 percent), the Chief Executive Officer (CEO), and the other director. Pied Piper is incorporated in Delaware, but the shareholders, officers, and directors all reside and work in California, and Pied Piper maintains its only office in California.
>
> At founding, Sam and Dave each entered into an identical stock purchase agreement with Pied Piper, which sets forth a vesting schedule for their shares. The agreements give Pied Piper the option to repurchase the unvested shares of any shareholder who is no longer an employee or director at the nominal par value of the shares.
>
> A dispute arose between Sam and Dave about the direction of the business, which resulted in Dave taking several antagonistic actions against Sam. First, Dave purported to "fire" Sam as an employee and remove him as a director. Thereafter, he also purported to cause Pied Piper to repurchase Sam's unvested shares in Pied Piper. He further removed Sam's access to any corporate information and excluded Sam from business decisions.
>
> Soon thereafter, Dave began to pay himself a salary, even though Dave and Sam had both agreed at founding that neither of them would receive a salary. Dave also caused Pied Piper to guarantee a loan for a different company he owns to buy a building. Dave then leased that building back to Pied Piper as office space.

> Sam retained Lisa Lawyer to understand whether Dave has violated Sam's rights, including whether Dave could lawfully fire Sam and remove him as a director, whether Pied Piper can force a repurchase of Sam's shares and whether Dave's salary, the loan guarantee and the lease constitute self-dealing. Sam also wants to know his options for forcing a sale of the corporation.

Next, we use this hypothetical to illustrate litigation strategies that Dave can pursue against Sam. The facts of this hypothetical do not change during our discussion.

III. Sources of Minority Shareholder Rights

Sam's rights as a minority shareholder arise from the corporation's governing documents and contracts, as well as by statute, case law, and equity.

A. Applicable State Law

The rule in Delaware and most other jurisdictions is that the law of the state of incorporation governs internal corporate affairs, which includes most issues that arise in a shareholder dispute, irrespective of where the corporation conducts its business.[2] As such, a Delaware court will typically apply its law as to issues relating to the internal affairs of a Delaware corporation, regardless of that corporation's primary place of business.

A corporation that conducts its business in a "foreign" state may, however, be subject to certain corporate laws of that state. For example, California's Corporations Code gives shareholders the right to inspect corporate records maintained in state, even if the corporation is incorporated elsewhere. Several provisions of the California Corporations Code may also apply, to the exclusion of the law of the state of incorporation, to "pseudo foreign corporations," that is, corporations that are incorporated elsewhere but primarily do business in California.[3] Some such provisions are favorable to minority shareholders but

2. *See generally* VantagePoint Venture Partners 1996 v. Examen, Inc., 871 A.2d 1108 (Del. 2005).

3. Under California Corporations Code section 2115 ("section 2115"), pseudo-foreign corporations are entities incorporated outside California, but that meet two tests: (1) the corporation transacts more than half of its business (as measured by various objective

are not the default provisions under Delaware law, including the right to cumulate votes at any election of directors, limits on the removal of a director over the objection of shareholders entitled to cumulate their votes, and broader inspection rights.[4]

Shareholders' and stock purchase agreements may also contain choice of law provisions, which a Delaware court will typically enforce if the jurisdiction selected bears some material relationship to the transaction, for example, if the corporation's principal place of business is in the chosen state, and the determination of a particular issue under the chosen state's law is not repugnant to Delaware's public policy.[5] Similarly, a California court will enforce a choice of law provision unless (1) some other state has a materially greater interest than the chosen state in the determination of the particular issue or (2) the chosen state's laws conflict with California's public policy.[6]

If the corporate laws of two different states arguably apply to a particular situation, the best practice is often to avoid taking an early position on which state's law applies. Practitioners should instead consider alleging the issue in the alternative, and over the course of the case, carefully weigh the advantages and disadvantages of each state's law.

Returning to our hypothetical, Pied Piper is arguably governed by the laws of both Delaware and California. Although Pied Piper is incorporated in Delaware, the shareholders, officers, and directors all reside and work in California, and Pied Piper maintains its only office in California. Accordingly, California would likely consider Pied Piper a pseudo-foreign corporation subject to various provisions of the California Corporations Code. On the other hand, a Delaware court is likely to still apply Delaware law as to any internal corporate governance matter. As we discuss later, this conflict of law presents some strategic considerations, including the importance of filing first to secure the preferred venue.

---

criteria) in California, and (2) a majority of the voting securities are held by California residents.

4. Cal. Corp. Code § 2115(b). The Delaware Supreme Court has declined to apply section 2115, suggesting that such "outreach statutes," which require certain foreign corporations to conform to a broad range of in state internal affairs provisions, violate the U.S. Constitution. *VantagePoint Venture Partners 1996*, 871 A.2d 1108. However, section 2115 has survived constitutional challenges in California. *E.g.*, Wilson v. La.-Pac. Res., Inc., 138 Cal. App. 3d 216 (1982); Greb v. Diamond Int'l Corp., 56 Cal. 4th 243, 251–52 (2013).

5. Bonanno v. VTB Holdings, Inc., No. 10681-VCN, 2016 Del. Ch. LEXIS 24, at *14 (Ch. Feb. 8, 2016) (collecting cases).

6. Colaco v. Cavotec SA, 25 Cal. App. 5th 1172, 1188 (2018) (collecting cases).

B. Governing Documents

The governing documents, which typically include bylaws and the articles of incorporation (also known as the charter), can be used to modify certain default procedural and substantive rights of shareholders. Examples of such provisions include:

- Dual class shares, which often provide that the majority shareholder, or occasionally a minority shareholder, has exclusive voting rights or other preferential rights, especially upon the sale or dissolution of the corporation;
- Supermajority voting (up to two-thirds of outstanding shares) to approve certain, specified transactions;
- Cumulative voting, which allows a minority shareholders to cumulate their votes for the election or removal of directors;
- The adoption of shareholder resolutions without a meeting or prior notice to all shareholders, if a majority of shares entitled to vote on such resolutions consent in writing; and
- Information rights that are broader than the rights afforded by statute.

State law delineates what rights can and cannot be modified. For example, in California, the bylaws arguably cannot alter the right to seek involuntary dissolution and several other important rights.[7]

C. Shareholders' and Stock Purchase Agreements

Shareholders' and stock purchase agreements modify procedural and substantive rights of shareholders who are parties to those agreements. (Often, the corporation is also a party to such agreements.) Examples of such provisions include:

- Buy/sell provisions, which may give the majority shareholder or the corporation the right to buy out the minority shareholder, or alternatively the minority shareholder the right to sell his interest back to the corporation or the majority shareholder;
- Control rights or dissention rights, for example, provisions that require a supermajority vote or the consent of a particular shareholder for dissolution or sale;

7. Cal. Corp. Code § 212.

- Minimum dividends, often fixed as a proportion of the corporation's profits or sufficient to cover tax obligations of individual shareholders in a pass-through corporation; and
- Limitations on management compensation.

In our hypothetical, Sam entered into a stock purchase agreement that gives Pied Piper the option to repurchase his unvested shares if Sam is no longer an employee or a director. Dave argues that as the majority shareholder, he has the power to fire Sam and remove him as a director, and under the stock purchase agreement Pied Piper could then force a repurchase of Sam's unvested shares. Without such an agreement, Dave and Pied Piper have no mechanism under Delaware or California law to "remove" Sam or compel him to sell his shares (other than through a sale of the entire corporation).[8]

D. Fiduciary Duties

Beyond statutory and contractual duties, minority shareholders are protected by fiduciary duties owed to them by majority shareholders, officers, and directors. When a majority shareholder, who is often also a director and/or officer, acts in those capacities, he owes the same fiduciary duties as any other officer or director. When he acts in his capacity as a shareholder, he may separately owe fiduciary duties in specific circumstances. And sometimes, a majority shareholder is arguably acting in both capacities. To determine if a majority shareholder has breached his fiduciary duty with respect to a challenged action, one must carefully consider which "hat" he was wearing with respect to that action.

1. Officers and Directors

A director and/or officer owes the fiduciary duties of loyalty and care to the corporation and its shareholders, included in which are the subsidiary duties of good faith, oversight, and disclosure. As explained by *Guth v. Loft*, one of the seminal Delaware cases on the issue, the fiduciary duties of officers and directors are among the strictest duties known under the law:

> While technically not trustees, [corporate fiduciaries] stand in a fiduciary relation to the corporation and its stockholders. A

8. *See generally* Del. Gen. Corp. Law (DGCL) ch. 1, subch. IX, §§ 251–267; Cal. Corp. Code chs. 11–13, §§ 1100–1313.

> public policy, existing through the years, and derived from a profound knowledge of human characteristics and motives, has established a rule that demands of a corporate officer or director, peremptorily and inexorably, the most scrupulous observance of his duty, not only affirmatively to protect the interests of the corporation committed to his charge, but also to refrain from doing anything that would work injury to the corporation, or to deprive it of profit or advantage which his skill and ability might properly bring to it, or to enable it to make in the reasonable and lawful exercise of its powers. The rule that requires an undivided and unselfish loyalty to the corporation demands that there shall be no conflict between duty and self-interest. The occasions for the determination of honesty, good faith and loyal conduct are many and varied, and no hard and fast rule can be formulated. The standard of loyalty is measured by no fixed scale.[9]

California law is similar.[10]

The fiduciary duties of directors and officers are intertwined with the business judgment rule.

> The business judgment rule exists to protect and promote the full and free exercise of [] managerial power. . . . The rule itself is a presumption that in making a business decision, the directors [and officers] acted on an informed basis, in good faith and in the honest belief that the action taken was in the best interests of the company.[11]

If there is no evidence of fraud, bad faith, or self-dealing, the court will usually presume that a director or officer reached their business judgment in good faith and "considerations of motive are irrelevant."[12] This presumption can only be rebutted by a showing of gross negligence.

However, the business judgment presumption is usually inapplicable to decisions or transactions in which the director and/or officer has a personal interest (i.e., a self-interested transaction), unless he obtains approval of the transaction by a majority of the disinterested directors or shareholders after fully disclosing to them the material facts.

---

9. Guth v. Loft, Inc., 5 A.2d 503, 510 (Del. 1939).

10. Bancroft-Whitney Co. v. Glen, 64 Cal. 2d (Cal. 1966).

11. Smith v. Van Gorkom, 488 A.2d 858, 872 (Del. 1985). While the business-judgment rule is based in common law, many states have codified the rule, including California. *E.g.*, Cal. Corp. Code § 309(a).

12. *Id.*

If the business judgment presumption is inapplicable, the burden shifts to the director or officer to prove that the transaction is entirely fair to the corporation and its shareholder. (The "entire fairness" standard is also referred to as "inherent fairness" or "intrinsic fairness" in some older Delaware cases and in other jurisdictions.)

Entire fairness has both a procedural and substantive aspect, which are found in the concepts of "fair dealing" and "fair price," respectively. Fair dealing "embraces questions of when the transaction was timed, how it was initiated, structured, negotiated, disclosed to the directors, and how the approvals of the directors and the stockholders were obtained."[13] "This element also embraces the duty of candor owed by corporate fiduciaries to disclose all material information relevant to corporate decisions from which they may derive a personal benefit."[14] Fair price focuses on whether the transaction generated the highest value reasonably available to the shareholders.[15]

The California rule is similar. When the challenged transactions are self-interested, the burden shifts to the fiduciary to prove both that he acted in "good faith" and that the transactions were "inherently fair" to the company.[16] The concept of good faith is analogous to fair dealing under Delaware law, while the concept of inherent fairness mirrors fair price.

It is essential to properly plead the case to maximize the likelihood that the court applies entire fairness, rather than the business judgment rule. This is one of the most important issues in prevailing on a breach of fiduciary duty claim because the rebutting business judgment presumption is very difficult.

In our hypothetical, Dave, in addition to being the majority shareholder, is also a director and an officer of Pied Piper, so he owes fiduciary duties to Sam as to his actions as a director and an officer.

Lisa should frame Sam's claims against Dave for removing Sam as a director and causing Pied Piper to repurchase Sam's unvested shares as self-dealing. Dave's actions resulted in him owning and controlling the entire corporation for a pittance, so Lisa can allege and argue that Dave personally benefited from the transactions. Any evidence of embezzlement would be self-dealing, as well.

---

13. Weinberger v. UOP, Inc., 457 A.2d 701, 711 (Del. Super. 1983).
14. Mills Acquisition Co. v. MacMillan, Inc., 559 A.2d 1261, 1280 (1988).
15. *Id.*
16. Jones v. H.F. Ahmanson & Co., 1 Cal. 3d 93, 108 (1969).

2. Majority Shareholders

A majority shareholder acting *only* in his capacity as a shareholder, and not as an officer or director, may still owe fiduciary duties to minority shareholders for certain transactions. Delaware's decisional law has not defined the exact scope of those duties, but it is closest to a duty of loyalty to act in the best interests of minority shareholders.

In the seminal case of *Sinclair Oil Corp. v. Levien* (1971), the Delaware Supreme Court held that a majority or controlling shareholder's self-interested transactions with the company is subject to entire fairness review.[17] The majority shareholder, Sinclair Oil Corp. ("Sinclair"), owned 97 percent of its subsidiary, Sinven, and elected all of Sinven's directors. Sinclair caused Sinven to enter into a sales contract with Sinclair's international subsidiary ("International"). Even though Sinclair subsequently breached that contract, Sinclair caused Sinven to waive the breach. Sinven's minority shareholder sued Sinclair for breach of fiduciary duty based on that action. The court found that the contract was a self-dealing transaction by Sinclair in part because of its "domination" of Sinven's management. Accordingly, the court held that Sinclair's decision to cause Sinven to not enforce the contract must be reviewed under the entire fairness standard, with Sinclair bearing the burden of proof.

Sinclair helpfully identified other situations that potentially violate a majority or controlling shareholder's fiduciary duty to minority shareholders. These include causing the company to declare dividends without a business purpose, structuring dividends in such a way so as to deprive the minority shareholders of their proportionate share, or usurping a corporate opportunity by reorganizing subsidiaries in a way that is advantageous to the majority shareholder but detrimental to the minority shareholder.

California has a similar standard. *Jones v. H.F. Ahmanson & Co.* is the seminal California case on a controlling shareholder's fiduciary duty to minority shareholders.[18] Defendants owned a controlling stake in a savings and loan association (the "Association") and controlled its management. For a number of reasons, there was no market for the stock in the Association. In order to take advantage of the bull market, defendants transferred their controlling stake into a new holding company and offered its shares to the public. The minority shareholders sued, arguing that with the creation of a holding company and with no

17. 280 A.2d 717, 719 (Del. 1971).
18. 1 Cal. 3d 93 (1969).

opportunity for the minority shareholders to participate, "it became a virtual certainty that no equivalent market could or would be created for the Association stock."[19] Thus, the court concluded

> defendants chose a course of action in which they used their control of the Association to obtain an advantage not made available to all stockholders. They did so without regard to the resulting detriment to the minority stockholders and in the absence of any compelling business purpose. Such conduct is not consistent with their duty of good faith and inherent fairness to the minority stockholders.[20]

Returning to our hypothetical, Dave separately owes fiduciary duties to Sam with respect to his actions as a majority shareholder. Those duties may be triggered if Dave acts in his capacity as a shareholder. For example, if Dave votes his majority interest to sell Pied Piper to one of his other businesses, he would likely have the burden of proving that such a sale is entirely fair to Sam under both California and Delaware law.

E. Inspection Rights

Most states give minority shareholders statutory rights to inspect the corporation's books and records. The scope of shareholder inspection rights is typically defined by statute but may be expanded by the bylaws or other governing documents. Governing documents may also purport to restrict information rights; however, under Delaware law, such restrictions are likely unenforceable unless specifically waived by contract.[21]

An inspection demand is a useful tool, which can be used early in a shareholder dispute. Such demands help "pin down" the universe of governing documents, shareholder agreements, and corporate actions in order to determine whether a majority shareholder's actions were procedurally and substantively proper. Inspection demands can also be used to obtain accounting records in order to obtain evidence of irregularities or fraud. Such evidence can be a powerful tool for settlement, so such records should be obtained as soon as possible.

---

19. *Id.* at 114.

20. *Id.*

21. *Compare* Gaskill v. Gladys Belle Oil Co., 16 Del. Ch. 289, 146 A. 337 (bylaws cannot abrogate statutory inspection rights) *with* Kortüm v. Webasto Sunroofs, Inc., 769 A.2d 113 (statutory inspection rights potential waivable by contract).

Many states, including Delaware, impose procedural and substantive limitations on the shareholders' right of inspection. Under Delaware law, a shareholder must provide a sworn affidavit setting forth facts supporting a "proper purpose" for the inspection, such as investigating alleged mismanagement, waste, or wrongdoing by fiduciaries.[22] (The bylaws or shareholder agreement may waive this requirement.) In contrast, California imposes fewer procedural hurdles for a shareholder inspection.[23]

If the demand is refused or ignored, such a response can be used as evidence of a majority shareholder's total control and breach of fiduciary duty. If the minority shareholder ultimately files a complaint that pleads some facts based on information and belief—which is often necessary in minority shareholder actions—the refusal of an inspection demand may help defeat a motion to dismiss on the grounds that the allegations in the complaint are insufficient or speculative.

In many states, if a minority shareholder prevails on a suit to enforce an inspection demand, he is entitled to have the corporation pay his attorneys' fees. This can be an effective tool to convince the corporation to comply with proper inspection demands.

A minority shareholder who is also a director has a much stronger claim to inspect the books and records. Directors usually have an *absolute* right to inspect *all* corporate books and records at any time and need not identify a proper purpose for their demand.

In our hypothetical, Lisa should consider advising Sam to make an inspection demand as a director and shareholder for Pied Piper's accounting books and records, governing documents, shareholder agreements, and corporate actions. Lisa could make such a demand as part of a lawsuit for breach of fiduciary duty or separately, before bringing such a suit, depending on the urgency of the situation. Lisa should determine whether Dave intends to take any action that would prejudice Sam and cannot be undone. If so, a full-blown lawsuit may be necessary immediately. If not, and Dave has not threatened any action that cannot be undone, then filing a special proceeding to enforce Sam's inspections rights before filing a lawsuit may be appropriate.

Either way, Lisa must follow the proper form when making the demand, by requesting the scope of inspection allowed by statute and nothing more. In one California case to enforce an inspection demand, the court found that the demand was improper because it asked that

22. City of Westland Police & Fire Ret. Sys. v. Axcelis Techs., Inc., 1 A.3d 281, 287 (Del. 2010).

23. Havlicek v. Coast-to-Coast Analytical Servs., Inc., 39 Cal. App. 4th 1844, 1851 (1995) (no "proper purpose" requirement in California).

books and records be sent to the shareholder, whereas California's inspection statute at that time only permitted inspection and copying of books and records at the corporation's office.[24] Lisa's demand should cite both the Delaware and California inspection statutes in the alternative. (Delaware's inspection statute applies to any Delaware corporation. California's inspection statute applies to any corporate books and records maintained in California, regardless of the state of incorporation.) Lisa should articulate a "proper purpose" in the demand to avoid any argument that the demand is deficient under Delaware law. A proper purpose could be that Sam is investigating Dave's embezzlement of corporate funds and other self-dealing, or that Sam seeks to value his shares.

IV. Violations of Minority Shareholder Rights

Once Lisa has a good understanding of the governing documents and shareholder agreements, and has possibly obtained information through an inspection demand, she can begin to identify actual or potential violations of Sam's rights. Next, we discuss examples of a majority shareholder's actions that potentially violate a minority shareholder's rights.

A. Self-Dealing

Self-dealing is any transaction through which a fiduciary, for example, the majority shareholder, gains a personal advantage at the expense of the corporation and its shareholders. Such transactions violate the fiduciary's duty of loyalty, which in turns requires the fiduciary to act in good faith and advance the best interests of the corporation and its shareholders. Self-dealing can range from outright embezzlement of corporate funds to more subtle business decisions that may appear proper but advantage the majority shareholder.

1. Examples of Self-Dealing Transactions

Common examples of the types of transactions that carry a presumption of self-dealing include:

- Payments to the majority shareholder and/or his friends and family, characterized as compensation or expense reimbursements

24. Jara v. Suprema Meats, Inc., 121 Cal. App. 4th 1238, 1263 (2004).

in the corporation's books. Examples of such payments include bloated salaries and reimbursements for health care premiums; car payments for personal vehicles; country club or similar membership dues; and personal travel, meals, and entertainment expenses.
- Salary advances.
- Loans to the majority shareholder, his friends and family, or an entity in which the majority shareholder or his friends and family hold an interest.
- Causing the corporation to guarantee personal obligations of the majority shareholder, his friends and family, or an entity in which the majority shareholder or his friends and family hold an interest.
- Causing the corporation to enter into a supposedly arms-length contract with a majority shareholder and/or his friends and family, or another entity in which they have a personal interest.

Such transactions are often not disclosed to or approved by disinterested directors or shareholders in cases where the majority shareholder has directly, or through individuals he controls, assumed complete control of a corporation.

Dave's actions to pay himself a salary, cause Pied Piper to guarantee a loan for one of his other businesses, and cause Pied Piper to enter into a lease with a company he owns are presumed to be self-dealing.

2. Standard of Review for Self-Dealing Transactions

As discussed earlier, the business judgment presumption is inapplicable to self-interested transactions for which the fiduciary failed to obtain the approval of a majority of the disinterested directors or shareholders, after fully disclosing to them the material facts of the transaction. In such cases, the burden shifts to the fiduciary to prove that the transaction is entirely fair to the corporation and its shareholders in both substance and process.

For Dave to take advantage of the business judgment presumption for his self-interested transactions, that is, his salary, the loan guarantee, and the lease, Dave would have needed the approval of a majority of either the disinterested directors or the disinterested shareholders. If Sam can establish that he could not be removed from the board of directors, he is the only disinterested director. Sam also holds the majority of the disinterested shares. Sam did not consent to these transactions, so the business judgment presumption is unlikely to apply here. Thus, Dave likely has the burden to prove that these transactions are entirely fair to Pied Piper in both process and substance.

The lease example is instructive for understanding the procedural and substantive aspects of entire fairness. If Dave bears the burden of proof, he would need to prove procedural fairness, that is, "fair dealing," by, for example, showing that he conducted a good faith investigation of alternatives and an arm's-length negotiation as to the lease terms. He would need to prove substantive fairness, that is, "fair price," by, for example, showing that there is a business purpose for the lease, and the terms of the lease are consistent with the market.

If Pied Piper had nominally independent directors who approved Dave's self-interested transactions, Dave would have a better argument that the business judgment rule protects those decisions. In that event, the relevant inquiry is whether the directors who voted to approve the salary are sufficiently independent and were sufficiently informed. The independence of a director is a fact-specific analysis. Dave's family members are generally not considered independent. However, Dave's friends may still be considered independent unless they are essentially "beholden" to Dave. Delaware courts are reluctant to find that directors are not independent merely because of long-standing personal or professional relationships with the defendant director/shareholder.

3. Statutory Restrictions on Self-Interested Transactions

Some states have codified specific rules regarding the necessary approvals for certain types of self-interested transactions. For example, California's Corporations Code provides that a corporation "shall not make any loan of money or property to, or guarantee the obligation of, any director or officer of the corporation or of its parent, unless the transaction . . . is approved by a majority of the [disinterested] shareholders."[25] If that provision applies to Pied Piper, Dave violated it by causing Pied Piper to guarantee a loan for his other company. In contrast, Delaware generally permits the board of directors to authorize loans to or guarantee the obligations of officers and directors, subject of course to their fiduciary duties.[26]

4. Voiding Self-Dealing Transactions

Under both Delaware and California statutory and common law, if the majority shareholder fails to meet his burden of proving that a

25. Cal. Corp. Code § 315.
26. DGCL § 143.

self-interested transaction is entirely fair to the corporation and its minority shareholders, those transactions are either void or voidable.

> Void acts are those acts that the board, or more generally the corporation, has no implicit or explicit authority to undertake or those acts that are fundamentally contrary to public policy. . . . Void acts include fraud, gift, waste, or *ultra vires* acts. No amount of shareholder ratification validates acts repugnant to public policy (e.g., fraud), and which are therefore void *ab initio*.[27]

In contrast, "voidable acts . . . [are] performed in the corporation's interest but beyond management's explicit authority."[28] A voidable act could be cured by informed shareholder or director ratification after the fact.

B. Termination of Dividends

In the absence of a specific agreement to pay dividends, such as a shareholders' agreement, a shareholder has no right under the law to dividends, even if the corporation has money to distribute.[29] If the board of directors in good faith decides against declaring a dividend, courts will generally not disturb that decision, with two major exceptions.

First, if a dividend is declared, it must be paid out pro rata according to share ownership. A majority shareholder cannot pay himself a dividend without paying a proportionate dividend to each of the other shareholders. This issue typically arises when there is a dispute as to the ownership of shares, such as in our hypothetical. For example, Dave argues that when he removed Sam as an officer and a director, Pied Piper had the right to and did buy back the majority of Sam's shares. Sam disputes that his removal and the repurchase were lawful. If Pied Piper declares a dividend now, Sam likely has a claim to his proportionate share of that dividend.

Second, if the corporation has a custom and practice of paying dividends and abruptly stops doing so after a shareholder dispute emerges, that decision arguably lacks good faith. This issue often arises when a majority shareholder causes the corporation to stop paying

27. Stephen A. Solomon v. Armstrong, 747 A.2d 1098, 1114 (Del. Ch. 1999).

28. *Id.*

29. *E.g.*, Baron v. Allied Artists Pictures Corp., 337 A.2d 653 (Del. Ch. 1975); Miller v. McColgan, 17 Cal. 2d 432, 436 (1941).

dividends to "starve" a minority shareholder as retaliation during a dispute. Many corporations have a custom and practice of paying, or contractual requirement to pay, regular dividends. For example, many corporations are pass-through entities for taxation purposes and customarily pay quarterly dividends sufficient to meet the shareholders' tax obligations.

C. Management Rights

A corporation is managed by its board of directors, unless otherwise provided in the certificate of incorporation or the bylaws. A minority shareholder who is also a director has a right to participate in the management of the corporation. This includes the right to review the corporation's books and records at any time and for any reason, attend board meetings, and vote on board resolutions.

The default rule is that each seat on the board of directors is elected separately, by a simple majority vote. Thus, an absolute majority shareholder, that is, a shareholder holding more than 50 percent of the voting shares, can out vote the other shareholders and secure every board seat for his slate of candidates. Occasionally, shareholder agreements or other governing documents may give a shareholder the right to appoint a director outside of the normal election process. This is common in venture-backed startups, where investors often condition their investment on having the right to appoint a director.

An important but often overlooked protection against this "tyranny of the majority" is cumulative voting. Cumulative voting is an opt-in provision under Delaware corporate law, and a nonwaivable right under California's Corporations Code, that gives shareholders the right to cumulate votes for the election of directors.[30] Under cumulative voting, each shareholder is entitled to one vote per share multiplied by the number of directors to be elected. Each shareholder can allocate those votes for any combination of candidates. The candidates receiving the highest cumulative votes are elected, up to the number of board seats.

In both California and Delaware, directors can be removed from office without cause by a majority vote of the shareholders. However, if cumulative voting applies, a director cannot be removed from office if the number of votes cast against his removal is sufficient to elect him as a director if voted cumulatively at an election of the directors.

30. *See* DGCL § 214; Cal. Corp. Code § 305.

In our hypothetical, Dave would have the power as majority shareholder to remove Sam as a director, unless cumulative voting applies, in which case Sam could not be removed because he can cumulate his votes to elect himself as a director. If Lisa files the lawsuit in California, and the court finds that Pied Piper is a pseudo-foreign corporation subject to California's cumulative voting rule (among other corporate laws), Sam should prevail on the dispute over whether he could be removed and bought out.

D. Involuntary Dissolution Rights

The right to seek judicial dissolution, that is, a liquidation or sale of the corporation or its assets, is a powerful tool for a minority shareholder. This is one area, however, in which state law significantly differs between jurisdictions. Delaware, known for its management-friendly business laws, does not give a minority shareholder the right to seek judicial dissolution. A shareholder could theoretically involve the attorney general, who has the authority to file a suit for dissolution for "abuse, misuse or nonuse of its corporate powers, privileges or franchises," but the bar is high. And, even if the attorney general cooperates or a shareholder can establish standing as a relator, Delaware courts have long been wary of exercising this power.[31]

In contrast, judicial dissolution is available in California under a variety of scenarios. The following persons may file for involuntary dissolution: (1) one-half or more of the directors, (2) any shareholder in a close corporation, or (3) shareholder(s) representing at least one-third of the outstanding shares (or the outstanding *dissenting* shares for reasons of fraud, mismanagement, abuse of authority, unfairness towards a shareholder, self-dealing, or waste). The grounds for such dissolution include:

- Abandonment of business for more than a year;
- The board of directors is effectively deadlocked;
- Those in control of the corporation have been "guilty of or have knowingly countenanced persistent and pervasive fraud, mismanagement or abuse of authority or persistent unfairness toward any shareholders or its property is being misapplied or wasted by its directors or officers"; or

31. Hall v. John S. Isaacs & Sons Farms, Inc., 39 Del. Ch. 244, 253, 163 A.2d 288, 293 (1960).

- "In the case of any corporation with 35 or fewer shareholders . . . liquidation is reasonably necessary for the protection of the rights or interests of the complaining [] shareholders."[32]

California's involuntary dissolution statute gives minority shareholders powerful leverage in negotiations over a business dispute with a majority shareholder. However, a minority shareholder should carefully consider alternatives before invoking involuntary dissolution because California Corporations Code section 2000 allows a majority shareholder to buy out the shares of a complaining minority shareholder who seeks involuntary dissolution at "fair value," which is often less than fair market value. Since Sam wants to sell the corporation, Lisa should consider seeking involuntary dissolution under California law when she files suit, as long as Sam can live with a buyout at "fair value" if Dave elects that option. (Note that the law is unsettled as to whether a California shareholder could seek involuntary dissolution of a Delaware corporation in California.)

E. Dissention Rights

Both California and Delaware recognize the right of a minority shareholder to challenge an exit event, such as when the corporation is being dissolved by action of the majority shareholder (known as voluntary dissolution), sold, reorganized, or merged with another corporation. Accordingly, minority shareholders should cautiously evaluate exit events for fairness.

Such exit events are presumed to be an exercise of business judgment by the approving directors, subject of course to their fiduciary duties to minority shareholders. As with any other transaction, however, the business judgment presumption may not apply, and the exit event may be subject to entire fairness review, if the approving directors have a conflict of interest, for example, a sale of the corporation to a director or an entity in which the director has a financial interest.

Shareholder-driven exit events are reviewed under a similar framework. For example, a majority shareholder holding at least a 50 percent voting interest has the right to dissolve the corporation, but if he does so in order to continue in the same line of business on his own behalf, that is, a usurpation of corporate opportunity, it is self-dealing.

---

32. Cal. Corp. Code § 1800.

Under special circumstances such as a merger or sale involving a "change in control," Delaware will apply an intermediate form of review commonly known as "enhanced scrutiny" or the "*Revlon/Unocal* duties," which require that the board of directors take efforts to achieve the highest value reasonably attainable for the stockholders, even if there is no conflict of interest.[33]

Delaware law provides that if a corporation is in the process of voluntary dissolution, any shareholder or director can apply to the Court of Chancery, which for good cause shown can appoint one or more directors of the corporation as a trustee, or one or more outside persons as a receiver, to take charge of the dissolution, and such person has a broad mandate, including to prosecute claims in the name of the corporation as necessary and proper.

California law somewhat differently provides that if a corporation is in the process of voluntary dissolution, any shareholder(s) of a close corporation or representing at least 5 percent of outstanding shares can petition the court to supervise the dissolution. The court then has broad equitable powers to supervise the dissolution to protect the rights of shareholders.

Another consideration is contractual dissention rights, for example, a majority shareholder's contractual right to veto a merger or sale of a corporation. Such contractual provisions are typically enforceable, but a majority shareholder may still be liable if he does not exercise that contractual right consistent with his fiduciary duty, and separately, consistent with the implied covenant of good faith and fair dealing.

F. Buy/Sell Rights

Absent a "buy/sell" or similar agreement, or in the event of a merger, consolidation, or reorganization, a shareholder cannot be forced to sell his shares, nor can he force a purchase of his shares. As such, many closely held corporations have shareholder agreements that give the majority shareholder the option to buy out a minority shareholder or the minority shareholder to sell his interest to the majority shareholder. Such agreements often require some kind of an appraisal of the minority interest by a neutral when the option is exercised, and they often specify the appraisal methodology. For example, the agreement may

33. Revlon, Inc. v. MacAndrews & Forbes Holdings, Inc., 506 A.2d 173 (Del. 1986); Unocal v. Mesa Petroleum Co., 493 A.2d 946 (Del. 1985).

call for an appraisal at fair market value, with or without a specified minority and other discounts, or may call for a liquidation value.

A common issue that arises in the operation of a buy/sell agreement is a minority shareholder's potential derivative claims. If a majority shareholder exercises an option to buy out the minority shareholder, the minority shareholder has an argument that the appraisal process should not continue until his derivative claims are resolved. If the minority shareholder prevails on his derivative claims and recovers on behalf of the corporations, the value of his interest in the corporation will correspondingly increase.

"Shotgun" agreements are a common method used to determine purchase price under a buy/sell agreement, especially where the minority shareholder's interest is closer to 50 percent. A shotgun agreement is exercised by one shareholder offering to purchase the other shareholder's interest. The shareholder receiving the offer then has the option of either (1) accepting the offer and selling his interests at the offered price or (2) flipping the offer and buying the offering shareholder's interests at the same price per share. Shotgun agreements are preferred by some parties because they can avoid a battle of appraisers or tying the purchase price to some other metric that is subject to manipulation. If the offering shareholder offers too low a price, he risks having to sell his own shares at the same price.

As with all contracts, a buy/sell agreement includes an implied covenant of good faith and fair dealing. If the agreement vests the majority shareholder with discretion as to a certain subject, the majority shareholder has an obligation to exercise that discretion consistent with the implied covenant of good faith and fair dealing. For example, suppose a buy/sell agreement allows the majority shareholder to buy out the minority shareholder if the minority shareholder fails to meet a capital call. The majority shareholder has, by his control of the corporation, the discretion to cause the corporation to make a capital call. If he does not exercise that discretion reasonably, for example, suppose the capital call has no business purpose, but is instead intended to force the minority shareholder into a default and trigger the buyout agreement, he is arguably violating the buy/sell agreement's implied covenant of good faith and fair dealing.

V. The Complaint

Once Lisa has identified potential violations of Sam's individual and derivative rights as a minority shareholder, she will need to decide on the jurisdiction and venue to initiate a lawsuit and draft the complaint.

A. Jurisdiction and Venue

Fiduciary claims against a majority shareholder can usually be brought in any state court that has personal jurisdiction over the majority shareholder. If, as is common, the minority shareholder asserts derivative claims on behalf of the corporation or contractual claims against the corporation, the court must have personal jurisdiction over the corporation as well as the majority shareholder. Fiduciary claims against a majority shareholder are often filed where the majority shareholder manages the corporation, because the management of the corporation within the state is typically sufficient to give the state personal jurisdiction over both the majority shareholder and the corporation.[34]

The state of incorporation also has jurisdiction over fiduciary claims against majority shareholders who are also directors or officers. Delaware's "implied consent" statute provides that a nonresident officer or director of a Delaware corporation consents to the exercise of personal jurisdiction over that individual "in all civil actions or proceedings brought in this State, by or on behalf of, or against such corporation, in which [he] is a necessary or proper party, or in any action or proceeding against [him] for violation of a duty in such capacity."[35]

It is increasingly common to find that shareholders' agreements require arbitration of claims by shareholders against the corporation or its officers and directors, which is typically enforced, subject of course to any limitations on the scope of arbitrable claims. Such provisions often dictate where the arbitration can be initiated and which state's law governs.

With respect to contractual claims against a majority shareholder, for example, a breach of an express provision in the shareholder's agreement as opposed to a fiduciary claim, the contract's choice of jurisdiction, law, and venue likely governs, unless the enforcement of those provisions would violate the forum state's statutory or decisional law. The contracts may also require arbitration of those claims.

Claims can be brought in federal court if the federal court has diversity jurisdiction over the matter. If the corporation is named as a defendant or nominal defendant, it is important to consider the citizenship of the corporation in determining whether diversity jurisdiction exists.

Pied Piper and Dave are subject to jurisdiction in Delaware as well as in California, where the corporation is principally based. Lisa should

---

34. *See, e.g.*, Openwave Sys. v. Fuld, No. C 08-5683 SI, 2009 U.S. Dist. LEXIS 48206, at *1 (N.D. Cal. June 6, 2009).

35. 10 Del. C. § 3114.

advise Sam to sue in California, because he has a good argument that Pied Piper is a "pseudo-foreign corporation" subject to California's cumulative voting rule, and that Dave's attempt to remove Sam as a director violates that rule. Sam may prevail on this argument in California, but he is unlikely to prevail on this argument in Delaware, which has declined to enforce California's pseudo-foreign corporation laws as unconstitutional. There is no diversity jurisdiction or arbitration provision in our hypothetical.

B. Direct versus Derivative Claims

Lisa should consider filing both "direct" claims for Sam's individual damages, as well as "derivative" claims on behalf of Pied Piper for damages from the unauthorized salary, loan guarantee, and lease. Chapters 2 and 3 address derivative claims.

C. Causes of Action

1. Breach of Fiduciary Duty

Most common types of misconduct by a majority shareholder can be characterized as a breach of fiduciary duty. This includes self-dealing, embezzlement, disproportionate distributions, excessive compensation, unauthorized expense reimbursements, and usurpation of corporate opportunity.

Depending on the pleading requirements of your jurisdiction, the best practice may be to plead breach of fiduciary as a single cause of action, brought individually and derivatively on behalf of the corporation, rather than pleading separate wrongs as separate causes of action. This preserves flexibility and may preclude the defendant from bringing partial summary judgment motions.

In our hypothetical, Sam might plead a single cause of action for breach of fiduciary duty against Dave, brought individually and derivatively, which would encompass all of Dave's wrongdoing.

2. Breach of Contract/Implied Covenant of Good Faith and Fair Dealing

If a majority shareholder has violated the bylaws or any other governing documents, the minority shareholder should plead causes of action for both breach of contract as well as, if applicable, breach of the implied covenant of good faith and fair dealing.

When the corporation itself is a party to a shareholder agreement or other governing document, it is important to consider whether the breach is by the majority shareholder or the corporation, or both, and plead accordingly. For example, if the agreement contains a minimum dividends provision and the corporation stops paying dividends consistent with the agreement, a minority shareholder's claim for breach of the agreement is arguably against both the corporation and the majority shareholder.

In our hypothetical, Sam seeks to invalidate Pied Piper's repurchase of his unvested shares pursuant to the stock purchase agreement. Lisa should thus consider including a claim against Pied Piper for breach of the stock purchase agreement and breach of the implied covenant of good faith and fair dealing therein.

3. Statutory Violations

Statutory violations can be asserted as separate causes of action, even though a violation of statutory corporate law may also be a breach of fiduciary duty. For example, if an inspection demand is improperly refused, a minority shareholder may want to include a cause of action to enforce the inspection demand as authorized by statute. As another example, in both California and Delaware a shareholder can assert a separate cause of action or file a separate lawsuit to try and determine the validity of any corporate election and the right of any person to be a director.[36]

In our hypothetical, Lisa should include a cause of action for violation of California Corporations Code section 315, which generally requires shareholder approval for loans to or guarantee of obligations of any directors or officers, and California Corporations Code section 303, which precludes the removal of a director over the objection of shareholders entitled to cumulate their votes. She should also consider a cause of action or an expedited proceeding to determine whether Sam is a director under California Corporations Code section 709.

4. Declaratory Relief

The minority shareholder should plead a declaratory relief cause of action if there are any disputes as to the interpretation and operation of a particular contractual provision, for example, what constitutes a

36. DGCL § 225; CAL. CORP. CODE § 709.

triggering event under a buy/sell agreement. The same is true for disputes as to the rights of the minority shareholder with respect to the majority shareholder or the corporation, for example, whether he is in fact a shareholder and how many shares he owns.[37] Statutory violations may also give rise to a declaratory relief claim.

In our hypothetical, Lisa should consider including a claim for declaratory relief that Sam remains a director of Pied Piper pursuant to California's statutory right to cumulate votes for the election or removal of a director, and that Pied Piper's repurchase of Sam's unvested shares was invalid pursuant to the stock purchase agreement.

5. Fraud

If the majority shareholder's conduct rises to the level of fraud, consider an individual cause of action for fraud. Although there are heightened pleading requirements for fraud, it may be useful if, for any reason, the court finds that the defendant does not owe a fiduciary duty with respect to certain actions. Moreover, the potential reputational harm from a judgment of fraud might help drive the litigation toward resolution. Lisa probably does not have a basis for a fraud claim here, unless she obtains evidence of fraudulent misrepresentations by Dave.

6. "Common Counts" and Other Equitable Causes of Action

The best practice is to accompany a breach of fiduciary duty cause of action with equitable causes of action for accounting, conversion and money had and received. If the court for any reason finds that the defendant does not owe a fiduciary duty, the common counts may still allow for recovery.

Common counts may also provide a further basis for broad discovery. For example, an accounting cause of action may support complete discovery into the corporation's books and records. Conversion and money had and received may support discovery into a majority

---

37. The Delaware Declaratory Judgment Act gives Delaware courts broad "power to declare rights, status and other legal relations whether or not further relief is or could be claimed." 10 Del. C. § 6501. Similarly in California, "[a]ny person interested under a written instrument . . . or under a contract, or "who desires a declaration of his or her rights or duties with respect to another" may seek declaratory relief. Cal. Code Civ. Proc. § 1060. However, the scope of permissible declaratory relief may be more limited in other states.

shareholder's personal finances if he is alleged to have embezzled corporate funds.

7. Quasi-Contractual Causes of Action

Depending on the jurisdiction, quasi-contractual causes of action are variously styled as unjust enrichment, breach of implied-in-fact contract, or restitution, and are predicated on the majority shareholder unjustly obtaining a benefit at the minority shareholder's expense.

Similar to the common counts, quasi-contractual causes of action are useful if the court were to find that the defendant does not owe a fiduciary duty with respect to a challenged transaction. As an example, a putative shareholder may have given the majority shareholder a sum of money believing that he was investing in the corporation, but the court instead finds that it was a loan.

D. Right to a Jury Trial

Under both Delaware and California law, litigants have a right to a jury trial for legal claims, but not equitable claims. In Delaware, the equity jurisdiction of the Court of Chancery as it existed prior to the separation of the colonies determines whether an action is legal or equitable. In California, the right to a jury trial is coextensive with that right as it existed in 1850 under English common law. In both states, there is generally no right to a jury trial for derivative claims by shareholders, which are considered equitable. An individual claim for breach of fiduciary duty may or may not entail a right to jury trial depending on the legal principles applicable to the claim, the mode of relief sought, and defendant's affirmative defenses. Similarly, statutory claims may or may not entail a right to a jury trial depending on the statutes and interpreting case law. An individual cause of action for breach of contract will usually entail a right to a jury trial. There is a substantial body of case law on these issues, which is beyond the scope of this chapter, but they are worth considering early if plaintiff or counsel have a preference for a jury trial or a bench trial.

VI. Common Majority Shareholder Defenses

Here we discuss the likely affirmative defenses Sam can expect Dave to plead.

A. Statute of Limitations and/or Laches

The statute of limitations for a breach of fiduciary duty claim is three years in Delaware and usually four years in California. Under the "discovery rule," the limitations period does not begin to run until discovery of the wrongdoing. This is coupled with the general rule that a shareholder has no affirmative duty to investigate a fiduciary's conduct until he reasonably should have suspected wrongdoing. In California, some courts have also tolled the limitations period so long as there is a continuing fiduciary relationship.

Laches is an equitable defense that applies to equitable common law claims as opposed to legal claims. The modern trend is for courts of equity to apply the analogous limitations period to equitable claims, although a court sitting in equity technically has the power to bar a common law claim brought before the analogous limitations period has expired.

A majority shareholder will often assert statute of limitations and/or laches where the minority shareholder seeks damages for conduct dating back a number of years, usually on the basis that the minority shareholder knew of or could have discovered the challenged conduct but delayed in filing suit. In our example, if Sam obtains accounting records and discovers that Dave is paying himself a salary without authorization, he typically cannot wait beyond the limitations period to file suit without risking that his claim, or some portion of it, will be time-barred. As such, Lisa should advise Sam to strongly consider initiating a lawsuit within a reasonable time after discovering wrongdoing, and by no later than the end of the limitations period.

B. Waiver and/or Estoppel

A waiver of a right arises where a minority shareholder's intentional words or conduct are inconsistent with his intent to enforce a legal right, whether or not he subjectively intended to relinquish that right. The related doctrine of estoppel prevents a minority shareholder from asserting a right that has come into existence by contract, statute, or other rule of law where, because of his conduct, silence, or omission, it would be unconscionable to allow him to do so.

Waiver and/or estoppel typically arises where a minority shareholder by words, conduct, or silence leads a majority shareholder to believe that the minority shareholder does not object to the challenged conduct. Returning to our example, if Dave shared with Sam that Dave was receiving a salary several years ago, and Sam did not object at first, but years later sues Dave over it, Sam has arguably waived and/or is estopped from asserting that claim.

C. Unclean Hands

Unclean hands is an equitable doctrine that allows the court to deny relief to a party who has done anything illegal or unethical in relation to the subject of the lawsuit. In the context of fiduciary claims, the unclean hands defense usually arises if the shareholder plaintiff has himself engaged in wrongdoing related to the transaction he challenges. In our example, if Sam, prior to Dave firing him, had himself engaged in self-dealing through Pied Piper, the unclean hands doctrine may arguably bar Sam's self-dealing claims against Dave.

VII. Positioning the Complaint for Trial

As the case progresses closer toward trial, Sam may want to consider streamlining his complaint.

First, if there is no apparent dispute as to whether Dave owes Sam a fiduciary duty with respect to each challenged transaction, then Sam should consider pursuing only a breach of fiduciary duty claim, which has the benefit of shifting the burden onto Dave to prove that his self-interested transactions are entirely fair to Pied Piper and Sam.

Second, if Sam desires a bench trial as opposed to a jury trial, then he should consider dismissing his legal claims. If the gist of Sam's claim is breach of fiduciary duty, a bench trial may be advantageous because a jury may have difficulty grasping the concepts of fiduciary duty, entire fairness, and burden shifting. For example, where a judge applying the law might find that a defendant fiduciary failed to meet his burden of proving the entire fairness of his self-interested transactions, a jury might be moved by facts that present the defendant fiduciary in a sympathetic light.

VIII. Conclusion

As illustrated by the Piped Piper hypothetical, a minority shareholder often has no recourse but litigation when a majority shareholder seizes complete control of a corporation, engages in self-dealing, or deprives the minority shareholder of his fair share the corporation's value. Under those circumstances, the best overall strategy to protect the minority shareholder's rights is to effectively plead and aggressively position the case for trial. And, this strategy is also effective if the minority shareholder's goal is to be bought out at a price that fairly compensates him for not only the value of his shares but also the value of his claims.

Lawyers pursuing this strategy are advised to carefully plan for the "end game" from the outset, considering how the positions they take in an early demand letter might impact, for example, the jurisdiction in which the client will need to initiate the lawsuit and how to plead the case to maximize or minimize the possibility of a jury trial.

Lawyers are also advised to counsel their clients on these issues early in the litigation process, so that clients understand the power imbalance that accompanies their status as minority shareholders and have realistic expectations about the likelihood of a favorable, early resolution.

Chapter 5

Fiduciary Duties in the Context of the Limited Liability Company

By Dale Schian, Dominick San Angelo, and Kortney Otten

I. Introduction

The ubiquity of the limited liability company as an entity form throughout the United States in the last several decades has often been described as a "much heralded development in corporate law."[1] This entity form, first made available in the state of Wyoming in 1977, offered the benefit of a limitation on personal liability (much like a corporation) for its "members," while enabling its members to treat the income generated from their interest as a pass-through for taxation purposes (much like a partnership). The limited liability company (LLC) statutes adopted throughout the United States thus created a hybrid entity that offers flexibility for the members and other participants in the entity to customize their relationships by contract. The LLC statutes established entities that "are creatures of contract, 'designed to afford the maximum amount of freedom of contract, private ordering and flexibility to the parties involved.'"[2] All 50 states and the District of Columbia have enacted LLC legislation.

1. *See, e.g.*, Rachel Maizes, *Limited Liability Companies: A Critique*, 70(3) St. John's L. Rev. art. 3 (1996), *available at* https://scholarship.law.stjohns.edu/cgi/viewcontent.cgi?article=1618&context=lawreview.

2. TravelCenters of Am., LLC v. Brog, 2008 WL 1746987, at *1 (Del. Ch. Apr. 3, 2008) (quoting *In re Grupo Dos Chiles, LLC*, 2006 WL 668443, at *2 (Del. Ch. Mar. 10, 2006));

The LLC entity form affords novelty and flexibility that create its own set of issues for determining whether certain actors within the entity are bound by fiduciary duties, and to whom. This chapter explores some of these unique issues in the LLC context, including the source of the fiduciary duty; a discussion of who owes fiduciary duties; to whom such duties are owed; how the duties differ in the context of "member-managed" versus "manager-managed" LLCs; and the extent to which statutory, common law, and the contractual agreements bind the LLC and its participants.

II. Fiduciary Duties

Fiduciary duties consist of the duty of loyalty and the duty of care. The duty of loyalty requires the fiduciary to act with undivided loyalty to the LLC. It mandates that the best interests of the company take precedence over any personal interests or individual advantages possessed by an officer, director, or member that are not shared by the company generally. Failure by such actors to fulfill a duty of loyalty usually includes some form of self-dealing or misuse of corporate office for personal gain.[3] Corporate decisions that confer a benefit (indirectly or directly) upon a participating director, officer, or member can implicate the duty of loyalty.

The duty of care requires fiduciaries of the LLC to act in good faith and exercise reasonable care in carrying out their obligations in dealing with the LLC's operations and activities. It requires that the fiduciary act with a degree of care that an ordinarily prudent person in a similar situation would use.[4]

III. Applicable Source of the Duty

An LLC possesses characteristics typically associated with both corporations and partnerships. The fiduciary duties of participants in an LLC arise from three sources: the authorizing statute, the common law, and the agreement of the parties. Whether a fiduciary relationship exists

see also CML V, LLC v. Bax, 6 A.3d 238, 250 (Del. Ch. 2010), *aff'd*, 28 A.3d 1037 (Del. 2011), as corrected (Sept. 6, 2011).

3. *In re* BH S & B Holdings LLC, 420 B.R. 112, 150 (Bankr. S.D.N.Y. 2009), *aff'd as modified*, 807 F. Supp. 2d 199 (S.D.N.Y. 2011) (internal citations omitted).

4. *In re* Sols. Liquidation LLC, 608 B.R. 384, 407 (Bankr. D. Del. 2019).

among the various parties is generally a question of fact.[5] Even where no duty exists, it is possible that, through a course of dealing or contract, a duty arises when an actor accepts responsibility for and takes actions that generate reliance on the part of the beneficiary.[6]

A. By Statute

The creation and formation of LLCs is governed by statute. State statutes vary substantially across the nation. When efforts began in 1992 to draft a uniform act, called the Uniform Limited Liability Company Act (ULLCA), nearly every state had already adopted legislation authorizing LLCs.[7] In 1996, the ULLCA was finally completed, but only six states adopted it. The ULLCA sought to codify fiduciary duties consistent with the approach taken in the Revised Uniform Partnership Act.

The ULLCA was substantially revised in 2006 and ten states adopted it. The 2006 revision recognized that the approach taken in 1996 was *too* reliant on the concept of good faith and fair dealing. The 2006 revision also sought to more fully define fiduciary duties using a "reasonableness under the circumstances standard" and defined that duty by reference to the well-known business judgment rule.

Efforts to harmonize the 2006 ULLCA with other uniform acts on unincorporated associations led to the current version of the revised 2013 ULLCA.[8] It has been adopted in nine states and the District of Columbia. Section 409 of the 2013 ULLCA deviates from the 2006 ULLCA in that it no longer expressly recognizes the business judgment rule that is a prominent measure of fiduciary duty for directors in the corporate context. The standard of reasonableness based on similar circumstances and references to fiduciary duty have also been removed. Instead, section 409(c) defines the duty of care as refraining "from

---

5. *See* Gemstar Ltd. v. Ernst & Young, 917 P.2d 222, 233 (1996).

6. *See* Spinella v. Apriva LLC, No. CV 2015-053104, 2016 WL 8939205, at *4 (Ariz. Super. Ct. Feb. 29, 2016) (citing Lloyd v. State Farm Mut. Auto Ins. Co., 860 P.2d 1304 (Ariz. Ct. App. 1992)); *see also In re* Sky Harbor Hotel Properties, LLC, 443 P.3d 21, 23 (Ariz. 2019) (describing the "fiduciary relation which results from the manifestation of consent by one person to another that the other shall act on his behalf and subject to his control, and consent by the other so to act") (quoting Restatement (Second) of Agency § 1 (Am. Law. Inst. 1958)).

7. Unif. Ltd. Liab. Co. Act (2006) (last amended 2013), Prefatory Note to ULLCA (2006), 6C U.L.A. 4 (2016). Unless otherwise indicated references in this chapter to the "uniform act" or "ULLCA" refer to the Uniform Limited Liability Company Act (2006) (last amended 2013).

8. 6C U.L.A. 1 (2016) (Harmonized) (last amended 2013) ("ULLCA (2013)"); *id.* at 7 (Prefatory Note to 2011 and 2013 Harmonization Amendments).

engaging in grossly negligent or reckless conduct, willful or intentional misconduct, or knowing violation of law."[9] The comment to section 409(c) states that "eliminating the label 'fiduciary' is merely semantics; no change in law is intended."[10]

Because some state statutes predate the uniform acts, they often rely on common-law or agency principals to establish and define the scope of fiduciary duties. Even the approach to address fiduciary duties in the 1996 ULLCA changed in the 2006 version, and then again in 2013. The purpose of the 2013 revision was "to harmonize, to the extent possible, all uniform acts pertaining to unincorporated associations."[11] Additional judicial development will be necessary to know if the different formulations and descriptions of the duties owed make a meaningful difference in the standard of conduct required for those who act for and on behalf of LLCs.

B. At Common Law

Many, but not all, state LLC statutes address the fiduciary duties owed by managers, members, and other parties to the LLC and to each other. Courts have analyzed the extent to which fiduciary duties apply at common law to LLCs in states without statutory provisions, and have generally held that such duties exist.[12] Courts have looked to the law of agency, contracts, and other areas of common law to conclude that fiduciary duties are present in the context of the LLC. The law continues to evolve in that area and states continue to amend their statutes to address fiduciary duties.

In 1992, Arizona adopted the pre-ULLCA version of the LLC act, which did not address fiduciary duties at all. The LLC act did however, provide that the principals of agency law applied to LLCs. The Arizona Supreme Court recently held that the Arizona LLC Act necessarily imposes fiduciary duties on members, managers, and the LLC because it incorporates the law of agency, which includes principals of fiduciary duty.[13] The court also determined that LLCs and their members *cannot* eliminate the implied covenant of good faith and fair dealing, which is present in every contract.[14]

---

9. 6C U.L.A. 107.
10. *Id.* at 109 (comment subsection (c)).
11. *Id.* at 7 (Prefatory Note to 2011 and 2013 Harmonization Amendments).
12. *E.g.*, Executive Ctr. v. Meieran, 823 F. Supp. 2d 883 (E.D. Wis. 2011).
13. *In re* Sky Harbor Hotel Properties, LLC, 443 P.3d 21, 22–23 (Ariz. 2019).
14. *Id.* at 24.

Delaware courts have relied on contract law, equitable conduct, and prior common law to find fiduciary duties in an LLC member context.[15] The Delaware LLC Act does not explicitly articulate that managers of Delaware LLCs owe common law fiduciary duties of care and loyalty in the same way that directors and officers do in the corporation context. Rather, Delaware law allows parties to an LLC agreement to restrict or expand fiduciary duties to the LLC or its members or managers. However, because there is an ability to *restrict* fiduciary duties, many contend that such fiduciary duties *must* exist for there to be something to restrict or eliminate by contract.[16] And although the LLC act does not expressly provide for fiduciary duties, Delaware courts have determined that *default equitable* fiduciary duties exist in an LLC context and are implicit in Delaware's LLC Act.[17] Even if an LLC agreement

> disclaims all statutory fiduciary duties of the directors, the directors' duties are limited to (i) those expressly set forth in the agreement and (ii) those that a court deems to arise under the implied covenant of good faith and fair dealing (which adheres to every contract and, by statute, cannot be waived or modified).[18]

Like Delaware, Florida relied on those same principles before amending and instating the Florida Revised LLC Act in 2015. Florida's Revised LLC Act now includes and addresses fiduciary duties that were previously lacking.[19] It specifically incorporates fiduciary duties of

---

15. *See* Gatz Properties, LLC v. Auriga Capital Corp., 59 A.3d 1206, 1214 (Del. 2012) and Auriga Capital Corp. v. Gatz Properties, 40 A.3d 839, 861 (Del. Ch.), *judgment entered sub nom.* Auriga Capital Corp. v. Gatz Properties, LLC (Del. Ch. 2012), *aff'd,* 59 A.3d 1206 (Del. 2012).

16. *Fiduciary Duties of Managers of LLCs: The Status of the Debate in Delaware*, American Bar Association (Feb. 28, 2012), *available at* https://www.americanbar.org/groups/business_law/publications/blt/2012/02/02_lazarus/.

17. *See Auriga Capital Corp.*, 40 A.3d 839; and *see* McWhinney Centerra Lifestyle Ctr. LLC v. Poag & McEwen Lifestyle Centers-Centerra LLC, 2021 WL 126572 (Colo. App. Jan. 14, 2021).

18. Gail Weinstein, Steven J. Steinman, Brian T. Mangino, Randi Lally & Maxwell Yim, *Fried Frank Discusses the Obligations of LLC Directors and Managers*, The CLS Blue Sky Blog (June 20, 2018), https://clsbluesky.law.columbia.edu/2018/06/20/fried-frank-discusses-the-obligations-of-llc-directors-and-managers/.

19. Louis T.M. Conti, *Un-Cabined Fiduciary Duties in Florida LLCs: The Common Law and Equity Opens the Door to Expanded Liability and the Manifestly Unreasonable Standard*, 91(8) Fla. Bar J. (Sept./Oct. 2017), https://www.floridabar.org/the-florida-bar-journal/un-cabined-fiduciary-duties-in-florida-llcs-the-common-law-and-equity-opens-the-door-to-expanded-liability-and-the-manifestly-unreasonable-standard/.

loyalty and care in the LLC context, relating to managers, members, and the LLC. Florida also applies a duty of good faith and fair dealing in the LLC context, which, like other states have found, cannot be waived.[20] Unlike other states, Florida's LLC Act expressly limits or prohibits all together the ways in which the fiduciary duties may be altered or eliminated.

Wisconsin's Limited Liability Company Law (WLLCL) does not expressly mention fiduciary duties, but it does provide that common law principles of agency apply to the members and/or managers of the LLC. Wisconsin courts have construed that provision to apply fiduciary duties in connection with LLCs. In doing so, Wisconsin courts have found that the WLLCL did *not* abrogate common law claims and defenses and that members and managers owe common law fiduciary duties to other members and the LLC.[21]

In summary, because LLCs are created by statute, it is appropriate to look "first, foremost, and primarily" to the statute to define fiduciary duties.[22] Yet, many states' LLC acts are ambiguous or incomplete when addressing fiduciary duties. Because of this ambiguity and incompleteness, many courts have looked to other states' LLC acts and drawn on other areas of law to fill in gaps where the applicable act is silent. The result is a growing body of case law that defines the contours of the fiduciary duties owed in various circumstances at common law.

C. By Agreement

Fiduciary duty obligations can also arise by agreement from a company's operating agreement.[23] One of the significant advantages of the LLC form over other entity forms is the flexibility of defining the relationships among the LLC's participants by contract. Most state statutes provide that, unless prohibited by law or superseded by a provision in an LLC's charter documents, an LLC may reduce or enlarge the fiduciary duties of certain actors through the company's operating agreement, or other agreement of the parties.

For imposition of fiduciary duties, the three versions of the ULLCA have been largely consistent concerning what is permissible to include in an operating agreement.[24] The differences between state statutes,

---

20. *See* Fla. Stat. § 605.04091 and Jeramie J. Fortenberry, *Florida LLC Law* (July 6, 2020), https://www.fortenberrylaw.com/llc-law/florida/#_Toc44947663.

21. Marx v. Morris, 925 N.W.2d 112, 124 (Wisc. 2019).

22. 800 S. Wells Commercial LLC v. Cadden, 103 N.E. 3d 875, 885 (Ill. Ct. App. 2018).

23. ULLCA (2013) § 105.

24. ULLCA (1996) § 103(b)(2)-(4); ULLCA (2006) § 110(c)(4)-(5), (9), (d), ULLCA (2013) § 105(c)(5)-(7), (11), (d).

state common laws, relevant state case law, and adopted ULLCA versions all determine what may be accomplished in an operating agreement in relation to expanding or eliminating fiduciary duties for an LLC's members, managers, or the LLC itself.

1. Expansions and Limitations on Fiduciary Duties by Agreement

Generally, an LLC can, by contract through its operating agreement, expand or limit the fiduciary duties of various actors within the LLC. Pursuant to the multiple versions of ULLA, operating agreements can define the standards of performance related to the fiduciary duties of members or managers as long as those standards are "not manifestly unreasonable."[25] For example, an operating agreement could enlarge the scope of the fiduciary duty to impose the same fiduciary duties owed by officers and directors to a corporation.[26] Conversely, an operating agreement may allow managers to engage in self-interested transactions.[27] In many states, an LLC can limit fiduciary duties of managers and other persons in its operating agreement with exculpatory provisions.[28] Further, an operating agreement can limit affirmative duties to take certain actions that would typically be required for a manager or other person to fulfill fiduciary duties, such as removal of the duty to provide information or the books and records of the LLC to its members.[29] Even Florida law, which is more restrictive in terms of the allowance of the elimination or modification of fiduciary duties than are other jurisdictions, permits *some* alteration of these duties within specified limits.

---

25. *Id.*

26. *See* Strebel v. Wimberly, 371 S.W.3d 267, 271 (Tex. Ct. App. 2012) (analyzing an operating agreement that provided that "the Managers shall have fiduciary duties to the Company and the Members equivalent to the fiduciary duties of directors of Delaware corporations" and applying substantive Delaware corporate law to determine whether there was a breach of fiduciary duty by the Manager).

27. *See, e.g.*, Synectic Ventures I, LLC v. EVI Corp., 294 P.3d 478, 485–86 (Or. 2012) (observing that Oregon law permits self-interested transactions that are authorized by operating agreement or that are approved by members).

28. *E.g.*, Kelly v. Blum, 2010 WL 629850 (Del. Ch. 2010) (discussing 6 Del. C. § 18-1101(e)).

29. Feeley v. NHAOCG, LLC, 62 A.3d 649, 664 (Del. Ch. 2012); *see also* J. William Callison & Maureen A. Sullivan, *Limited* Liability Companies: A State-by-State Guide to Law and Practice, Ltd. Liability Co., Fiduciary Duties § 8:7 n.45 (2020 ed.) (collecting cases).

2. Limitations (and Limitations on Limitations) on Fiduciary Duties Imposed by Law

Many jurisdictions provide that the covenant of good faith and fair dealing is imposed by law and part of every contract. The ULLCA has consistently prohibited attempts to eliminate the covenant from operating agreements.[30] Courts generally will give effect to an operating agreement's language that establishes, limits, or sometimes eliminates fiduciary duties. Delaware and other states permit the complete elimination of fiduciary duties, but not the implied contractual covenant of good faith and fair dealing.[31]

Although parties have the legal right to make whatever contracts they desire, they cannot contract for illegal purposes or against public policy.[32] The majority of the courts that have analyzed fiduciary duties in the LLC context have found that parties cannot contract around the covenant of good faith and fair dealing and that the attempt to do so is against public policy or contrary to law. Generally, a contract that cannot be performed without violating applicable law is illegal and void, and thus unenforceable.[33] Thus, while most states permit the elimination or modification of fiduciary duties as applicable to LLCs and its members or managers, some restrictions and prohibitions uniformly remain across the states in that regard.

IV. The Individuals Who May Have Fiduciary Duties

The roles of shareholders, partners, officers, and directors are more easily defined in corporations and partnerships than in the LLC context. LLCs are creatures of customization by contract, coupled with a myriad of choices afforded to parties to alter their roles and relationships

30. ULLCA (1996) § 103(b)(4); ULLCA (2006) § 110(c)(5); ULLCA (2013) § 105(c)(6).

31. *See, e.g.*, TM2008 Investments, Inc. v. Procon Capital Corp., 323 P.3d 704, 708 (Ariz. Ct. App. 2014); Feeley v. NHAOCG, LLC, 62 A.3d 649, 664 (Del. Ch. 2012).

32. ULLCA (1996) §§ 103(b)(3), 409(c); ULLCA (2006) § 110(d)(3); ULLCA (2013) § 105(c)(7).

33. E & S Insulation Co. of Arizona v. E. L. Jones Const. Co., 591 P.2d 560, 562 (Ariz. Ct. App. 1979); *see also* Mountain States Bolt, Nut & Screw Co. v. Best-Way Transp., 568 P.2d 431 (Ariz. Ct. App. 1977) ("(I)f the acts to be performed under the contract are themselves illegal or contrary to public policy, or if the legislature has clearly demonstrated its intent to prohibit maintenance of a cause of action, then recovery should be denied.").

as members and managers. This contributes to the unique flexibility of LLCs, but makes defining the roles and relationships among members, managers, officers, and other role players in the LLC more complex. Because of that, it is difficult to make generalized statements of the law for actors within the LLC. This is especially true with respect to fiduciary duties of these actors in the LLC context. Moreover, state statutes vary across the nation. And, many states, like Delaware, have more case law to draw from to address these issues, versus other states that have had less opportunity to deal with LLC roles and fiduciary duties and thus little case law or analysis to look to for clarification.

A. Officers

Officers of an LLC sometimes owe fiduciary duties in the same way as they would in a corporation.[34] Yet, when the officers are supervised by the LLC's manager(s), some courts have held that such officers may not have fiduciary duties.[35] In an Illinois case, an LLC brought suit against its officer (a vice president) for breaching its fiduciary duty to its members and the LLC by diverting corporate opportunities, improperly transferring assets, and improperly allocating expenses.[36] Because the LLC was expressly a manager-managed LLC, the court determined that where activities are exclusively controlled by an LLC's manager, the duties owed to the company reside in the manager, and *not* in the officer. It held that an officer does not owe any fiduciary duties to an LLC (or its members) simply by being an officer of the LLC.

B. Managers in a Manager-Managed LLC

When an LLC is not managed by its members, but elects to have its affairs directed by one or more managers, managers are analogous to directors and officers in a corporation and tend to have similar fiduciary duties. Although the scope of the fiduciary duties may be enlarged or limited by an operating agreement, it will be subject to the covenant of good faith and fair dealing, as discussed earlier.[37]

Without a contrary provision in the operating agreement, the manager of an LLC owes duties of loyalty and care to the members of the

34. *See In re* BH S & B Holdings LLC, 420 B.R. 112 (Bankr. S.D.N.Y. 2009).
35. 800 S. Wells Commercial LLC v. Cadden, 103 N.E.3d 875, 886 (Ill. Ct. App. 2018).
36. *Id.*
37. *Supra* Section III(c)(ii).

LLC.[38] Many states that have adopted statutory provisions about managerial duties "require managers to act in *good faith* and with such care as an ordinarily prudent person would exercise in similar circumstances (i.e., a *reasonableness standard*)."[39]

C. Controlling Members

Controlling members hold an ownership interest that permits them to make decisions for the company, even where those decisions may be contrary to the wishes of other members and where a decision may be detrimental to the interests of the company or other members. Most courts treat controlling members the same as controlling shareholders[40] in a corporation.[41] This differs from a passive LLC member, who has an ownership interest but does not actively participate in or control the company's decisions or its operations.

Controlling members are generally found to owe fiduciary duties to the LLC and minority members of the LLC in the same vein as managers of an LLC do.[42] Delaware courts have held that members who control an LLC owe fiduciary duties to the LLC *and* noncontrolling members.[43] Managing members[44] of an LLC owe fiduciary duties to the LLC and its member investors, thus, a managing member must act with the utmost good faith and loyalty in managing the LLC.[45]

---

38. Bay Ctr. Apartments Owner, LLC, v. Emery Bay PKI, LLC, C.A. No. 3658-VCS, 2009 WL 1124451, at *8 (Del. Ch. Apr. 20, 2009).

39. Callison & Sullivan, *supra* note 29, § 8:7.

40. A controlling shareholder is a shareholder who owns the largest number of a corporation's shares or one who has control over the company's affairs for reasons other than share ownership percentage. *See, e.g.*, Kahn v. Lynch Commc'n Sys., Inc., 638 A.2d 1110, 1113 (Del. 1994).

41. *See* Kelly v. Blum, CA. No. 4516-VCP, 2010 WL 629850, at *12 (Del. Ch. Feb. 24, 2010).

42. Glidepath Ltd. v. Beumer Corp., No. CV 12220-VCL, 2019 WL 855660, at *18 (Del. Ch. Feb. 21, 2019), *judgment entered* (Del. Ch. 2019) ("Buyer owed fiduciary duties as a controlling member."); Kelly v. Blum, 2010 WL 629850 (Del. Ch. 2010).

43. *See* Klein v. Wasserman, 2019 WL 2296027 (Del. Ch. 2019) (control can be established through ownership or through showing of actual control over LLC's business and affairs through general control or specific control); Glidepath Ltd. v. Beumer Corp., 2019 WL 855660 (Del. Ch. 2019) (LLC controller owes fiduciary duties); Cancan Dev. v. Manno, 2015 WL 3400789 (Del. Ch. 2015); *In re* Atlas Energy Resources, 2010 WL 4273122 (Del. Ch. 2010) (controlling members in member-managed LLC owe minority members the traditional fiduciary duties that controlling shareholder owes to minority shareholders).

44. A managing-member is a member who is designated to make decisions for the company regardless of their ownership interest percentage in the LLC.

45. 51 Am. Jur. 2d Limited Liability Companies § 11 (Nov. 2020 update).

D. Members

Generally, absent an agreement, members of an LLC do not owe fiduciary duties to each other solely by virtue of being a member.[46] Yet, in Arizona and some other states, members will be found to have fiduciary duties to the LLC and the other members if the LLC is member managed.[47]

In a manager-managed LLC, neither common law nor the law of corporations or partnerships expressly imposes a fiduciary duty on members of an LLC without a duty being imposed through an operating agreement.[48] The caveat here is that this general statement assumes the member is passive and not controlling, and that the member has not undertaken to act on behalf of the LLC. As discussed earlier, a controlling member has fiduciary duties to noncontrolling members.[49] Further, a member who controls or acts on behalf of the LLC may have fiduciary duties to the other members.[50]

E. The LLC

The LLC itself does not generally have fiduciary duties to its members, but this is an evolving area of law.[51] Note that an LLC can have fiduciary duties to members of other LLCs, if, for example, the LLC is the manager or controlling member of another LLC.[52]

---

46. *In re* Tsiaoushis, 2007 WL 2156162 (E.D. Va. 2007) (nonmanaging members of manager-managed LLCs owe no fiduciary duties).

47. Ariz. Rev. Stat. § 29-3409.

48. TM2008 Investments, Inc. v. Procon Capital Corp., 323 P.3d 704, 708 (Ariz. Ct. App. 2014).

49. Controlling members are prohibited, for example, from engaging in oppressive conduct. *See* ULLCA § 701(5)(b); *see also* Sports Imaging of Arizona, L.L.C. v.1993 CKC Tr., No. 1 CA-CV 05-0205, 2008 WL 4448063, at *19 (Ariz. Ct. App. Sept. 30, 2008).

50. Evergreen W. Bus. Ctr., LLC v. Emmert, 296 P.3d 545, 552 (Or. 2012), *rev'd on other grounds*, 323 P.3d 250 (Or. 2014) (en banc) (finding that a member had "entered into a relationship of confidence with the company that required him to act 'in good faith and with due regard to the interests of the one reposing the confidence'") (quoting Starkweather v. Shaffer, 497 P.2d 358 (Or. 1972) (en banc)).

51. *See* Khoobehi Properties, LLC v. Baronne Development No. 2, L.L.C., 16-506 (La. Ct. App. 5th Cir. 3/29/17), *writ denied*, 2017-0893, 227 So. 3d 288 (La. 9/29/17) (LLC was not liable for breach of fiduciary duty for not disclosing material information to member before member sold interest).

52. Generally, courts will differentiate between parties who serve in multiple capacities, such as a member and a creditor. *See, e.g.*, Bootheel Ethanol Investments, L.L.C. v. Semo Ethanol Co-op., 2009 WL 398506 (E.D. Mo. 2009) (no fiduciary duties owed by member who failed to make capital contributions with respect to nonpayment of LLC's debt to other member allegedly resulting); *In re* South Canaan Cellular Investments, LLC, 427 B.R.

V. To Whom Is a Fiduciary Duty Owed?

A. To the Limited Liability Company

More case law is developing that indicates fiduciary duties *are* owed to the LLC itself, either by managers, members, or both. North Carolina has found that an LLC manager's obligation to discharge his duties in good faith, with the care an ordinary prudent person in a like position would exercise under similar circumstances, and in the manner the manager reasonably believes to be in the best interests of the LLC, is owed by the manager *to the company*, rather than to other members.[53]

In *Flippo v. CSC Assocs.*,[54] the Virginia Supreme Court affirmed that a member of an LLC was directly liable for a breach of fiduciary duty *to the LLC.*[55] *Flippo* involved a claim for breach of fiduciary duty against the member-manager of an LLC for conveying assets to another business entity for the member-manager's personal benefit.

B. To the Limited Liability Company's Members

Whether members owe fiduciary duties to each other appears to be expanding with the implementation of new state statutes and supplemental case law. As discussed, many states impose equitable fiduciary duties among members that can be altered based on agreement, and, whether a member owes fiduciary duties to other members will normally depend on the type of LLC involved—including whether the LLC is member or manager managed, and whether the LLC member has any control or management responsibilities. Passive members will generally not owe fiduciary duties to other members. However, when members *are* found to owe each other a fiduciary duty, they are the typical fiduciary duties discussed herein: the duty of loyalty and of care.

Members may enforce these rights on behalf of the LLC itself. The ULLCA has consistently recognized the right of members to maintain actions at law and in equity to enforce their rights under the operating

85 (Bankr. E.D. Pa. 2010) (member could become LLC creditor and could use information provided by LLC); Christopher's Partner, LLC v. Christopher's of Colonie, LLC, 69 A.D.3d 1275, 893 N.Y.S. 2d 689 (3d Dep't 2010) (member as secured creditor).

53. Kaplan v. O.K. Technologies, L.L.C., 675 S.E.2d 133 (N.C. Ct. App. 2009), *review denied*, 690 S.E.2d 699 (N.C. 2010).

54. 547 S.E. 2d 216 (Va. 2001).

55. *Id.* at 219.

agreement and to assert derivative rights on behalf of the LLC.[56] The 1996 ULLCA recognized the right to bring derivative actions, but did not protect against unreasonable restrictions in operating agreements until the 2006 version of ULLCA was enacted.[57] The 2013 amended version of ULLCA carried forward the preservation of derivative actions in operating agreements.[58] The act prohibits eliminating or unreasonably restricting the right to bring such claims.

Nevertheless, the right to bring an action on behalf of the LLC may not provide the remedy the member seeks. In *Gowin v. Granite Depot*,[59] the Virginia Supreme Court permitted a member to bring a derivative action against the manager for a breach of his fiduciary duty to the LLC. Although it was acknowledged that one reason for action was to terminate the interest of the other member, the court found the action did not have any impact on the LLC and denied recovery.

C. To the Limited Liability Company's Creditors

As discussed in more detail in Chapter 12, at times, fiduciary duties may be owed to creditors. This is particularly so when an entity is *insolvent*. Some states have held that managers of insolvent LLCs have fiduciary duties to creditors of the LLC.[60] The Delaware court in *Gheewalla* held that when a corporation is insolvent, "creditors become the principal constituency injured by any fiduciary breaches that diminish the firm's value."[61]

That said, it is not always clear that a creditor could bring an action to enforce its rights. Some courts have held that creditors cannot bring a direct action against managers breaching a fiduciary duty owed to a creditor.[62] And other courts, such as the Delaware court in *CML*,

56. ULLCA (1996) §§ 1101–1104; ULLCA (2006) §§ 901–906; ULLCA (2013) §§ 801–806.

57. ULLCA (2006) § 110(a)(9).

58. ULLCA (2013) § 105(c)(11).

59. 634 S.E.2d 714 (Va. 2006).

60. *In re* Senior Cottages of America, LLC, 482 F.3d 997 (8th Cir. 2007) (fact that fiduciary duties might also run to creditors does not prevent bankruptcy trustee from making claim on LLC's behalf); *In re* McCook Metals, L.L.C., 319 B.R. 570 (Bankr. N.D. Ill. 2005) (managers of insolvent LLCs owe fiduciary duties to LLC creditors; manager usurped LLC opportunity by acquiring asset into another LLC); JPMorgan Chase Bank, N.A. v. KB Home, 632 F. Supp. 2d 1013 (D. Nev. 2009) (Nevada law would extend corporate insolvency exception to LLCs so that managers have fiduciary duties to creditors).

61. N. Am. Catholic Educ. Programming Found., Inc. v. Gheewalla, 930 A.2d 92, 102 (Del. 2007).

62. *In re* Mooney, 2007 BNH 29, 2007 WL 2403774 (Bankr. D. N.H. 2007) (although managers of insolvent LLC have similar fiduciary duties as officers and directors of an

have held that derivative claims *cannot* be brought by creditors in the context of an LLC.[63] "Creditors are often protected by strong covenants, liens on assets, and other negotiated contractual protections."[64] To limit creditors to their bargained-for rights and deny them a *new* right to sue derivatively on behalf of an insolvent entity tracks the LLC act's contractarian environment.[65]

All versions of the ULLCA have taken a fairly restrictive approach to third parties, including creditors, interfering with the operation and management of LLCs. Although derivative actions are authorized in all three versions of the act, each limits the "proper plaintiff" to "a member of the company when the action is commenced."[66] The statutory language, the policy of defining relationships by agreement of the parties, and the philosophy of encouraging parties to know their partners, and *not* compelling members to admit outsiders, suggests that creditors who are not parties to the operating agreement are unlikely to be permitted to assert rights and urge duties owed to the LLC by its managers and members.

VI. Conclusion

The LLC entity form offers flexibility in the fiduciary duty realm. The ability of members to control which fiduciary duties and to whom they are owed is a significant advantage of the LLC form to a savvy drafter at the inception of the entity. Although state statutes and courts nationally have tended to find fiduciary duties in the LLC context, there is still much opportunity to control those duties by expanding, limiting, or eliminating them through the operating agreement. When creating an LLC, the drafter of an operating agreement should carefully consider the LLC's members and what fiduciary duties are appropriate, if any. Additionally, the drafter should consider the LLC's state statutes, recent court decisions, and the latest version of the ULLCA in order to have a full understanding of how fiduciary duties may be determined should an issue arise down the road with the LLC or its members.

---

insolvent corporation, creditors cannot bring direct action against managers).

63. CML V, LLC v. Bax, 6 A.3d 238, 250 (Del. Ch. 2010), *aff'd*, 28 A.3d 1037 (Del. 2011), as corrected (Sept. 6, 2011).

64. *Id.*

65. *Id.*

66. ULLCA (1996) § 1102; ULLCA (2006) § 903; ULLCA (2013) § 803.

Chapter 6

Fiduciary Duty Claims Involving Investment Advisers and Other Financial Professionals

By Stephen L. Brodsky

I. Introduction

The financial services industry can be confusing. The nearly $75 trillion industry is filled with different types of professionals and companies. For example, there are investment advisers, financial advisers, financial planners, wealth managers, and investment consultants. There are also brokers, broker-dealers, and brokerage houses. Many advise their clients on investments and strategies, invest on their clients' behalf, and manage their clients' portfolios as they deem fit. Others execute trades and make investments as their customers instruct. Still others may recommend a financial plan based on investment objectives and a current financial position. Despite all these different types of financial professionals who may do different things, nearly half of all retail investors in the United States believe that all owe the same duties and are subject to the same standards of care. That is incorrect. As discussed in this chapter, investment advisers and certain others owe fiduciary duties to their clients, while others do not.

At the same time, financial professionals themselves must ensure they understand and satisfy their legal obligations, which have evolved over the years. This is due in large part to proposed regulations that may or may not be finalized and enacted and agency statements that clarify or expand upon existing law. One example is the Department of Labor's (DOL) Fiduciary Rule. The DOL proposed the Fiduciary Rule in April 2015, intending that it mandate fiduciary obligations for all professionals in the retirement industry, in addition to ERISA plan fiduciaries. Though the Fifth Circuit Court of Appeals struck down the Fiduciary Rule in 2018, the DOL proposed a modified version in 2020. Another example is Regulation Best Interest (Reg BI), which the Securities Exchange Commission (SEC) adopted in early June 2020. Reg BI enhanced the standard of conduct for broker-dealers beyond existing suitability obligations, and clarifies that broker-dealers must act in the "best interest" of their customers.[1] It is not yet clear whether Reg BI helped or made matters worse—both for investors and financial professionals—and although the Second Circuit Court of Appeals upheld Reg BI, vigorous public and industry debate over Reg BI is ongoing.

With this backdrop in mind, in this chapter we discuss the duties that investment advisers and other financial professionals owe to their clients and customers. First, we discuss the different types of services that various financial professionals provide. Then, we review the legal framework underlying the duties and standards of care for these professionals—statutory, regulatory, and at common law. We then discuss why investment advisers owe fiduciary duties to their clients, why others are typically subject to lesser, nonfiduciary standards of care, and when those professionals may be deemed to owe fiduciary duties to their retail customers. We also discuss breach of fiduciary duty claims that investment advisers and broker-dealers may face, when and why such relationships may arise, and the considerations courts may assess and weigh when resolving the claims.

Finally, we address the ongoing industry debate whether all financial service professionals should owe fiduciary duties to those they service. We consider the unintended result that the United Kingdom experienced after it banned commissions for all professionals, and analyze the different types of professional relationships in the industry that sit on opposite ends of a spectrum—the fiduciary relationship of the investment adviser/client relationship on one end, and the contractual relationship of the broker-dealer/customer on the other.

1. *See* Financial Insurance Regulatory Authority (FINRA) Rule 2111, as amended by SR-FINRA-2020-007.

II. Financial Professionals

A. Investment Advisers

1. Services

Broadly speaking, investment advisers (also spelled "advisors") provide investment advice and related financial advisory services to their clients on an ongoing basis. They may recommend investment strategies and types of investments to their clients, execute transactions on their clients' behalf, and manage their clients' investment portfolios and other financial affairs. They may also provide related financial services such as tax advice, recommendations as to insurance coverage and products, and even "home office" services. Their recommended investments and strategies may derive from their own education, professional experience, and even their particular investment models and philosophies. Over time, and in response to market or other events, they may adjust their clients' investments as they believe appropriate and in the interest of their clients.

Certainly, the relationships that investment advisers may have with each of their clients can differ greatly. Some clients may demand to be involved in all decisions and strategies. Others may not have the time or desire to be engaged in this manner; they may simply want an annual report and a telephone call about the prior year's performance and recommendations for the next year. Investment advisers understand that, in their roles as "trusted advisers," they may need to say things to their clients they may not want to hear, to protect their clients from making unwise, emotional, or reactive decisions. Bill Hammer Jr., founder and CEO of Hammer Wealth Group, states, "Over a lifetime, a few big mistakes can dramatically change where you end up financially. That's why having an adviser who isn't afraid tell you the uncomfortable truth is so important. I believe part of my duty is to tell my clients uncomfortable truths to protect them."

The investment adviser/client relationship is a fiduciary one. Clients place their trust and confidence in their advisers, relying upon them for their knowledge and skill. Advisers, in turn, take on a position of superiority, control, and authority over their clients. Stacy Francis, president and CEO of Francis Financial, a firm that serves divorced and widowed women, states,

> I equate the faith that a person puts in an investment adviser to the confidence that a patient places in her physician. The patient is not a medical expert and relies on the doctor to give

> the best possible advice for her overall well-being and health. This relationship is built on a solid foundation of trust, confidence, and reliance. The same is true of an investment adviser and her client.

Avani Ramnani, managing director with Francis Financial, adds that "It is also essential to educate your clientele. To some, financial terms can be challenging to understand and overly complicated. An investment adviser must explain these terms, concepts, and recommendations as neglecting to do so can lead to misunderstandings, misinterpretations, or misguided advice."

Trust is an intrinsic aspect of the relationship. Edward J. Mooney, senior family wealth strategist with BNY Mellon Wealth Management, states, "So when I think about the fiduciary standard, I come at it as being somewhat akin to the standard of a trustee where you review the terms of the trust and discuss with the beneficiaries their risk tolerances and income needs to determine the appropriate course of action." He adds,

> But more personally I think of the fiduciary standard as being a question of trust in its most basic sense, trust in that as the investment adviser you are taking on the management of what could be only a small amount of client's wealth to fulfill a distinct investment allocation or it may be managing the bulk of a client's life savings. In either case, the stewardship of the client's funds is an enormous responsibility.

Larry Heller, the president of Heller Wealth Management, echoes this sentiment, adding that, "Our clients can think of us as the quarterback of their team, coordinating the players for a successful retirement. This is one of our chief roles as a trusted financial adviser to our clients."

2. Compensation

As compensation for their services, investment advisers typically charge a percentage of assets under management (AUM), a fixed hourly fee, or a combination of both. These compensation arrangements are considered transparent and most unlikely to result in bias or conflicts of interest, and, therefore, they are considered most appropriate for investment advisers.

Investors who retain investment advisers generally pay more than investors who use the services of broker-dealers and financial planners. This is not surprising, given the comprehensive, ongoing advisory and other services investment advisers provide. It is important to note that many investors may not need, desire, or be able to afford an investment adviser. For them, broker-dealers and financial planners are sufficient and at the right price point.

3. Licenses

U.S. investment advisers must be licensed, as any other financial professional. FINRA and the North American Securities Administrators Association (NASAA) oversee securities licensing procedures and requirements. Investment advisers and others who provide investment advice on a percentage of AUM or hourly fee require at a minimum a Series 65 license issued by NASAA, which is needed to provide any financial advice or service on a noncommission basis.

4. Designations

One may notice three- or four-letter designations, such as CFP®, ChFC®, or CFA®, after an investment adviser's name. The letters denote certifications that an adviser received, which are granted based on degrees, coursework, work experience, and/or examinations. The CFP board oversees the Certified Financial Planner (CFP®) certification, while the American College of Financial Services renders the Chartered Financial Consultant (ChFC®) certification. The CFA Institute grants the Chartered Financial Analyst (CFA®) certification for financial analysts, as opposed to financial advisers.

B. Broker-Dealers

1. Services

Broker-dealers execute investments and other securities transactions on behalf of their retail customers, as they instruct. They may also recommend investments to their customers, based on their customers' investment objectives and financial circumstances.[2] It is important to note that the duties that broker-dealers owe to their customers depends in large part on the scope and nature of their authority. For example, those who trade in a nondiscretionary account for their customers owe

2. Broker-dealers provide the same broker services for their customers and also may invest on their own account. The terms "broker" and "broker-dealer" will be used interchangeably.

no fiduciary duties. Their duties are limited to faithfully and competently executing transactions and providing accurate, unbiased, and complete information when making investment recommendations or dealing with other matters within their purview. As discussed later in the chapter, Reg BI expanded broker-dealer duties and mandates that a broker-dealer act in the "best interest" of its customer. This best-interest obligation, however, is still a nonfiduciary duty.

Nonetheless, there are times when a broker-dealer may be deemed to owe fiduciary duties to its customer. For example, many state courts hold that a broker who trades in a discretionary account for its customer will owe fiduciary duties to its customer, by virtue of the agency authority that the customer has given to the broker-dealers. Apart from this rather bright-line case, it is always possible that the particular facts and circumstances may implicate fiduciary obligations. Certainly, when and why a fiduciary relationship may arise is immensely fact specific.

2. Compensation

Brokers-dealers are usually compensated by commissions, which may be based on the investment products sold to the customer and/or the transactions executed. Reg BI was intended to address the possibility that broker-dealers may have an incentive to recommend trades or investments that benefit them. Therefore, Reg BI enhances the disclosures that broker-dealers must undertake and the considerations they must weigh, before recommending any trade or investment to their customers.

3. Licenses

Brokers, at a minimum, require a Series 7 license issued by FINRA. A Series 7 license authorizes licensees to sell virtually any type of individual security, except for commodities futures, real estate, and life insurance. It is known in the industry as the general securities' representative license.

C. Financial Planners and Other Professionals

The range of services that different financial professionals provide is beneficial. There is no one size fits all. One investor may want an investment adviser for ongoing portfolio management and oversight, while another may want a broker to execute trades for it, and still another may want someone to provide a financial plan. FINRA makes clear that the last group of professionals, known as "financial planners," may come from a variety of backgrounds and offer a variety of services.[3] Financial planners could be brokers, investment advisers, insurance agents, or accountants, or they may have no financial credentials at all. The scope of services a financial planner may provide will vary; while some may create comprehensive plans that address every aspect of an individual's financial plans, others may have a much more limited focus. They are regulated in relation to the "other" services they provide. A financial planner who is also a registered investment adviser will be regulated by the SEC or the state regulatory in which he or she does business, while an accountant who also prepares financial plans will be regulated by the state Board of Accountancy for the state in which the accountant practices.

Like the range of services available to investors, it is helpful to view the relationships between financial professionals and their clients or customers on a spectrum. On one end is the limited, "arm's-length" relationship between a broker-dealer and a retail customer. The broker-dealer's duty to its customer is fundamentally contractual in nature, though augmented by governing regulations. On the other end is the special relationship of trust and confidence between an investment adviser and its client. The investment adviser owes a fiduciary duty to its client (the strictest duty recognized at law), due to the faith and reliance that the client places in the adviser, and the position of superiority, control, and discretionary authority the adviser has over its client's affairs. To best understand the bases for these duties and standards of care, we should understand their legal underpinnings.

III. Statutory and Regulatory Framework

A. Investment Advisers Act

Congress enacted the Investment Advisers Act of 1940 (IAA) in response to a 1935 report by the SEC after the stock market crash of 1929 and the ensuing Great Depression. The IAA provides the statutory framework for monitoring those who provide investment advice to individuals, institutions, and pension funds.[4] It defines an "investment adviser"

3. *See* https://www.finra.org/investors/learn-to-invest/choosing-investment-professional/financial-planners.

4. *See* 15 U.S.C. §§ 80b-1 *et seq.*

as a "person or firm that, for compensation, is engaged in the act of providing advice, making recommendations, issuing reports, or furnishing analyses on securities, either directly or through publications."[5] Among others, the IAA excludes banks, attorneys, and any broker or dealer whose performance of advisory services is "solely incidental" to their business and who receive no "special compensation" for those services.[6]

The IAA mandates that investment advisers register either with the SEC or state regulators based upon certain AUM thresholds. In July 2020, the Dodd-Frank Wall Street Reform and Consumer Protection Act and SEC rules increased the IAA's monetary thresholds. Presently, investment advisers with $110 million or more AUM must register with the SEC. Those with less than $110 AUM must register with the state securities authority for the state in which the adviser has its principal place of business.[7] Registration is not meant to reflect an endorsement or recommendation by the SEC or state authority. It simply means that the investment adviser has fulfilled all of its registration requirements, including providing certain information, and that it is subject to the jurisdiction and regulation of the SEC and/or state regulator. An investment adviser registered pursuant to the IAA is commonly known as a "registered investment adviser," or "RIA." Often, such advisers refer to themselves by this term.

The IAA imposes broad fiduciary duties on investment advisers. Notably, the IAA does not itself expressly state that investment advisers are fiduciaries to their clients. The U.S. Supreme Court, however, has held that an investment adviser's fiduciary duties are both mandated and apparent, in light of the IAA's overall framework and legislative history,[8] its antifraud provisions in section 206,[9] and the very nature of

5. 15 U.S.C. § 80b-2(a)(11).

6. *Id.* § 80b-2(a)(11)(A)-(C).

7. *See also* Form ADV, App. B.

8. SEC v. Capital Gains Research Bureau, Inc., 375 US. 180, 191–92 (1963) (the IAA "reflects a congressional recognition 'of the delicate fiduciary nature of an investment advisory relationship,' as well as a congressional intent to eliminate, or at least to expose, all conflicts of interest which might incline as investment adviser—consciously or unconsciously—to render advice which was not disinterested."); Transamerica Mortgage Advisors v. Lewis, 444 U.S. 11 (1970) ("The Act's legislative history leaves no doubt that Congress intended to impose enforceable fiduciary obligations.").

9. Santa Fe Indus., Inc. v. Green, 430 U.S. 462, 472, n.11 (1977) (the IAA "prohibits, as a 'fraud or deceit upon any client,' a registered investment adviser's failure to disclose to his clients his own financial interest in his recommendations). Although Capital Gains involved a federal securities statute, the Court's references to fraud in the 'equitable' sense of the term were premised on its recognition that Congress intended the Investment Advisers Act to establish federal fiduciary standards for investment advisers."). *See also* Hollerich, v. Acri,

relationship between an investment adviser and its client.[10] The seminal decision by the U.S. Supreme Court, *Capital Gains Research*,[11] has been interpreted to establish a federal fiduciary standard for investment advisers based upon the IAA. The SEC, which oversees and regulates the IAA, has issued its own guidance concerning the fiduciary duties of investment advisers. As discussed later, the SEC issued its final "interpretation" of the fiduciary duties owed by investment advisers to their clients in Release No. IA-5248, Commission Interpretation Regarding Standard of Conduct for Investment Advisers ("Release IA-5248").[12]

B. Investment Companies Act

At the time that Congress enacted the IAA, it also enacted the Investment Company Act of 1940 (ICA). The ICA regulates investment companies (such as mutual funds) and provides the statutory basis for the fiduciary duties that investment advisers owe to these companies. The fiduciary duties reflect the unique relationships that investment advisers have to investment companies.[13] The ICA addresses other matters, such as financial disclosures, retail investment products, accounting and recordkeeping, changes to investment policies, and actions in the event of fraud or a breach of fiduciary duty. As with the IAA, the SEC oversees and regulates the ICA.

C. DOL's Fiduciary Duty Rule

In April 2015, the DOL proposed new legislation concerning professionals in the retirement industry. The DOL's proposal was in response to the Obama administration's call to clarify the duties and obligations of retirement industry professionals. The DOL's intended legislation, which became known as the "fiduciary rule," expanded the definition of an "investment advice fiduciary" in the Employee Retirement Income

---

259 F. Supp. 3d 806 (N.D. Ill. 2017); Morris v. Wachovia Securities, Inc., 277 F. Supp. 2d 622 (E.D. Va. 2003).

10. *Capital Gains Research*, 375 U.S. at 191–92.

11. 375 U.S. 180, 191–92 (1963).

12. Release IA-5248 became effective on July 12, 2019.

13. For example, a mutual fund is a pool of assets, typically consisting of securities, that belong to the investors, or shareholders, who hold shares in the fund. Burks v. Lasker, 441 U.S. 471, 480 (1979). Mutual funds usually have no employees of their own. Typically, an investment adviser sets up the mutual fund, selects the fund's directors, manages the investments and provides other advisory services for a fee. Jones v. Harris Assocs., L.P., 559 U.S. 335, 346 (2010).

Security Act of 1974 (ERISA). In so doing, the fiduciary rule sought to make all who work with retirement plans or provide retirement planning advice "fiduciaries." However, it thereby imposed new fiduciary status upon retail service providers in the retirement industry, including brokers, dealers, and insurance agents who sell annuities to IRAs. The fiduciary rule resulted in extremely vigorous public and industry debate, and even controversy. The Trump administration ultimately delayed implementation of the fiduciary rule to allow for additional analyses of its potential impact. During that time, six court actions were filed that challenged the fiduciary rule's validity and lawfulness.

On June 21, 2018, the Fifth Circuit Court of Appeals, in *Chamber of Commerce v. U.S. Dep't of Labor*, struck down the fiduciary rule *in toto*.[14] While the DOL did not contest the Fifth Circuit's ruling, then DOL Secretary Alexander Acosta announced plans to present a redrafting of the rule in the future. On June 29, 2020, the DOL issued a new modified, proposed "fiduciary rule" to regulate "investment advice fiduciaries" under ERISA. This has resulted in yet another strident debate. One issue is whether the DOL's proposal comports with the distinctions between fiduciary conduct and nonfiduciary conduct, in the manner that the Model Regulation of the National Association of Insurance Commissioners (NAIC) and Reg BI do. Another issue is that the DOL's proposal confers ERISA fiduciary status and standards to rollover recommendations not previously viewed as fiduciary advice. It is unclear whether the DOL's "new" fiduciary rule will be adopted in its present form.

D. SEC Release IA-5248: Investment Adviser's Fiduciary Duties under the IAA

On June 5, 2019, the SEC adopted Release IA-5248, in which the SEC commented upon and gave guidance concerning the fiduciary duties of investment advisers pursuant to the IAA. Release IA-5248 has also become known as the SEC's "final interpretation" of the IAA. The SEC issued the final interpretation after it had reviewed over 150 comment letters to an April 18, 2018, proposed interpretation of the IAA. The

---

14. *See* Chamber of Commerce, 885 F.3d 360 (5th Cir. 2018). The Fifth Circuit held that the DOL's new definition of "fiduciary" was inconsistent with ERISA, the Internal Revenue Code, and common law meanings of the term, predicated on a special relationship of trust and confidence. It also held that Fiduciary Rule impermissibly created private rights of action against brokers and insurance agents with no congressional authorization. Therefore, it vacated the fiduciary rule, on the ground that it was arbitrary and capricious abuse of power by the DOL. 885 F.3d at 388.

comment letters provided to the SEC were submitted by individuals, investment advisers, trade and professional organizations, consumer advocacy groups, law firms, and bar associations.

In Release IA-5248, the SEC stated that the IAA set a federal fiduciary duty for investment advisers based upon common law principles and the nature of the adviser/client relationship, which the SEC described as one of "trust and confidence." The fiduciary duty the SEC enunciated encompasses an overarching obligation to serve the best interests of its client, such that the adviser may never place its own interests ahead those of its client. Moreover, the fiduciary duty is comprised of two components: the duty of care and the duty of loyalty. The duty of care requires the investment adviser to provide investment advice in the best interest of its client, based on its client's objectives. The duty of loyalty obligates the adviser to eliminate or make full and fair disclosure of all conflicts of interest that might incline the adviser—consciously or unconsciously—to render advice that is not impartial and disinterested. This is so that the client may provide informed consent to any conflict.

The fiduciary duty, the SEC stated in Release IA-5248, equally applies whether the client is a retail investor with limited assets, experience, and knowledge or an institutional client with exceptionally large portfolios and substantial knowledge, experience, and analytical resources. However, the SEC elaborated that the fiduciary duty has "sufficient flexibility" to address the various types of relationships that advisers may have with different clients based on the services rendered. Thus, the investment adviser's fiduciary duty must be viewed in the specific context of the agreed-upon scope of the relationship between the adviser and client.

An investment adviser's fiduciary obligations flow from the role and functions that the adviser, as agent, has agreed to assume for the client, as principal. As a result, the obligations of an investment adviser providing comprehensive, discretionary advice in an ongoing relationship with a retail client (including, for example, portfolio monitoring and periodic realignment, with very limited restrictions) will differ significantly from those of an adviser to a registered investment company or private fund, where the advisory agreement defines the adviser's scope of services, and the limitations on its authority, with substantial specificity (for example, a mandate to manage a fixed income portfolio subject to specified parameters). In sum, while application of an investment adviser's fiduciary duty may vary with the scope of the relationship, the relationship in all cases remains a fiduciary one.

"[A]n adviser's federal fiduciary duty may not be waived, though it will apply in a manner that reflects the agreed-upon scope of the relationship."[15] By this statement in its final interpretation of the IAA, the SEC appears to acknowledge that an adviser and client may, by contract, circumscribe the matters as to which the fiduciary duty may apply, but they may not waive the fiduciary duty altogether. Thus, a contract provision purporting to waive the adviser's federal fiduciary duty generally would be inconsistent with the IAA. Examples of impermissible waivers might include (1) a statement that the adviser will not act as a fiduciary; (2) a blanket waiver of all conflicts of interest; or (3) a waiver of any specific obligations under the IAA.

As significantly, the SEC stated in Release IA-5248 that "[t]he Final Interpretation does not take a position on the scope or substance of any fiduciary duty that applies to an adviser under applicable state law." The SEC's apparent distinction between a federal fiduciary duty and a state fiduciary duty may yield conflicting law, or at least ambiguity. Because the IAA does not itself set forth the contours of an investment adviser's fiduciary duty—other than through the antifraud provisions of section 206, and the SEC's own "interpretation" of that duty—courts may apply state common law principles to determine if a breach of a fiduciary duty has occurred. The SEC's final interpretation may result in doctrinal tiers as to whether fiduciary duties may be contractually waived: one where courts apply "federal law" and render waivers unenforceable, and another, where courts apply "state common law" fiduciary duties and contract principles to enforce a waiver or disclaimer.

E. Reg BI's "Best Interest" Standard for Brokers and Dealers

Along with its final interpretation of the IAA, the SEC also adopted "Regulation Best Interest" for brokers and broker-dealers.[16] Reg BI, as it is commonly known, enhances the standard of conduct for brokers and broker-dealers beyond existing suitability obligations, to make it clear that they may not put their financial interests ahead of the interests of retail customers when making recommendations. Under Reg BI, a broker-dealer is required to act in the best interest of a retail customer when making a recommendation of any securities transaction or investment strategy involving securities to a retail customer.

---

15. 17 C.F.R. part 276, Commission Interpretation Regarding Standard of Conduct for Investment Advisers, Release No. IA-5248, *available at* https://www.sec.gov/rules/interp/2019/ia-5248.pdf.

16. 17 C.F.R. § 240.15l-1.

Reg BI sets forth a general, overarching "best interest obligation," which mandates that broker-dealers and those associated with them, when recommending a securities transaction or investment strategy,

> shall act in the best interest of the retail customer at the time the recommendation is made, without placing the financial or other interest of the broker, dealer, or natural person who is an associated person of a broker or dealer making the recommendation ahead of the interest of the retail customer.[17]

Two points are immediately clear. First, Reg BI does not define "best interest" in its text. Second, Reg BI does not mandate a broker-dealer to place its customer's interests ahead of its own. For comparison, an investment adviser's fiduciary duty to its client requires the adviser to place its client's interests ahead of its own interests. In this manner, Reg BI's "best interest" rule requires more than the previously applicable "suitability" standard of care, but less than an investment adviser's fiduciary duty. While an adviser owes a fiduciary duty to its client, a broker-dealer owes a lesser, nonfiduciary duty to its customer.

Reg BI sets forth four composite obligations that, together, comprise the "best interest obligation." These are the (1) "disclosure obligation," (2) "care obligation," (3) "conflict of interest obligation," and (4) "compliance obligation." Under Reg BI, if a broker (or dealer or associated person) satisfies these four obligations, the broker is deemed to have acted in the "best interest" of the customer.

The "disclosure obligation" requires a broker, before or when recommending a securities investment or strategy to a customer, to disclose in writing "all material facts" related to (1) the scope and terms of the broker's relationship with the customer, including the broker's fees and costs and the scope of services provided to the customer, and (2) conflicts of interests associated with the recommendation.[18]

The "care obligation" mandates a broker to exercise "reasonable diligence, care and skill" when making recommendations based on an understanding of the potential risks, rewards, and costs, and the broker must have a reasonable basis to believe (1) the recommendation could be in the best interest of some customers; (2) the recommendation is in the particular customer's best interest, in light of its investment profile and the potential risks, rewards, and costs associated with the recommendation; and (3) a series of recommended transactions, even if in the

17. *Id.* § 240.15l-1(a)(1).
18. *Id.* § 240.15l-1(a)(2)(i).

customer's best interest in isolation, are also in the customer's best interest and are not excessive when viewed together.[19]

The "conflict of interest obligation" requires a broker to establish, maintain, and enforce written policies and procedures reasonably designed to address conflicts of interest and mitigate against their occurrence.[20]

Finally, the "compliance obligation" requires a broker to establish, maintain, and enforce written policies and procedures reasonably designed to achieve compliance with Reg BI.[21]

The purpose and intent of Reg BI is clear. Reg BI does not intend to alter an arm's-length contractual, relationship between a broker and its customer. Rather, it seeks to reinforce this contractual relationship by ensuring a level playing field for the customer. For this reason, Reg BI focuses on enhancing a broker's disclosures obligations, obligations of care when making investment recommendations, obligations to avoid conflicts of interest, and compliance obligations. The goal of Reg BI is to buttress and support an equality of bargaining power between the customer and broker. In other words, Reg BI recognizes the bifurcation of the fiduciary duties owed by investment advisers to their clients and the nonfiduciary, contractual duties owed by broker-dealers to their customers. This is appropriate. Many investors do not need nor desire the comprehensive, portfolio management services of an investment adviser. Moreover, as noted, many investors simply cannot afford the services of an adviser.

F. Form CRS–Relationship Summary Form

Finally, along with Reg BI, the SEC also expanded and revamped the types of disclosures that investment advisers and brokers-dealers must make to their clients and customer, through a new "Form CRS." Form CRS includes information about the adviser's or broker-dealer's services, fees, costs, conflicts of interest, the applicable legal standard of conduct and any disciplinary history of the firm and its professionals. The SEC intended Form CRS to provide investors with simple, easy-to-understand information about the nature of their relationship with their financial professional. While facilitating layered disclosure, the format of the relationship summary allows for comparability among

19. *Id.* § 240.15l-1(a)(2)(ii).
20. *Id.* § 240.15l-1(a)(2)(iii).
21. *Id.* § 240.15l-1(a)(2)(iv).

the two different types of firms (investment advisers versus broker-dealers) in a way that is distinct from other required disclosures.

IV. Differing Duties among Financial Professionals

A. Fiduciary Duty versus Contractual Duty

As is evident from the preceding, investment advisers and broker-dealers have different duties and standards of care. Differing duties and standards do not reflect inconsistency in the financial industry, as some may contend. Rather, they are warranted and appropriate in light of different kinds of relationships at opposite ends of a spectrum. On one side is the fiduciary relationship between an investment adviser and client, where the client reposes its trust and confidence in its adviser who is in a position of authority and control over its client. Given the trust and confidence reposed by the client in its adviser, and the conversely superior position of the adviser, the adviser is obligated not to abuse is superior position and to safeguard the interest of its client. On the other side is an arm's-length, contractual relationship between a broker-dealer and its retail customer. In this relationship, full disclosure, objectivity, and reasonableness are important to maintain an equal playing field between the parties. When viewed in this manner, the different standards simply reflect the different types of relationships in the investment industry.

The IAA and SEC's final interpretation recognizes the fiduciary nature of the investment adviser/client relationship and the resulting obligations that apply. The investment adviser/client relationship is not unique. It is merely one of many fiduciary relationships of trust and confidence recognized under the law. The examples are many: a trustee is a fiduciary of a trust; corporate officers and directors are fiduciaries for their corporations; a privately held company's majority shareholders owe fiduciary duties to the minority shareholders; and partners are fiduciaries to each other.

Importantly, Reg BI does not change the fundamental arm's-length nature of the broker/retail customer relationship into a fiduciary relationship of trust and confidence. It does not require the broker to place its customer's interests ahead of its own. To the contrary, it seeks to maintain the nature of the relationship by enhancing the broker's obligation to provide the customer with appropriate facts so that the customer may make its own informed decisions. To address concerns as to possible conflicts of interest, Reg BI "enhances" broker duties as to disclosures, obligations of reasonable care, and compliance.

B. Should All Financial Services Professionals Be Fiduciaries?

There is debate presently roiling the financial services industry over whether all financial services professionals should be subject to fiduciary standards of care. Some contend that imposing fiduciary duties upon all financial services professionals is the only way it can be ensured that all investors receive unbiased and unconflicted services. They contend that the SEC's Reg BI did not go far enough to expunge the potential for conflicts of interest. Based on this line of thought, broker-dealers who are presently subject to Reg BI's "best interest" standard of care (nonfiduciary standard) should instead be subject to fiduciary standards such as those mandated by the IAA for investment advisers. Others caution, however, that mandating fiduciary duties for all financial services professionals may result in a situation where the cost of financial services rises across the board, and a segment of investors no longer able to afford the available services are left unable to access any—the so-called guidance gap.

Sheila Murphy, an expert with Bates Group and consultant with more than 30 years of legal, insurance, regulatory, and compliance experience, notes that this potential unintended consequence of a universal fiduciary rule is not merely speculative. She cites studies after the United Kingdom banned commissions for all retail investment advice:

> While not a replica of the U.S. rule, the U.K.'s Retail Distribution Review (RDR) is close enough to be informative as to areas that the U.S. may want to monitor. Professor Andrew Clare of London's Cass Business School is the principal author of two studies: "The Guidance Gap" and "The Impact of the RDR on U.K.'s Market for Financial Advice." These studies provide insights as to what may happen in the U.S. Based on the studies' results, what we may see is a bifurcation of financial advice. High net worth clients are more likely to receive more transparent information and improved advice from a smaller force of better-qualified and less-conflicted advisers. But an unintended consequence of RDR and similar acts would likely be that the lower and middle-market investors may have limited access to investment advice, and the guidance gap will expand.

According to Professor Clare's studies, the RDR in the United Kingdom had both positive and negative results: improved investment advice for high-net-worth investors and no investment advice for certain other investors.

Other commentators have the same concerns. Charlotte Baumanns, at Oxford University Commercial Law Centre, referenced the United Kingdom's experience after the RDR when she contemplated a rule banning commissions for investment advice in Germany:

> [T]he RDR reforms led to a higher quality of advice, and higher business standards in the financial services sector; however, the UK now faces an advice gap with many investors now finding investment advice unaffordable, and a significant number of banks advising high-income investors only. Though it might be argued that no advice is better than biased advice, in the face of the current low-interest phase and the April 2015 introduction of pension flexibility in the UK, a significant number of people will be exposed to the risk of making ruinous investment decisions.[22]

Lastly, Emma Wall, a commentator for Morningstar, wrote the following about the state of financial services in the United Kingdom after the RDR:

> It is now harder for investors with small portfolios to get advice post-RDR. Many advisers have segmented their advice depending on the size of investor portfolios, meaning that for investors with small portfolios, it's very hard to get bespoke advice.[23]

Thus, two intractable questions remain. First, can a universal fiduciary standard of care be mandated for all financial professionals in the United State without causing a "guidance gap"? Second, is affordable nonfiduciary financial advice better than none?

---

22. Charlotte Baumanns, The UK Ban on Commissions Relating to Retail Investment Advice—A Good Example for German Law? (Oxford Commercial Law Centre, May 29, 2017).

23. Emma Wall, *How RDR Has Changed the Advice Landscape* (Morningstar, May 11, 2017).

V. Claims for Breach of Fiduciary Duties

A. Claims under the IAA

While the IAA mandates that an "investment adviser" owes fiduciary duties to its client, the IAA does not provide a client with a private cause of action against its adviser for damages for a breach of fiduciary duties. The SEC may impose sanctions, including monetary fines and/or registration revocation, upon the adviser. But a client has only a limited private remedy under the IAA for rescission of the adviser contract and recovery of consideration paid. Nonetheless, clients may sue their investment advisers for monetary damages predicated on state common law breach of fiduciary duty claims. If an investment adviser is registered with the SEC, the adviser will be deemed, as a matter of statutory and regulatory law, a fiduciary of its clients. Courts have even gone beyond the application of the IAA, holding that the investment adviser/client relationship in and of itself is a fiduciary relationship as a matter of law.

Because of IAA's federal fiduciary standard for registered investment advisers, some courts facing alleged breaches by investment advisers have sought to rely upon "federal common law" when determining whether a breach occurred. Other courts, however, have relied upon state common law. These courts observe that, although they may look to federal law for the statement of the investment adviser's fiduciary duty and the standard to which investment advisers are to be held, they must still view a cause of action against an investment adviser for breach of fiduciary duty as springing from state law, because no federal cause of action for damages is permitted.[24] As is apparent, this results in unnecessary, conflicting legal doctrine, even though the results are the same. If the investment adviser breached its fiduciary duty to its client, the adviser is liable, and damages may be awarded to the client for the breach.

B. Claims under Common Law

Aside from the IAA, an investment adviser (or any other financial professional, for that matter) may face liability and damages for breach of

24. Belmont v. MB Inv. Partners, Inc., 708 F.3d 470, 501–04 (3d Cir. 2013) (explaining that some state courts have looked to the federal standard to determine whether there is a fiduciary relationship in the investment-adviser context, but others apply both state and federal standards).

fiduciary duty if a fiduciary relationship arose between the professional and its client or customer. Registration under the IAA is not necessary for the professional to be deemed a fiduciary. Fundamental principles governing a fiduciary relationship may always apply, given the circumstances. The existence of an investment advisory contract is not determinative. If the client reasonably relied upon the financial professional, reposing its trust and confidence in it, while the financial professional knowingly assumed a position of superiority and control over the client's affairs (for example, by assuming discretionary authority to manage the client's investment account and trade on behalf of the client), a fiduciary relationship may exist between the two. The totality of the evidence may demonstrate that a professional was either rendering investment advice to the investor or was otherwise in a position of trust and confidence to its client.

At times, there may be multiple groups of investors and investment advisers with varying interactions among them. An investment adviser also may stand in different roles with regard to investors and firms. As a result, whether an investment adviser may face liability for a breach of fiduciary duty will turn on the specific relationships that the adviser had with each of the various parties. The legal analysis becomes extremely fact intensive. Some relationships may be advisory, while others may not. At issue is whether an investor was an advisory client of the adviser, either by virtue of an advisory agreement or because the adviser had assumed an advisory role with regard to that investor. Courts will first examine who had an investment advisory contract with whom. If there is no advisory contract, courts will then examine other facts, such as communications among the parties involving investment advice. The goal is to tease apart the relationships and determine who was the "client" to whom the adviser was rendering advice.

Even if a court determines that an investment adviser or other financial professional owes a fiduciary duty to its client, it still must determine whether the adviser breached its fiduciary duty. Courts have relied upon "the prudent investor" standard to assess the adviser's conduct. Understandably, there is no precise formula as to what constitutes "imprudence." Generally, whether an investment adviser breached its fiduciary duty to its client is a factual determination to be made by the trial court. Courts may engage in a balancing analysis of the investment adviser's considerations and its actions, considering the history of each individual investment, viewed at the time of its action or its omission to act. If the adviser acted prudently, considering all the information available to it at the time, an error of judgment alone is not a breach of fiduciary duty. In other words, it is not enough that hindsight may suggest that another course would have been more beneficial.

C. Breach of Fiduciary Claims under the ICA

As noted, an investment adviser typically will set up a mutual fund, select the fund's directors, manage its investments, and provide other advisory services for a fee. The law acknowledges that, given the unique nature of the relationship between the adviser and the mutual fund, it is difficult, if not impossible, for the two to maintain an arm's-length, independent relationship. For this reason, the ICA imposes a fiduciary duty upon an investment adviser with regard to the compensation for its services.[25] Unlike the IAA, the ICA additionally grants mutual fund shareholders a private right of action for damages for breach of an investment adviser's fiduciary duty with regard to its compensation.[26] The clam is generally limited to alleged excessive compensation, and does not encompass broader issues, such as personal misconduct or general malfeasance.

The Supreme Court in *Jones v. Harris Assocs. L.P.*[27] set the standard for a mutual fund adviser's breach of fiduciary duty. An investment adviser to a mutual fund breaches its fiduciary duty if it charges an advisory fee that is so disproportionately large that it bears no reasonable relationship to the services rendered and could not have been based on arm's-length bargaining. When evaluating the amount of the fee, courts consider all relevant circumstances, including, for example, the fees of similarly situated funds, profitability, and economies of scale. However, the court cannot second-guess informed board decisions or engage in precise fee calculations. Instead, the court should simply determine whether the fees themselves are excessive.

In *Jones*, the Supreme Court also approved use of the Second Circuit's multifactor test in *Gartenberg v. Merrill Lynch Asset Mgmt., Inc.*[28] to assess whether a fee is excessive. Under that test, breach of fiduciary duty claims by mutual fund shareholders against their funds' investment advisers have failed, for example, when the funds' boards were independent, qualified, and they engaged in a robust, or even adequate, process to approve the advisers' arrangements and fees; the advisers' fees were within the range of comparable funds, including competitors; the advisers provided high-quality services; and the shareholders failed to show that economies of scale were not shared with shareholders or that the advisers had received significant other benefits.

---

25. 15 U.S.C. § 80a-35(b)(1)-(2).
26. *Id.*
27. 559 U.S. 335 (2010).
28. 694 F.2d 923 (2d Cir. 1982).

D. When a Broker-Dealer May Owe a Fiduciary Duty to a Retail Customer

A broker for a nondiscretionary account, in the ordinary course of business, does not owe a fiduciary duty to its customer. In such a case, the broker is simply executing transactions that the customer instructs it to make. It is the customer, rather than the broker, who determines which purchases and sales to make. Certainly, the broker's duty of care, set forth in Reg BI, bears on the appropriateness of any investment recommendation or series of recommendations. Apart from Reg BI's mandates, when assessing the broker's duty with regard to a nondiscretionary account, each transaction is viewed singly. Generally, the broker owes its customer duties of diligence and competence when executing a nondiscretionary customer's trade orders. The broker must execute upon the customer's orders promptly, in a manner best suited to serve the client's interests. The broker's obligation to the customer ceases when the transaction is closed. Some courts have referred to the broker's duty to appropriately execute a customer's trade as a fiduciary duty; that is, the broker has a fiduciary duty limited to the narrow task of consummating the transaction requested. Notably, other courts may consider such a narrow "fiduciary duty" as duplicative of the broker's contractual obligation.

In contrast, a broker that manages a discretionary account for its customer may owe a fiduciary duty to its customer. The facts and circumstances may establish the broker's practical control over the customer's account, which, in turn, may give rise to fiduciary duties. Courts will consider evidence that the customer placed his or her trust and confidence in the broker, with the broker's knowledge, to manage the customer's account for the customer's benefit. For example, if the customer relinquishes control over his or her brokerage account to its broker, the broker may owe a fiduciary duty to the customer to manage the account in accordance with the customer's needs and objectives. The broker's failure to manage the customer's discretionary account may give rise to a breach of the broker's fiduciary duty if it failed to exercise due care, skills, and diligence to protect the customer's interests. A fact finder, such as a jury, must assess the facts.

E. General Principles Regarding Fiduciary Duties Always Apply

It is apparent that one must always be mindful of both fundamental legal principles governing fiduciary relationships and the specific facts in the given case, to discern whether a fiduciary duty exists. Investment advisers are fiduciaries to their clients not merely because the IAA mandates them to be. The investment adviser/client relationship is fiduciary by its very nature. It is not unique though. Indeed, this book discusses many other fiduciary relationships that arise in other contexts and industries, for example, the relationships of trustees to trust beneficiaries, of directors and officers to their corporations, and of the majority shareholders to the minority shareholders in a private corporation.

VI. Conclusion

We have repeatedly acknowledged the well-known, ongoing debate whether all financial professionals should owe fiduciary duties to their clients and customers. Some contend that Reg BI does not go far enough, and that the potential for conflicts of interest cannot be expunged unless fiduciary obligations are mandated upon all financial professionals. It is submitted that the varying fiduciary and nonfiduciary duties are appropriate for the different types of services rendered in the financial industry. Having different types of financial services professionals, some with fiduciary obligations and others with nonfiduciary contractual obligations (as enhanced by the SEC's Reg. BI), may not be as bad as some contend.

There may be no one size fits all for consumers of investment services. Certain investors may want and can afford an investment adviser for comprehensive ongoing portfolio management. The adviser may have full discretionary authority and control over its client's portfolio to make investments and changes, while its client goes about his or her life and daily activities, working, eating, sleeping, relying upon and trusting its adviser to handle things. Others with may simply desire a professional to provide general recommendations and place investments based upon an agreed financial plan. Undeniably, investors also have different price points for what they want to spend or, indeed, can afford for financial services. Finally, there is support for caution that if all financial services professionals were made fiduciaries, the price for investment advice may rise across the board, and some investors will end up with none. There may be no ideal solution. Freedom of choice and access for all may be the next best thing.

Chapter 7
Partnership Claims

By Suzanne Spaulding Orza and Robert Charles Ward

Starting a business partnership[1] is exciting because it is generally filled with shared vision and the celebration of small successes. During the good times, a partnership is easy. But what happens when the honeymoon period is over and partners start to disagree? This chapter deals with some of the more common disputes that arise in partnerships and some of the steps you can take to avoid or resolve those disputes.

The disputes between partners are varied, but they often involve disagreements over how the business is managed, how the profits and risks of the business are allocated, and decisions concerning the admission or termination of partners who are deemed to be useful or harmful. These disputes can lead to two kinds of litigation between and among partners: (1) the partnership can sue a partner for breach of a partnership agreement or violation of a duty to the partnership that results in harm to the partnership, and (2) a partner can sue the partnership or another partner for legal or equitable relief to enforce the partner's rights.

This chapter is guided by the Revised Uniform Partnership Act of 1994, or RUPA, as it is typically called. RUPA went through several iterations before being "finalized" in 1994, and it was amended in 1997 to include the limited liability partnership. Despite its name, however, RUPA has not been enacted uniformly across all states; just a majority of them,[2] and state law varies significantly depending on when

1. There are three types of partnerships: general partnerships, joint ventures, and limited partnerships. Unless otherwise noted, "partnership," as used in this chapter, shall refer to a general partnership. Generally speaking, however, joint ventures are usually treated the same as general partnerships under the law.

2. All of the following states have, in some form or another, adopted RUPA: Alabama, Alaska, Arizona, Arkansas, California, Colorado, Connecticut, Delaware, District of Columbia, Florida, Hawaii, Idaho, Illinois, Iowa, Kansas, Kentucky, Maine, Maryland, Minnesota, Mississippi, Montana, Nebraska, Nevada, New Jersey, New Mexico, North

the state adopted the act.[3] Because some states adopted the act prior to its final 1997 incarnation, practitioners should never assume that a RUPA state has a statute consistent with the 1997 version. For that reason, counsel should *always* review state-specific statutes and related commentary and case law before advising partners or a partnership.

I. When Does a Relationship Give Rise to a Partnership?

Because this chapter is about partnerships, it seems appropriate to preface the chapter with an explanation of when a relationship actually gives rise to a partnership, especially because—unlike other entities—a partnership can be formed inadvertently.

A partnership is generally defined as an association of two or more persons who carry on as co-owners of a business for profit. One of the advantages to forming a partnership is how easy it is to form. Sometimes, it does not even matter whether the people intended to be partners or to form a partnership. As long as they receive—or expect to receive—their fair share of the profits, they are presumed under the law to be partners in the business.[4] So, assuming another business form such as a corporation or limited liability company has not been intentionally sought, a partnership will arise *by default*, and the relationship between the partners, as well as the means and manner by which that business relates to third parties, will be governed by partnership law.

No partnership agreement is required to form a partnership. Of course, in an inadvertent partnership, a written partnership agreement will not exist, and the default provisions of RUPA will provide a skeletal partnership agreement. However, because RUPA does not impose a writing requirement in order to modify its default rules, a contrary partnership agreement may arise orally or from course of conduct, as discussed later in the chapter. In addition, notwithstanding the absence of a writing requirement under RUPA, the applicable Statute of Frauds

---

Dakota, Ohio, Oklahoma, Oregon, Pennsylvania, South Dakota, Tennessee, Texas, Utah, Vermont, Virginia, Washington, West Virginia, Wisconsin, and Wyoming.

3. For example, Texas adopted a version of RUPA that is substantially similar to the 1997 version. Connecticut, West Virginia, and Wyoming, by contrast, adopted versions of the 1992/1994 RUPA.

4. A relevant consideration as to whether a partnership existed can be found based on how the business is reported to the IRS. For example, if the income of the purported partners was reported on K-1s, that will support a finding that a partnership existed.

will still apply where, for example, the agreement relates to the sale or transfer of real property, including contributions of real property to a partnership.

II. The Importance of a Partnership Agreement

Although you do not have to put anything in writing for a partnership to form, the importance of having a written partnership agreement cannot be overstated. Indeed, one of the best ways to avoid partnership disputes is to clearly delineate the rules in writing (preferably from the start), because that will help to manage the partners' expectations pertaining to the partnership operations and the other partners. A good partnership agreement will provide partners with a clear understanding of their partnership rights and obligations, how the partnership assets and liabilities will be managed, how to handle partnership withdrawals and buyouts,[5] and how disputes will be resolved.[6]

The partnership agreement is *the* crucial document in any partnership dispute and it should be the first place to turn to understand the roles, rights, and obligations of the partners. The agreement will control the relationships among the partners, and between the partners and the partnership. If, however, the partnership agreement is silent on any issue, practitioners should keep in mind that the default rules of RUPA will govern. It is also worth noting that, while partners are generally free to draft the partnership agreement as they see fit, a partnership agreement may *not* do any of the following:

- Vary the rights and duties of the partners regarding the execution, filing, and recording of statements with the Secretary of State, with the exception of the requirement that copies of such statements be provided to each partner;
- Unreasonably restrict the rights of partners to access the partnership's books and records;

5. The default rules under RUPA for handling a dissociation (i.e., partner withdrawals) or dissolution are relativity clumsy. A good partnership agreement will therefore include an agreed upon valuation mechanism to buy out a withdrawing partner and payment terms that allow a buyout to be consummated over time.

6. Many partnership agreements now have an arbitration provision. Arbitrations are a good way to keep any partnership disputes that may arise out of the public eye. Arbitrations also tend to be the more efficient dispute resolution option. And an arbitrator can craft more flexible and tax-efficient resolutions that usually are not allowed when proceeding in court pursuant to statute.

- Eliminate the duty of loyalty, except that the agreement may, if not manifestly unreasonable, (1) identify specific kinds of acts that do not violate the duty of loyalty, and/or (2) provide that the partnership may, after full disclosure of all material facts, ratify an act that would otherwise violate the duty of loyalty;
- Unreasonably limit the duty of care;
- Eliminate the duty of good faith and fair dealing (but the agreement may set reasonable standards for judging performance of that obligation);
- Vary the power for a partner to dissociate as a partner (except the notice requirement);
- Vary the right of a court to expel a partner;
- Vary the requirement to wind up the partnership business;
- Restrict the rights of third parties with respect to the partnership; or
- Vary the law applicable to a limited liability partnership.

III. Partners Owe Fiduciary Duties to the Partnership and to Their Partners

A partnership is a fiduciary relationship. As you can imagine, it is important for partners to be able to trust and rely upon each other to promote the best interests and success of the partnership—and to be able to hold partners accountable when they do not so act. Under RUPA, all partners owe a fiduciary duty to both the partnership and the other partners. The duties among partners are often viewed as duties governing the relations among equals, and each partner is therefore expected to adhere to and discharge such duties in both the conduct and winding up of the partnership. If a partner fails to do so, he may be held legally responsible for breaching those duties. Indeed, disputes between partners often involve claims for breach of fiduciary duty and the obligation of good faith and fair dealing. Actions that have traditionally triggered claims of a breach of a partner's fiduciary duty include (1) using partnership property for nonpartnership purposes, (2) engaging in self-dealing transactions, (3) engaging in activities deemed competitive with the partnership, and (4) diverting opportunities belonging to the partnership.

Of all RUPA provisions, none has proven more controversial than the formulation of the fiduciary duties of partners, and none has been the subject of greater variation among adopting jurisdictions. An example of the subtle but important state variations in the fiduciary duty area can be found in the modifications of RUPA's section 404(a) language: "The only fiduciary duties a partner owes to the partnership and the other partners are the duty of loyalty and the duty of care set forth in subsections (b) and (c)." California and Idaho, for example, have deleted the word "only" from the uniform language. Illinois and Kentucky deleted the word "only" and substituted "include" for "are," making the text read: "The fiduciary duties a partner owes to the partnership and the other partners include the duty of loyalty and the duty of care set forth in subsections (b) and (c)." Colorado and Texas eliminated the fiduciary characterization and the "only" qualifier.

RUPA's fiduciary duty provision represents fundamental change from the prior regime, change that has not been uniformly adopted. Accordingly, practitioners should carefully examine section 404 in comparison to the prior regime it was drafted to replace, and carefully review the state-by-state variations in the adopted versions of section 404. Doing so may offer potential argument opportunities. For example, in a case where the jurisdiction had an unfavorable common law rule, it would be critical to understand that section 404 is intended to displace the common law. In another jurisdiction, it might be equally important to understand that some of the state variations of section 404 are not intended to displace the common law, and that others leave open the argument. In cases where a version of a section 404 provision clearly applies, understanding RUPA drafters' thinking in the context of the changes from the prior regime, or the state drafters' thinking in the context of a change from the uniform language, might provide persuasive insight into the meaning of the statutory provision at issue.

Generally speaking, partners owe a fiduciary duty of loyalty, a fiduciary duty of care, and a nonfiduciary obligation of good faith and fair dealing.[7] These duties impose upon the partners the highest standards of care; the duty to act for the common benefit of all partners in transactions relating to the business; and the duty to refrain from taking advantage of one another by any misrepresentation, concealment, threat, or adverse pressure relating to the partnership and its business. Practitioners should be mindful of the fact that the burdens of proof vary based

7. Remember—some states have modified RUPA language in ways that make, or at least arguably make, the fiduciary formulation non-exclusive either by making the statutory listing of fiduciary duties nonexclusive or by making the definitions of the listed duties nonexclusive.

on whether the claim is based on a breach of the duty of loyalty or the duty of care, and those burdens also vary from state to state.

At the risk of getting a little too technical, the duty of loyalty includes three specific responsibilities: (1) the duty to account to the partnership and hold for its benefit any property, profit, or benefit a partner receives from the conduct or winding up of the partnership's business or from use of partnership property or information;[8] (2) the duty to refrain from dealing with the partnership as or on behalf of a party having an adverse interest to the partnership; and (3) the duty to refrain from competing with the partnership's business before the partnership is dissolved. A partner's duty of care requires partners to refrain from grossly negligent or reckless conduct, intentional misconduct, or a knowing violation of law in connection with the conduct and winding up of the partnership.

A partner is also required to discharge his duties to the partnership and the other partners under the statute and the partnership agreement, and to exercise any rights he has as a partner, consistent with an obligation of good faith and fair dealing. What is meant by the imposition of good faith and fair dealing obligations upon partners has been the subject of significant dispute. RUPA does not detail what this obligation encompasses, but it does provide that the obligation is not breached simply because a partner benefits from certain conduct. Nor does a partner violate the obligation under RUPA or the partnership agreement merely because the partner's conduct furthers the partner's own interest. The intent in drafting RUPA was not to set up a separate duty. Rather, the obligation is a contract concept, imposed as an ancillary responsibility whenever a partner discharges a duty or exercises a right under RUPA or the partnership agreement.

Importantly, a partner's fiduciary duties are subject to a wide range of modifications by agreement of the partners. For example, under RUPA, partners are permitted to make broad contractual modifications of the statutory duty of loyalty, both in type and sweep, as long as the modifications do not completely eliminate the duty. Partners can even identify categories of activities that do not violate the duty of loyalty as

8. This includes partnership opportunities, so a partner may take advantage of a business opportunity that is reasonably incident to the partnership's business, but only if he first presents that opportunity to the partnership.

long as those categories are not "manifestly unreasonable."[9] The only limitation with respect to the duty of care under RUPA is that partners cannot "unreasonably reduce" the duty. Because modifications are allowable, practitioners should always look at the fiduciary duty provisions in the partnership agreement and then confirm that any modifications to the duties in the agreement are consistent with the state-specific rules for modifications.

IV. Who Has the Authority to Act?

One of the more common disputes that arise in partnerships are disputes about who has the authority to act. A partnership may begin with co-equal management and the partners intending to reach decisions together, but things can change over time and disagreements can arise over who has authority to make decisions on behalf of the partnership. Can any partner act on behalf of the partnership? When is the consent of the other partners required? Like most legal issues, the authority of a partner to act on behalf of the partnership will depend on the situation.

Historically, one of the key advantages to conducting business through a partnership is the ability of the partners to define their relationship by agreement. Partners are afforded considerable freedom to contract. For that reason, the first place to look in dealing with authority disputes is always the written partnership agreement. In most cases, however, if a disagreement has arisen over a partner's authority to act on behalf of the partnership, it is unlikely that the written partnership agreement clearly spells out that partner's right to act in the way that he did. So, for purposes of this section, we will assume (1) that there is no written partnership agreement providing authority to act on behalf of the partnership, or (2) that the partner's actions on behalf of the partnership are contrary to the written agreement.

Generally speaking, each partner is an agent of the partnership for the purpose of the business, and each partner is meant to have equal rights in the management and conduct of the business. Absent an

9. The ability to modify the fiduciary duties is important because for many types of partnerships, such as real estate investment partnerships, the partners may well be invested (partnered) in other projects that could be considered to be in competition with the partnership.

agreement as to how management responsibilities will be apportioned, the default rule is that any act in the ordinary course of business may be decided by a majority of the partners, while any act outside of the ordinary course of business requires unanimous consent of all partners. What constitutes an act in or outside of the ordinary course of business will necessarily depend on the nature of the business.

In practice, many partnerships do not follow this default rule. For example, in a small partnership, one partner may be tasked with negotiating with customers and suppliers, while another is tasked with maintaining the books. Or maybe each of the partners wish to remain active in the small business, so the partners may prefer to have every business decision be made by unanimous consent, not just decisions involving acts outside of the ordinary course of business. In large partnerships or in limited liability partnerships, the partnership may elect to have one or more managing partners manage the day-to-day business of the partnership.

In situations where there is no written agreement, or when a partner acts in a way that contradicts the writing, it is still possible for a partner to be deemed to have the authority to act on behalf of the partnership by virtue of an oral or implied agreement among the partners. In those situations, practitioners should look to the relevant state common law on contract modification because those principles remain applicable to partnership agreements, that is, both oral agreements and course of conduct may supplement or even contradict a written agreement, even one that purports to be exclusively in writing and that precludes oral and/or course of conduct modifications.

For example, partners will often assign tasks or areas of responsibility to particular partners. In so doing, it may be unclear whether such a delegation is intended to be a binding part of the "partnership agreement," or a more temporary arrangement or accommodation. Practitioners should examine the partners' communications and course of conduct in analyzing this factual issue. Because a partnership agreement may not address the entire scope of partnership management, and may be written, oral, and/or implied by the partners' conduct, a dispute over management authority sometimes involves analysis of voluminous evidence regarding the duties of particular partners. Written evidence, including informal communications between the partners, can go a long way to protect a partner's rights—or to confirm an agreement to allocate responsibilities in a more permanent way that changes the default of majority control in a situation where there is no written agreement.

Another important wrinkle for practitioners to consider when there is a dispute over a partner's authority to bind the partnership in contract with a third party is whether the third party with whom the partner was dealing knew or had received a notification that the partner lacked authority to bind the partnership. If the third party had such knowledge, then the partnership cannot typically be held liable for breach of said contract.

V. Disagreements about Money

Financial disputes are another one of the more common disagreements that arise in partnership businesses. These disputes often emerge from day-to-day management of the company, such as how money should be used or allocated. The disputes always worsen when the company undergoes financial difficulties, and the question of each partner's liabilities and profit distribution can turn into a disagreement if it is not clearly stated in the partnership agreement.

To avoid disagreements about money, there are a number of things partners should always do at the outset of the relationship, even if the partners are good friends and deeply trust each other. For example, it is good practice for partners to discuss and agree upon the amount and type of contributions, including cash, assets, services, and the percentage ownership in the partnership. The partnership agreement should clearly define any property that is being contributed to the partnership in kind, including the address, the type of interest, and the value of the property contributed.[10] The partnership agreement should also address the responsibility for any taxes, mortgages, utilities, and insurance costs associated with the agreement. Partners should also discuss at the outset whether each partner will share equally in the profits and losses, or whether some other allocation is preferable. They should also decide how distributions will be made. Depending on each partner's financial situation, it may make sense to permit a distribution of the profits to each partner quarterly. In other situations, it may be preferable to distribute profits at the end of the year.

10. It is also good practice for the contributing partner to represent in the partnership agreement that he has the authority to contribute the property and that it is free and clear of any encumbrances, except permitted encumbrances.

These are all things partners *should* discuss and include in a partnership agreement, because when they don't, disagreements tend to arise. That begs the question: What happens when there is no agreement in place—how do you resolve who gets what?

In terms of the partnership's profits and losses, unless otherwise agreed, partners share equally (i.e., per capita, not based on contributions) in profits and they share losses in proportion to the partner's share of the profits.[11] Each partner is also deemed to have a capital account that is credited with the partner's share of the profits and charged with the partner's share of the losses.[12] Distributions are made from each partner's capital account in accordance with the partner's account balance. For example, if at the time of distribution a partner's capital account balance is negative, that partner will be required to contribute funds to bring the balance to zero.

In terms of compensation, unless otherwise agreed, a partner is not entitled to any compensation for services provided to the partnership other than reasonable compensation for winding up the partnership's affairs after dissolution. A partner may, however, be entitled to reimbursement from the partnership for payments made or to indemnify[13] a partner for liabilities incurred in the ordinary course of the partnership's business or for the preservation of its business property.[14] A partner is also entitled to reimbursement for any advance he provides to the partnership beyond the amount of capital the partner agreed to

11. Unlike the principals of some other business forms, partners are not shielded from liability for the partnership debts; all partners are liable jointly and severally for all obligations of the partnership unless otherwise agreed by the partners or provided by law.

12. Disagreements can arise over capital calls, that is, when a partner is asked to respond to a call to contribute to the capital of the partnership deemed necessary to keep the partnership afloat. Ideally, a partnership agreement would address when such capital calls are required and what happens if a partner does not contribute. For example, the partners should agree that a failure to respond to the capital call would result in a reduction of such partner's proportionate interest in the partnership.

13. Under RUPA, the partnership "shall indemnify each partner in respect to payments reasonably made and personal liabilities reasonably incurred by the partner in the ordinary and proper conduct of the business of the partnership or for the preservation of its business or property." RUPA § 401(c). Although mandatory, this is not one of the subjects described in Section II in this chapter, so it can be modified in the partnership agreement.

14. Questions can arise over what property belongs to the partnership and what property is the personal property of a partner. Generally speaking, property belongs to the partnership if (1) it was acquired in the name of the partnership, or (2) it was acquired in the name of one or more partners, and the instrument transferring ownership indicates that the partner acquired the property in his capacity as a partner or otherwise indicates the existence of a partnership.

contribute. Keep in mind that any payment or advance under these circumstances constitutes a loan to the partnership, which accrues interest from the date of payment or advance.

VI. Dissociation and Dissolution Disputes

"Dissociation" is RUPA's term for when a partner withdraws from or leaves a partnership. Dissociation can be voluntary on the part of a partner, or involuntary through action of other partners and possibly the court. For obvious reasons, the latter is the more difficult situation to deal with.

Let's start with the basics: What happens when a partner wants out of the partnership? Maybe the partner is ready to retire, or maybe he simply wants to go in a new direction with his career. Can a partner leave whenever he wants to? The answers to these questions depend on the term of the partnership.

A partnership can take one of three forms: (1) at will, (2) for a particular term, or (3) for a particular undertaking. A partnership "at will" is considered the default classification and is one in which any partner may withdraw at that partner's volition and terminate the partnership. Absent an agreement to the contrary, there is no liability for terminating an at will partnership. Conversely, where a partnership is for a defined term, or where the partnership has a defined undertaking, it is no longer a partnership at will if there is an agreement to remain partners for that period of time. Absent an agreement to remain partners, the partnership remains one at will. In those instances where there is an agreement to remain partners, while a partner may be able to withdraw from the partnership, the partner will be liable for damages for the early withdrawal.[15]

In amicable situations, the other partner or partners will likely support the decision of a partner to withdraw from the partnership, and all that will remain is to determine how to wind up the partnership[16] or

15. It is good practice for the intent of the partnership to be clearly stated in the partnership agreement because it will have a material impact upon the rights and duties of the various partners. Those believing themselves to be partners in a partnership at will and exercising what they believe to be the no fault right to withdraw will be unpleasantly surprised when that partnership is *ex ante* defined as one for a particular term or for a particular undertaking with that withdrawal now giving rise to a claim for damages.

16. Under RUPA, not every partner dissociation causes a dissolution of the partnership. But if the partnership is made up of only two partners, the dissociation of one partner will

buy out the departing partner's interest so that the partnership can continue in that partner's absence.[17] If going with the latter, and assuming there is no partnership agreement in place providing otherwise, the net buyout price is typically calculated by determining the dissociated partner's share of the sale or liquidation value of the partnership as of the date of dissociation, minus any damages for withdrawing early.[18]

Unless otherwise agreed, upon buyout of a dissociated partner, the partnership is required to indemnify the dissociated partner against all partnership liabilities, past and future. There is an important exception to this for certain post-dissociation conduct by the dissociated partner that binds the partnership. For example, when a dissociated partner is bought out from the partnership but he continues to hold himself out as an agent of the partnership, and third parties reasonably believe that the dissociated partner is a current partner, the dissociated partner can be held liable to the partnership and to the third parties as if he is still a partner.

The more contentious dissociation situation occurs, when, for example, the partnership wishes to expel a partner because they believe he has behaved wrongfully, or when a partner wishes to dissolve the partnership due to disagreements over how to operate the business. A contested departure can be particularly complicated if there is no partnership agreement. In a contested departure or dissolution, there is typically animosity and suspicion between the partners, which may make it difficult to reach an amicable resolution.

RUPA includes a laundry list of events that cause a partner to dissociate from a partnership, including the partner's expulsion pursuant

---

necessarily result in a dissolution of the partnership. This may cause some problems if the remaining partner wants to continue operating the business, for instance, as a sole proprietorship or some other type of business entity.

17. In a perfect world, the partnership agreement will delineate how a partner can be bought out. In drafting this section of the partnership agreement, special consideration should be given to the amount of the buyout price for any disassociated partner. For example, it may be appropriate to limit the buyout price to the amount currently existing in the partner's capital account. Or perhaps the partnership may decide that a partner is entitled to receive his or her share of partnership profits up to and until the time at which disassociation occurs. Adequate thought should also be given to the procedure to remove a partner involuntarily and the buyout price associated with involuntary removal. For example, it may be appropriate in larger partnerships to have a majority of the partners consent to involuntarily disassociating a partner. Alternatively, smaller partnerships may find it more appropriate to require unanimous consent.

18. If the dissociated partner and the partnership are unable to agree on a net buyout price or on any other terms of the buyout, the dissociated partner may file suit against the partnership.

to the partnership agreement,[19] the partner's expulsion by unanimous vote of the partners, certain bankruptcy events affecting the partners, the death or incapacity of the partner, the distribution of a trust's entire transferable interest in the partnership, and the partner's expulsion by judicial decree on application of the partnership or other partners.

To expel a partner by judicial decree (or decree of an arbitrator where the agreement so provides), the partnership must show (1) that the partner engaged in wrongful conduct that materially harmed the partnership business, (2) that the partner willfully or persistently breached fiduciary or contractual duties to the partnership, or (3) that the partner engaged in conduct (not necessarily wrongful conduct) that made it not reasonably practicable to carry out partnership business with that partner. Practitioners should keep in mind that, even when expelled by judicial decree, the partnership still has to compensate the dissociated partner for the partner's share of the partnership, but the partnership can reduce any such compensation by any damages to the partnership.

Maybe expelling a partner isn't enough and the desire is instead to dissolve the partnership. The occurrence of any of a number of events can trigger dissolution. An at will partnership can dissolve if at least half the partners decide to dissolve, that is, by majority rule. For a term partnership, the majority rule remains in effect throughout that term, that is, the partnership will dissolve after a death or wrongful dissociation of a partner unless a majority of the partners vote to continue. An event that makes it unlawful to continue the business also dissolves the partnership. If needed, a partner can also seek judicial dissolution based on any of the following grounds: (1) the economic purpose of the partnership is likely to be unreasonably frustrated, (2) another partner has engaged in conduct making it not reasonably practicable to carry on the business of the partnership, or (3) it is otherwise not reasonably practicable to carry on the business in conformity with the partnership agreement.

19. Where a partnership agreement permits expulsion (and they typically permit expulsion without cause), courts have held that a partnership may expel a partner for purely business reasons, including to protect business relationships, a partner's alcoholism, contentious behavior during firm meetings, and speech that is offensive to a major client, if doing so will resolve a fundamental schism in firm, lack of productivity, and even policy disagreements. Expulsion for these reasons does not generally constitute bad faith, and the burden is on the expelled partner to show bad faith; otherwise the court would, in effect, be placing the burden on the partnership to justify expulsion, which would translate into a requirement of showing cause.

If dissolved, the partnership continues to exist for the purpose of winding up its business, after which it is terminated. A partner who has not wrongfully dissociated may participate in the winding up of the partnership's business. If there are disagreements over how to wind up the business, any partner or any partner's legal representative may, for good cause shown, apply to a court (or arbitrator) for judicial supervision of the winding up.

Unless otherwise agreed, the payment scheme under RUPA in connection with winding up and liquidating a partnership is: first to creditors, which may include partner creditors; and second, to partners. In determining each partner's share, profits and losses of the partnership resulting from the liquidation are credited and charged to the partners' capital accounts.[20] A partner with a positive balance in its account is entitled to receive a distribution equal of such balance. In contrast, a partner with a negative balance must contribute to the partnership an amount necessary to bring the balance to zero.

VII. Conclusion

Although this chapter is by no means a comprehensive examination of the disputes that can arise in partnerships, the takeaway should be that no matter the dispute, practitioners should always look to the partnership agreement first, and if there is no agreement in place—or if the partnership agreement is silent on any issue—practitioners should look to the relevant state-specific statutes and related state-specific commentary. The vast majority of states follow a version of RUPA, which as discussed herein, provides important rules regarding the authority of a partner to act on behalf of the partnership, how the profits and risks of the business are allocated, the admission or termination of partners who are deemed to be useful or harmful, and the dissolution of a partnership.

20. Dissolution under RUPA requires liquidation of the partnership's assets and does not allow for distributions in kind, which can be more tax efficient. This is yet another reason why dissolution should be specifically addressed in the partnership agreement and the dissolution should be overseen by an arbitrator rather than a court.

Chapter 8
Trust Claims

By Sonia E. O'Donnell, Robert A. O'Donnell, and Donald E. Christopher

I. Introduction to Trust Issues

This chapter will briefly address some issues surrounding trusts, but it is not intended to be a comprehensive summary of trust law. That law is complex and often spills over to probate, guardianship, and other proceedings.

A trustee must satisfy an entire edifice of expectations developed over centuries of Anglo-American practice. Often these are codified in detailed statutory schemes. From the moment the position is accepted, a trustee undertakes specific, delineated duties owed to others. For example, under a revocable trust, the trustee generally owes duties to the settlor of the trust; under an irrevocable trust, the trustee generally owes duties to the trust's beneficiaries, as well as to the settlor, and in every instance is bound by the charter of the trust. In addition to revocable (which allows the trust creator to retain control, make changes, and remove trust assets) and irrevocable trusts (under which assets cannot be removed and the trust cannot be amended), there are testamentary trusts that do not come into being until death of the settlor and are created by means of a will that spells out the trust's terms.

More than half of the states have adopted some variation of the Uniform Trust Code (2000) (the "Code"). States that continue to maintain their own idiosyncratic law of trusts quite often will enact provisions that have their analogue within the Code. The Code contains 11 articles and details, including, among other things, the role of the courts in overseeing trusts, representation, creation, validity and termination of trusts, creditor's claims, revocable trusts, duties and powers of a trustee, liability of a trustee, and rights of persons dealing with a trustee. In general, most states agree that upon assuming a position as trustee, that trustee must administer the trust faithfully and prudently, carrying out the trust's purposes as set forth in the trust. The trustee must administer the trust faithfully and disinterestedly, avoiding any self-dealing. In administering the trust, a trustee must do so transparently, accounting for and reporting periodically concerning trust assets. A trustee must administer the trust competently, preserving trust property, making it productive, and defending the trust from invasion or attack.

A. Duty to Administer Trust Faithfully to the Trust's Purpose

A trustee has a duty to administer a trust in a manner faithful to the trust's original terms and stated purposes.[1] As an example, in one case in Florida, a trust specified that the school expenses of the beneficiary would be paid. The trustee was found to be in breach of duty, and liable to the beneficiary when contrary to the settlor's written directive in the trust, the bank neglected to pay the beneficiary's costs during his junior and senior years at the university.[2]

The trustee's duty to administer a trust faithfully and prudently includes a duty to call upon any special skills the trustee might have.[3] A trustee must also perform duties personally; although a trustee may delegate tasks to another if those tasks have a definite scope and the trustee reviews the agent's work periodically.[4] Trustees are typically expected to make decisions that involve a fair amount of discretion or that may not be strictly prescribed in the trust documents.[5] To that end, for example, the Florida Supreme Court has acknowledged a "general rule that a trustee in whom there is vested discretionary powers involving personal confidence cannot delegate his powers and shift his responsibility."[6]

1. *See, e.g.*, FLA. STAT. ANN. § 736.0806; CAL. PROB. CODE § 16000; VA. CODE § 64.2-763.

2. Kritchman v. Wolk, 152 So. 3d 630 (Fla. 3d DCA 2014).

3. *See, e.g.*, N.Y. CONSOL. LAW EPT § 11-2.3(b)(6); CAL. PROB. CODE § 16014, TEX. PROP. CODE § 117.004(f); FLA. STAT. ANN. § 736.0806.

4. *See, e.g.*, FLA. STAT. ANN. § 736.0807; *cf.* TEX. PROP. CODE § 113.018.

5. *See, e.g.*, CAL. PROB. CODE § 16012(a); Matter of Saxton, 274 A.D. 2d 110, 120 (Sup. Ct. App. 3d Dep't NY, 2000).

6. Thomas v. Carlton, 143 So. 780, 785 (Fla. 1932).

B. Duty of Loyalty

A trustee owes a duty of exclusive loyalty to the trust and its beneficiaries.[7] Courts will intervene if it can be shown a trustee has acted out of personal interest. State statutes and case law address a wide range of abuses in which trustees may have improperly dealt themselves benefits. Trustee mischief is as old as trusts. State statutory codes have constantly evolved so that the written law has come to anticipate and explicitly prohibit the most common breaches. As a matter of general principle, a trustee's duty of loyalty is so well-established that the Florida Supreme Court confidently held, a century ago, that a trustee "could not assume as an individual and in his own right a position antagonistic to that of his *cestuis que trustent* [*id est.*, the trust's beneficiaries]. That a trustee cannot so act is too elementary to require citation of authority."[8]

Usually, a trustee who breaches the duty of loyalty does so by benefiting from being a trustee (other than by receiving fair-market-value compensation).[9] In New York, for instance, a trustee was found to have breached his fiduciary duty by allowing his own family to occupy trust property without paying rent at fair market rates.[10] A trustee can even breach the duty of loyalty in instances in which self-dealing does not actually injure the trust.[11] For example, a trustee who buys assets from a trust, or sells to it, will generally be deemed to have breached the

---

7. "To the *cestui que trust* a trustee always owes *uberimma fides*" State *ex. rel.* Oklahoma Bar Ass'n v. Clausing, 224 P.3d 1268, 1274 (Okla. 2009)

8. Crawford v. Crawford, 176 So. 838, 841 (Fla. 1937).

9. *See, e.g.*, CAL. PROB. CODE § 16004(a). California recognizes a legal presumption of a breach of fiduciary duty for any trustee who profits in some manner (aside from his regular compensation) by means of his work he does for the trust. CAL. PROB. CODE § 16004(c). *See also* Martin v. Dieringer, 108 P.3d 234, 240 (Alaska 2005).

10. Matter of Silverstein v. Goodman, 827 N.Y.S.2d 50 (S. Ct. 1st Dep't NY 2006).

11. *See, e.g.*, Hutchings v. Louisville Trust Co., 276 S.W.2d 461, 464 (Ky. Ct. App. 1954) (a trustee, in this case a corporate fiduciary, has violated the trust as soon as he puts himself in a position in which his interests may conflict with the beneficiary, "regardless of whether or not the transaction seemed at the time to be fair or unfair.") *Cf.* Cardozo's foundational opinion, in Meinhard v. Salmon, 249 N.Y. 458 (N.Y. Ct. App. 1928) that is cited across jurisdictions. *See also* UNIF. TRUST CODE § 1003(a) (2010), whose comment reads: "the principle on which a trustee's duty of loyalty is premised is that a trustee should not be allowed to use the trust as a means for personal profit other than for routine compensation . . . not all cases of personal profit involve a breach of trust. Subsection (a) . . . holds a trustee accountable for any profit made, even absent a breach of trust. . . ." *See, e.g.*, Uzyel v. Kadisha, 188 Cal. App. 4th 866, 906 (Cal. App. 2 Dist. 2010) ("it is no defense that the trustee acted in good faith, that the terms of the transaction were fair, or that the trust suffered no loss or the trustee no profit").

fiduciary duty of loyalty, even if the transaction involved a fair market price.[12] Even some dealings between a trustee and a beneficiary that do not concern trust property may still be suspect in some jurisdictions.[13]

A trustee's good faith is not often an adequate defense.[14] In such circumstances, the law will usually afford a beneficiary the opportunity to void the transaction. When a trustee has obtained use of a property, or an interest in property from a trust, the beneficiaries can then seek damages.

Some common exceptions absolve the trustee from liability for various forms of self-dealing. Such instances include if the terms of the trust authorize the self-dealing transaction;[15] if a court approved the transaction; if the beneficiary of the trust, after being fully instructed as to her rights, knowingly consented; or if the self-dealing was a result of a contract initiated before the trustee had become or had ever contemplated becoming trustee. In these instances, the self-dealing transaction may survive a challenge.[16]

For example, an attorney who owns an office complex enters into a ten-year lease with a nonprofit corporation owned by a trust. Three years later, during the lease term, the original trustee of the trust seeks to resign, and approaches the attorney to act as the successor trustee. If the attorney agrees to serve as trustee, an argument may be made that the lease, although an agreement that obviously transfers wealth from the trust to the attorney, its trustee, should be allowed to stand.

For another example, assume an endowment held in trust for the benefit of the New Universe Symphony exists to provide replacement parts for the orchestra. Michael Tomlinson, artistic director, along with the Symphony board, learns that the owner of the music shop where

---

12. Tex. Prop. Code § 113.053(a)(1); often a court will analyze such a transaction as both a violation of a specific prohibition against selling to or buying from the trust, and as an instance of a conflict of interest. Estate of McCredy, 323 Pa. Super. 268, 292 (Pa. Super. Ct. 1993).

13. Va. Code § 64.2-764(d): "a transaction between a trustee and a beneficiary that does not concern trust property but that occurs during the existence of the trust or while the trustee retains significant influence over the beneficiary and from which the trustee obtains an advantage beyond the normal commercial advantage from such transaction is voidable by the beneficiary unless the trustee establishes that the transaction was fair to the beneficiary."

14. *See, e.g.*, *In re* Weinz's Will, 59 N.Y.S.2d 576, 584 (Surr. Ct. Westchester, N.Y. 1945).

15. *See, e.g.*, *In re* Estate of Stevenson, 605 N.W.2d 818, 821 (S.D. 2000) ("A trustee is allowed to participate in any transaction concerning the trust in which he has an interest, present or contingent, adverse to that of his beneficiary if the instrument creating the trust expressly grants permission to the trustee . . .").

16. *See, e.g.*, Va. Code § 64.2-764(B)(5); Fla. Stat. Ann. § 736.0802(2)(e).

they traditionally buy their new reeds and strings happens to be a respected lawyer. The lawyer is a man of unimpeachable reputation, as well as a rather savvy investor—everything one could want in a trustee. The Symphony needs a new trustee, because the current one is moving to the Bahamas, and intends to resign.

Normally, the lawyer serving as successor trustee could be found to be self-dealing if he manages the trust so that it continues to buy replacement parts from the music shop the lawyer owns. But everyone at the Symphony agrees that the lawyer's music shop is the best, and that it would be in the Symphony's best interests to continue to buy from that shop. The lawyer now serving as trustee and being the shop owner might explain to the Symphony board that continuing to buy from his shop would cause him to operate under a conflict of interest because he would stand to benefit from his administration of the trust. Even though such transactions are traditionally voidable, the directors of the Symphony might under the circumstances, having been fully informed as to the law, decide that the best interests of the trust—whose purpose, after all, was to provide good quality repairs for the orchestra—to continue to deal with the shop owned by the attorney. What could otherwise be said to amount to a conflict of interest would be most beneficial for the trust. The board's informed consent could well release the trustee from liability for what would otherwise be a breach of fiduciary duty, assuming the board was fully informed. Of course, the attorney/trustee's failure to disclose the conflict could result in liability.

In addition to prohibiting a trustee from obtaining favors from the trust, most states prohibit a trustee who manages multiple trusts from privileging one over another. Similarly, a trustee may not favor one beneficiary over another in a manner contrary to the trust agreement.[17] So, for example, a trustee manages a trust for a very wealthy widow who has passed away. The trustee hates both of the widow's surviving daughters. They are the only heirs to her substantial estate. The trustee manages to convince one daughter to back him as personal representative and in return begins to distribute sizeable sums from the trust to her while denying her sister anything. The widow's will and the terms of the trust make clear her intent that both her daughters be treated equally.

A good argument may be made that the trustee has breached a fiduciary duty by preferring one daughter over the other and, even worse, by benefiting in the process. To avoid such preferential treatment, states also tend to prohibit a trustee's purchase and sale of assets from one trust to

---

17. *See, e.g.*, Cal. Prob. Code § 16003.

another. In most circumstances, a trustee is also forbidden to make or receive loans to or from a trust the trustee manages.[18]

C. Duty of Loyalty and the Question of Undue Influence

In assisting a settlor to establish a trust, a person might arrange to have themselves named as trustee in the trust documents. Such a trust might be set up so that there is no effective oversight of the trustee. An unscrupulous trustee could then make decisions that are in the trustee's own interest, not in the best interests of the beneficiary.

A person who has unduly influenced the formation of a trust so that they are appointed trustee may face liability for breach of fiduciary duty if an interested party can show that the trustee unduly influenced the creation of the trust and the appointment as trustee. A complaint will likely need to show that the trustee had sufficient control or undue influence over the settlor such that the settlor was not making free choices in decisions concerning the trust. The law of trusts has yet to develop a great deal of precedent on this particular issue. In the case of a self-serving trustee who influenced the trust's formation, a challenge to that trust therefore may likely proceed by analogy using theories of duress, coercion, and undue influence borrowed from contract law and the law of estates.

It is easy to appreciate an argument that borrowing the common law protections against coercion and undue influence from contract and estate law is appropriate. This is especially so in the case of a dead or incapacitated settlor. Challenging a trust that has been created under improper influence indeed seems nearly indistinguishable in principle from a challenge to a will. In either case, some impropriety must be shown in the drafting of a legal instrument that survives the benefactor's death or incapacity.

Each state's laws can focus on different areas of emphasis and each state's courts will manifest differing degrees of willingness to overturn legal instruments on the basis of undue influence. Despite this, the governing analysis is still fairly uniform concerning an interested party's

18. *See, e.g.*, Keye v. Gautier, 684 So. 2d 210, 211 (Fla. 3d DCA 1996) ("when a trustee loans trust funds to himself, the transaction deserves special scrutiny due to the conflicting interests that a trustee has as a representative of the trust and as a debtor. These conflicting interests make it nearly impossible for a trustee's estimation regarding the adequacy of the security offered in exchange for the loan of the funds to himself, for his own benefit, to be impartial.").

burden in challenging a *will*:[19] A presumption of undue influence can arise when one who stands to benefit from the challenged instrument had a relationship[20] with the testator intimate enough to exert coercion over the testator's decisions.[21] Courts look for the ability of one party to dominate the other, or situations in which one party is dependent in some way upon the other.[22]

Typically, however, once a person successfully establishes that a confidential relationship existed between the parties in question and that the party who would benefit from the grant of authority or property procured the instrument making such a grant, courts tend to shift the burden to the party challenged as receiving the benefit to demonstrate that he did *not* unduly influence the settlor, grantor, or testator by virtue of their confidential relationship.[23]

Some states will apply greater scrutiny to certain types of legal instruments over others. Wyoming courts, for example, acknowledge that one standard of analysis is appropriate to determine undue influence over a will, yet another standard for assessing undue influence over an *inter vivos* grant. Once a challenger has shown that a defendant enjoyed a confidential relationship with the grantor of property or power and that the defendant benefited from that grant of property or power, however, Wyoming courts will recognize the usual burden shift.[24]

---

19. The argument is fairly obvious, but probably should be brought explicitly to the court's attention early on, and almost certainly will face a challenge from the defendant.

20. *See, e.g.*, Tobias v. Korman, 141 S.W.3d 468, 475 (Miss. Ct. Ap. 2004) ("a confidential relationship alone . . . is not enough to raise a presumption of undue influence"; the court will look for a relationship in which "a special confidence is reposed on one side with a resulting influence on the other"); *see also* Duerbusch v. Karas, 267 S.W. 3d 700, 708 (Mo. App. 2008) ("presumption of undue influence arises when substantial evidence shows (1) a confidential or fiduciary relationship; (2) that the fiduciary obtained a benefit; (3) some additional evidence that supports an inference of undue influence"); *see also* Virginia law, where a confidential relationship will arise when one party relies substantially on the other. Ayers v. Shaffer, 286 Va. 212, 286 (Va. 2013); Gerber v. Glock, 293 Va. 497, 529 (Va. 2017).

21. Some states—Florida, for example—have a more expansive test, and may ask for evidence that the one whose influence is in question actively procured the instrument or had some part in the drafting.

22. A confidential relationship that gives rise to the presumption of undue influence "can be shown . . . by evidence that one party is under the domination of another . . . a grantor's dependence on the grantee may also create a confidential relationship." Johnson v. Keiger, 93 P.3d 992, 996 (Wyo. 2004).

23. *See, e.g.*, *In re* Estate of Carpenter, 253 So. 2d 697 (Fla. 1971).

24. Marchant v. Cook, 967 P.2d 551, 557 (Wyo. 1998) ("once the person who is seeking to void the transaction on the basis of undue influence has established that a confidential relationship existed between the grantor and the grantee, the burden of proof shifts to the recipient of the property to prove the transaction was fair and conducted in good faith").

Wyoming courts impose a more rigorous test for undue influence on an *inter vivos* transaction as opposed to the creation of a will. This more stringent standard for *inter vivos* transactions is based on the rationale that one needs one's property (and, presumably, the right to control one's person) during one's life, but that, in contrast, a bequest upon death is a normal gift expected to be made, whereas parting with one's property before death is less common.[25]

The Wyoming theory that *inter vivos* transactions require greater scrutiny has obvious implications for trusts established during a settlor's lifetime. If courts will closely scrutinize gifts to a trustee given without consideration during a grantor's lifetime, so might other transfers of authority or property that a settlor might make to a trustee during the settlor's lifetime be subject to similar heightened scrutiny. The analysis should little differ. The court would be asked to presume that no one would lightly transfer his own power or property to another during one's lifetime. Transfer to a trust—especially one that survives the settlor's incapacity—perhaps should be understood as merely a species of such assignment.

D. Duty to Disclose and Inform

A trustee must keep the trust's beneficiaries informed of the trust's administration.[26] In the case of an irrevocable trust, the trustee must usually provide an annual accounting of the trust assets and their market value to all beneficiaries.[27] Shortly after the creation of an irrevocable trust, the trustee normally has a duty to notify the beneficiaries of the trust's existence, as well as of the beneficiaries' rights to a copy of the trust, to annual accountings, and to the expectation of a fiduciary privilege of confidentiality[28] with respect to the trustee and to any attorney engaged by the trust.[29]

States tend to uniformly impose upon trustees a duty to provide an annual accounting.[30] A trustee must furnish rigorous and detailed annual

---

25. Willey v. Willey, 385 P.3d 290, 298 (Wyo. 2016) ("a person having need of property, or at least a desire to retain it during life, is not likely to part with it . . .").

26. *See, e.g.*, TEX. PROP. CODE § 113.151(a); VA. CODE § 64.2-775(B); *In re* Enger's Will, 225 Minn. 229, 239 (Minn. 1948) ("it is the trustee's duty to disclose to the beneficiary fully, frankly, and without reservation all facts pertaining to the trust").

27. *See, e.g.*, VA. CODE § 64.2-775(c).

28. *Cf.* N.Y. CONSOL. LAW EPT § 13-A-4.1, where the duty of confidentiality is more generally delineated as a duty of a fiduciary, but is more explicitly determined in case law.

29. *See, e.g.*, FLA. STAT. ANN. § 736.0813(1)(b).

30. *See, e.g.*, Shannon v. Frost Nat'l Bank of San Antonio, 533 S.W. 2d 389, 397 (Ct. Civ. App. of Tx., San Antonio 1975); IOWA TRUST CODE § 633A.4213(1); GA. CODE

accountings reflecting the disposition of all trust assets. Some states, like Florida, include within their written statutes the specific requirements for an acceptable accounting. The trust's annual accounting must be reasonably understandable,[31] must disclose all cash and property transactions during the accounting period,[32] and must identify assets held, including both the assets' carrying value and estimated current value.[33] The accounting must also show other significant transactions, such as name changes in investment holdings and changes of custodial institutions.[34] A trustee's failure to prepare an accounting is usually considered a breach of fiduciary duty.[35]

Concomitant with the trustee's ongoing duty of disclosure to the trust's beneficiaries is the trustee's duty to keep clear records of the trust's administration and his duty to avoid commingling trust property with non-trust assets. In the case of a trustee who breaches his duty and commingles trust funds with his own, if a portion of the commingled assets rise in value, that increase is presumed to be an increase of the value of the *trust's* assets. Should a portion of the assets decline, however, that portion is presumed to be a decline in the *trustee's* assets.

A trustee who improperly commingles funds tends to leave a court with a bit of arithmetic to do. See, for example, the *soi-disant* "lowest intermediate balance rule,"[36] which is used across many jurisdictions to determine what becomes of trust assets when a trustee has withdrawn money from a commingled account. Under the rule, a court analyzes commingled assets using the following parameters:

> the trustee withdraws non-trust funds first, thus maintaining as much of the trust's funds as possible . . . if the amount on deposit . . . has at all times equaled or exceeded the amount of the trust, the trust's funds will be returned in their full amount . . . if the commingled fund has been depleted entirely, the trust

§ 53-12-243(b)(1); Az. Trust Code § 14-10813(B); S.C. Code § 62-7-813.

31. *See, e.g.*, Fla. Stat. Ann. § 736.08135(1).

32. *See, e.g.*, Cal. Prob. Code § 16063(a)(1); Fla. Stat. Ann. § 736.08135(2)(b).

33. *See, e.g.*, Tex. Prop. Code § 113.152(3); Fla. Stat. Ann. § 736.08135(2)(c).

34. *See, e.g.*, Fla. Stat. Ann. § 736.08135(2)(d). California specifically demands that the trustee disclose the agents the trustee hired along with their compensation and their relationship (if any) to the trustee. Cal. Prob. Code § 16063(a)(4).

35. McCormick v. Cox, 118 So.3d 980, 986–87 (Fla. 3d DCA 2013); Ditta v. Conte, 298 S.W. 3d 187, 191 (Tx. 2009).

36. *See, e.g.*, Universal C.I.T. Credit Corp. v. Farmers Bank of Portageville, 358 F. Supp. 317, 325 (E.D. Mo. 1973); Ellefson v. Centech Corp., 606 N.W.2d 324, 336 (Iowa 2000); Ayers v. Fay, 102 P.2d 156, 159 (1940). *See also* Simonson v. McInvaille, 166 N.W.2d 155, 159 (Wis. 1969); Hurst v. Hurst, 405 P.2d 913, 917 (Ariz. Ct. App. 1965); Matter of Miller's Estate, 594 P.2d 167, 170 (1979); LaBarbera v. LaBarbera, 452 N.E.2d 684, 689 (1983).

> is considered lost . . . if the commingled fund has been reduced below the level of the trust fund but not depleted, the claimant is entitled to the lowest intermediate balance in the account. In no case is the trust permitted to be replenished by deposits made subsequent to the lowest intermediate balance.[37]

E. Duty to Preserve Trust Property, Make It Productive, and Defend It against Attack

A trustee is expected to invest trust assets with the duty of care that the finance community expects of a prudent investor. Most states have adopted a nearly identical standard for what characterizes the behavior of a prudent investor.[38] The trustee is expected to take investment positions at a level of risk appropriate to the distribution requirements, purposes, and terms of the trust.[39] So, for example, a New York trustee who retained an abnormally high concentration of IBM stock in the portfolio of a conservative beneficiary was found to have breached a fiduciary duty by choosing a portfolio mix that was manifestly inappropriate to the needs of the beneficiary.[40] If a trust has more than one beneficiary, the trustee must invest trust assets taking into account the differing interests of the multiple beneficiaries.[41]

Courts will evaluate a trustee's performance based upon the prudence and wisdom of investing behavior with respect to the trust's entire investment portfolio. Therefore, an investment portfolio that takes some positions in risky assets may nonetheless be considered a prudently designed portfolio if the risky assets can be shown to have a low correlation with other assets in the portfolio, or to be balanced by other low-risk, imperfectly correlated assets.

Risky trading alone is not a breach of duty. A Virginia court, before finding a breach of fiduciary duty for reckless investing, made sure to clarify that mere risky plays are not of themselves breaches of duty. It explained "this Court does not find that margin trading and day trading are per se violative of the duty of care of a prudent investor."[42]

---

37. *In re* Dameron, 155 F.3d 718, 724 (4th Cir. 1998) (citations omitted); see also https://cw-cpa.com/how-does-the-lowest-intermediate-balance-rule-for-tracing-work.

38. *See, e.g.*, MT CODE § 72-38-901; TX. PROP. CODE § 117.004(a); VA. CODE § 64.2-781; ME. TRUST CODE § 901; *cf.* LA. REV. STAT. § 9.2127.

39. *See, e.g.*, FLA. STAT. ANN. § 518.11(1)(e).

40. *In re* Estate of Saxton, 179 Misc. 2d 681, 685 (Surr. Ct. Broome Cnty. 1998).

41. *See, e.g.*, FLA. STAT. ANN. § 736.0803.

42. Higgerson v. Farthing, 2017 WL 9887512, at *3 (Cir. Ct. Va. 2017).

The codes of most states instruct courts to evaluate the performance of a trust's portfolio by looking at the portfolio's overall returns, including yet unrealized capital appreciation. Courts are required to evaluate a trustee's investment decisions based upon whether the facts and conditions at the time of the investment warranted the trustee's decisions.[43] A trustee has a duty to continue to monitor and rebalance the trust's investment portfolio as changes in the value and volatility of different aspects of the portfolio affect the portfolio's overall risks and inter-asset correlations.[44]

F. Actions upon Breach of a Trustee's Duties

A breach of trust (failure to meet standards imposed by the actual trust instrument) or breach of fiduciary duty (failure to meet standards imposed by statute or the common law governing fiduciaries) is characterized either as a tortious act of negligence or an intentional tort, depending upon the facts of the case and the jurisdiction.

The Wisconsin Supreme Court, for instance, stated that a breach of fiduciary duty is best understood as an intentional tort because of the nature of the relationship; the trustee made an active choice to accept heightened duties. That court reasoned that a trustee's breach of duty therefore "connotes disloyalty or infidelity."[45] Since a trustee has assumed that role, his failure to meet his duty is intentional in Wisconsin. Nevertheless, whether found to be intentional or not, generally, a trustee may nevertheless be liable personally under a negligence standard for his breach of fiduciary duty. A trustee may be found liable in the form of income the trust should have received but lost because of a failure to discharge his fiduciary duty and may be forced to return to the trust income received as a result of that breach of duty.[46]

In the case of a trustee's breach of fiduciary duty, a court has additional measures at its disposal besides a mere monetary sanction.[47]

---

43. *See, e.g.*, N.Y. Consol. Law EPT § 11-2.3(b)(1).

44. *See, e.g.*, Fla. Stat. Ann. § 518.11(1)(d).

45. Zastrow v. Journal Commc'ns, 291 Wis. 2d 426, 445 (Wis. 2006). Confer: Corya v. Sanders, 155 So. 3d 1279, 1285 (Fla. 4th DCA 2015).

46. *See, e.g.*, Fla. Ann. Stat. § 736.1002(1), Tex. Prop. Code § 114.001(c).

47. Fla. Ann. Stat. § 736.1001(a-b); § 736.1001(e); § 736.1001(f-g). Hostility between a trustee and his beneficiary is not usually enough on its own to warrant the trustee's removal, because hostility is not necessarily a breach of fiduciary duty. Forbes v. Forbes, 341 P.3d 1041, 1065 (Wy. 2015). However, if the trustee has to exercise discretion in a way that may injure his beneficiary, or if his hostility reaches to a point that the court feels the relationship is untenable, a court will usually appoint a new trustee. Walker v. Cox, 531 So. 2d 801, 804 (Miss. 1988).

Numerous equitable remedies, including compelling or enjoining specific trustee actions, appointing a special fiduciary to oversee the trust, and suspending or removing the trustee may be employed to address the breach of duty.[48]

If an interested party challenges a trustee's misbehavior as proscribed by the statutory standards, the trustee may still marshal a defense based upon authority granted in the trust documents or by the beneficiary's past behavior. A trustee generally will not face liability for a breach of fiduciary duty if that breach occurred because the trustee reasonably relied upon the terms of the trust instrument.[49] The trustee may also be absolved if it can be shown that the beneficiary, knowingly and fully apprised of her rights, and being competent to do so (and not subject to undue influence), consented to or ratified the conduct constituting the breach.

While the trust documents may relieve the trustee from liability for some negligent behavior,[50] the trust documents cannot disclaim or eliminate a trustee's duty to act in good faith.[51] An exculpatory clause in the trust can be voided. It requires proof that the clause relieving the trustee of liability resulted from the trustee's abuse of a confidential relationship with the settlor.[52] For example, the settlor's attorney also acting as a trustee cannot advise the settlor to commit to trust documents that simultaneously appoint the attorney as trustee and relieve the attorney of the duties of care. Such an exculpatory term in the trust is presumed invalid unless the attorney/trustee can prove that the clause is fair under the circumstances, and that its terms were adequately communicated to the settlor.[53]

II. Conclusion

Discussing in this summary chapter the numerous issues that can arise in trust litigation is simply not practicable. For example, an entire chapter might be written on what court is a proper court to entertain a trust challenge when a probate proceeding has been instituted following the

48. Even a trustee who has openly breached his fiduciary duty might not be removed if the court finds that having the trustee remain in his position is in the best interest of the beneficiaries of the trust. Schildberg v. Schildberg, 461 N.W.2d 186, 191 (Iowa 1990).

49. *See, e.g.*, Cal. Prob. Code § 16040(b); Fla. Stat. Ann. § 736.1009.

50. *In re* Schoenewerg's Estate, 277 N.Y. 424 (1938).

51. Tex. Prop. Code § 114.007; Va. Code § 64.2-799; Fla. Stat. Ann. § 736.1001(1).

52. *Id.*

53. *See, e.g.*, Fla. Stat. Ann. § 736.1011(2).

death of a settlor. The issue of whether probate court or a separate civil action is proper can depend on, for example, whether the trust is deemed to be incorporated by reference into the decedent's will. Determining whether a trust is incorporated by reference usually depends on the specific language used.[54] Other issues, such as, for example, whether trust litigation can be brought in federal court under diversity jurisdiction are also beyond the scope of this chapter. Although trust litigation is often brought in state court, and probate issues are generally considered matters for state courts, there are many reasons to consider federal courts for trust litigation, including the absence of law clerks in state courts; in some instances, the lack of experience of state court judges, which could inhibit analysis of complex issues; and the crowded dockets of state courts that sometimes can overwhelm state court judges. Trust litigation, like all complex litigation, will present expected and unexpected challenges that will require, as all litigation, careful analysis and research. The authors here simply hope to present an overview of some trust concepts.

54. Bravo v. Sauter, 727 So. 2d 1103 (Fla. 4th DCA 1999).

Chapter 9
Estate Litigation

By Siobhan Briley

It's your first week at your new firm in your new town, a small Midwest city. You moved here a couple months ago after your wife got the job of her dreams running a mid-size company in her hometown, to which she had long wanted to return. You'd met in law school and moved to a major city, where you'd both been practicing high-stakes commercial litigation. You were both on the verge of making partner at your Am Law 100 firms, but your wife had been looking for months for a position in-house. When she found one, you had no qualms about changing your plans and making a go of it in a new environment.

Now, 12 years out of law school, you're the new guy in the office, trying to figure out how you're going to build a practice that necessarily includes representing plaintiffs as well as defendants, individuals as well as small businesses, nonlitigation as well as litigation. You were fairly lucky to get the job you got. So you readily agree to do whatever is needed to be successful.

One of the firm's three partners, Peter, comes to you with a large file. He explains that he has a client, Cleo, whose mother Tessa recently died. He wants you to open the probate proceeding, something you've never done, although you're peripherally familiar with the process because you've worked on large trust litigation in the past. Peter points you to the statute you need to review and some examples of the documents you'll need to prepare in the firm's document management system. The file is well-organized, thanks to Peter's excellent assistant, so you don't think you'll have trouble finding the information you need. Then, as Peter is walking out of your office, he turns to you and says, "There might be an issue with the client's brother, Bennie. Cleo thinks he might have stolen some money from their mother. Cleo and Bennie are estranged and she doesn't know the details of his relationship with the mother—who apparently had dementia. See if you can figure out what happened. Let's talk in a week or so about next steps. Thanks."

Now, besides having to figure out what property the mother had, how much it's all worth, and who the possible heirs (in addition to beneficiaries) might be,[1] you also have to determine whether Bennie did anything improper or illegal. You pull out the folder labeled "Will" and find that there are two wills in there, one dated about two and a half years before Tessa's death and one dated about 15 years earlier. The later will appoints Cleo executor, and provides that the residue of Tessa's estate is to be distributed to all three of her children (Cleo, Bennie, and Esther) equally, except that Tessa's house is to go to someone named Ivan, "because of his devotion to Bennie and to me, and to compensate him for his extraordinary kindness and care during the final years of my life." Ivan does not appear to be related to the family. Peter's notes from the initial client meeting indicate that he asked about Ivan but Cleo doesn't know who he is. On the notepad you've placed next to the file, you jot down, *Ivan's relationship with Bennie?*

Other than the house, nothing seems odd about the will. It's properly executed and witnessed, under your new state's law, and nothing on its face suggests any other reason to conclude that it's not valid. You then review the earlier will. Like the later will, the earlier will names Cleo executor and bequeaths the mother's property to her three children, in equal shares. However, the earlier will didn't separately bequeath Tessa's home. Finally, and most interestingly, the earlier will references promissory notes signed by Bennie and states clearly that they are to be included in the mother's estate.

You thumb through the file and find the referenced notes. There are five of them, executed over a couple years, long ago. They total $325,000. You search the file for documentation that the notes had been satisfied but find none and nothing in Peter's notes indicates he asked Cleo about them. You jot down, *Ask Cleo whether notes have been paid.*

Other folders in the file contain Tessa's bank statements for the last few years, a couple of investment accounts, a deed transferring a small piece of farmland to Bennie last year, and an annuity opened around the time the farmland was transferred. Finally, there are a couple of general powers of attorney, giving the agent authority over Tessa's finances. The latest, executed a week before the later will, names Bennie as the mother's attorney-in-fact. The earlier one, executed about

1. This is a distinction you haven't thought about since your first-year property law class. You might need to dig up some first-year outlines to refresh your understanding and comply with your obligation to provide competent representation with regard to the probate filings.

five years ago, named Cleo. *Did Cleo know about new POA? Did she know about new will?*

Flipping through the bank statements, you notice another oddity: until two years ago, the average monthly balance in Tessa's checking account was consistently between $10,000 and $15,000. Then, over the two years before her death, the average balance began dwindling until it reached $572 the month before she died, despite deposits and income remaining the same. You run through the transactions to locate the cause and see increasingly frequent cash withdrawals, which grew significantly in the few months before her death. *Ask about Tessa's expenses in last year.*

You check the bank statement around the date the farmland was transferred to Bennie for evidence that he paid for the land. You find that $400,000 was deposited to the mother's checking account the day the deed was signed. But then, a couple days later, the $400,000 was transferred out of the checking account to another financial institution. Since the amount matches the deposit into the annuity, purchased so close in time to the land transfer, you pull out the annuity paperwork and, indeed, find that the $400,000 was almost immediately transferred to the annuity account. Surprisingly—or not so surprisingly—Bennie and Ivan are the only beneficiaries of the annuity proceeds. The paperwork purchasing the annuity is signed by Tessa but her signature is shaky and hard to read. *Contact institution re: purchase of annuity circumstances. Was Bennie present? What about Ivan?*

When you meet with Peter again, you have most of the answers to your questions. You explain to him that, by all appearances, Bennie (with or without Ivan's help) has behaved improperly. He never paid back the money he borrowed from Tessa. Although he paid for the farm ground the mother transferred to him, it seems he caused Tessa to use that money to purchase an annuity, the proceeds of which would go to him and Ivan only. Further, if Tessa's dementia were sufficiently advanced when she sold the farm ground to Bennie, it is possible that she was not competent to enter into the contract. The standard for competence to make a contract is higher than the standard for competence to make a will, so even if it turned out that Tessa had testamentary capacity when the transaction occurred, she nonetheless could have lacked the capacity to agree to sell the farm ground.[2]

2. *See* Algoe v. Johnson, No. 09-1678, 2010 WL 2598326, at *6 (Iowa Ct. App. June 30, 2010) ("A higher degree of mental competence is required for the transaction of ordinary business and the making of contracts than is necessary for testamentary disposition of property.") (internal quotation marks and citation omitted).

You have not yet figured out Ivan's role in the situation. Cleo told you she hasn't spoken to Bennie directly for probably a decade. When she and Bennie were in communication, he never mentioned anyone named Ivan. You learned a bit more from Tessa's caretaker, Carrie, whom you interviewed briefly over the phone. Carrie did not know the details of Ivan's relationship with Bennie or Tessa but said he was usually with Bennie when Bennie visited Tessa. As far as Carrie could tell, Tessa was comfortable with Ivan, referring to him most of the time as "dear."

Carrie also told you that, over the last two to two-and-a-half years, Tessa's mental faculties had been in sharp decline. Carrie has spent the last 12 years working as a caretaker specifically for patients with dementia and her observations about Tessa's decline were specific and detailed. Carrie's description revealed that by the last six months of her life, Tessa had almost no short-term memory and rarely knew where she was. Although Carrie did not manage any of Tessa's finances, she reported that she would have been surprised if Tessa had not lost the ability to do even basic math a year ago.

"What about the withdrawals?" Peter asks. When you spoke with Cleo, she had no idea that money was being withdrawn from Tessa's account. Tessa didn't have many bills and, in any event, Cleo had set up automatic bill pay for her mother a few years ago. Cleo had never received notification that any of these automatic payments failed. She doesn't know who made the withdrawals or what the money had been used for, but she says she wouldn't be surprised if Bennie had taken it. She is certain her mother had not purchased anything out of the ordinary in the last couple years. When you asked her why, she told you: "My mother would never buy anything without consulting me first. She never trusted Bennie or Esther the way she trusted me." For the time being, you decided, you would accept her statement at face value.

"So, what's left in the estate?" Peter wonders. Basically nothing, you tell him. The $572 in the checking account, a few pieces of somewhat valuable furniture in the house, and a couple thousand dollars in a savings account. You tell Peter that, but for Bennie's conduct, you could distribute the property by affidavit or through a small estate proceeding. "Couldn't we do that anyway, and go after Bennie in a separate proceeding?" Not if Cleo wants to contest the will. That will need to be done in the probate proceeding because the probate statute in your state governs will contests and contains a limitations period for such actions.[3]

3. *See* Iowa Code § 633.308 (2020) ("Any interested person may petition to set aside the probate of a will by filing a written petition in the probate proceedings."); Iowa Code § 633.308 (2020) (action must be commenced "within the later to occur of four months

There might be other claims she can bring, such as tortious interference with bequest, that could be brought in independent litigation, but, based on your research, you recommend filing a will contest on the grounds that Tessa lacked testamentary capacity and that Bennie and Ivan unduly influenced her to bequeath her property to them.

Peter then wonders aloud whether Cleo can also claim tortious interference with bequest. You haven't researched that possibility but agree to do so before your next meeting, at which you'll outline for Peter the elements of the claims available to Cleo and what evidence you'll need to prove them.

I. Testamentary Capacity

At the next meeting, you tell Peter that there is enough evidence to support a will contest on the ground that her mother lacked testamentary capacity when she signed the second will. During a follow-up call with Cleo, you learned that Tessa had begun to show signs of dementia several years before, and that about three years ago, she was no longer able to take care of herself all the time, so Cleo had hired Carrie to come in every day. Then, about 18 months ago, Carrie began living with Tessa. Cleo regretted that she was unable to move with in with Tessa, but her business as a prominent local developer made substantial demands on her time. She would not have been able to provide the care Tessa needed, and Tessa had grown very fond of Carrie over the years. Carrie seemed to share that fondness. She told you that the mother was a "kind, kind woman," and loved her family dearly. "She would do anything for them. Anything."

You asked Carrie whether she had seen anything that caused her concern when Bennie visited, and she told you that, in the last several months, the mother had started to believe Bennie was her dead husband, who had taken care of all the finances when he was alive. So, whenever Bennie asked the mother to sign papers, she would. The caretaker had not mentioned it to anyone because she didn't believe it was any of her business and no one had asked her about it. She was surprised to hear that Cleo and Bennie were estranged.

Peter asks whether you think the caretaker will make a good witness. You do. She's straightforward and has a solid recollection of the events that had transpired during the years she cared for the mother.

---

from the date of second publication of notice or one month following the mailing of notice to all heirs of decedent and devisees under the will").

Her ability to describe the details of Tessa's mental decline and her experience with dementia will be very helpful to show that Tessa probably was not competent to make a will, let alone to enter a contract to sell real property or purchase an annuity.

"What else do you we need to do to prove the mother lacked testamentary capacity? How is the standard different from being mentally incompetent?" You have the advantage of being a litigator, which Peter is not, so you know what is required to prove a claim in court and how to get the evidence admitted. You explain that it will be your client's burden to prove lack of testamentary capacity, which will be easier if the medical records clearly show Tessa's decline. You've already prepared a subpoena for the records. Once a proceeding is started—whether in probate or a separate litigation—you'll get it served and get the records. You've also called Tessa's physician and left a message that you need to speak with her as soon as possible. If she confirms Tessa's decline over the last two years, she likely can provide expert testimony on the mother's capacity at the time the second will was executed.[4]

Before laying out the elements of a claim that Tessa lacked capacity to make a will, you note that, except where a testator is subject to conservatorship, the law presumes she has the mental competence to make a will.[5] Thus, the law assumes that Tessa (1) knew and understood that she was executing a will; (2) knew the nature and extent of her property; (3) knew the "natural objects of her bounty," or her would-be heirs-at-law; and (4) knew how and to whom she wanted to distribute her property.[6] Since all of these elements must have been present when Tessa signed the will,[7] a showing that even one was not present is sufficient. Given that (of course) Tessa is not available to testify about any of these things, you'll have to prove them by circumstantial evidence.[8] Evidence of the condition of Tessa's mind at other times "may be allowed if it throws light on the mental competence at the time the will was made."[9] Tessa's medical records and her doctor's testimony, if

---

4. *See, e.g.*, Pearson v. Ossian, 420 N.W.2d 493, 495 (Iowa 1988). Even if a treating physician is not permitted to testify as an expert in the state where you practice, the mother's doctor could testify as a fact witness. The doctor's lay testimony would likely be just as effective as expert testimony.

5. *See, e.g.*, *In re* Estate of Boman, No. 16-0110, 2017 WL 512493, at *9 (Iowa Ct. App. Feb. 8, 2017).

6. *See, e.g.*, Matter of Estate of Henrich, 389 N.W.2d 78, 81 (Iowa 1986).

7. *Id.*

8. Like undue influence, testamentary capacity "usually is proven by circumstantial evidence." *See* Matter of Adams' Estate, 234 N.W.2d 125, 128 (Iowa 1975).

9. *Pearson*, 420 N.W.2d at 495.

supportive, will also be persuasive, but they might not be sufficient because the standard for competency to make a will is lower than the standard to show mental competency.[10]

If you can prove lack of testamentary capacity, you will also be able to prove that Tessa was not competent to enter into contracts or engage in ordinary business transactions.[11] However, even if you cannot prove that Tessa lacked testamentary capacity, you could still prove that she was incompetent to sell the farm ground or purchase the annuity if you can show that she had "no reasonable perception of the nature and terms of the contract."[12] This will depend in large part on what the medical records reveal and whether Tessa's physician can opine about what Tessa could understand when she signed the deed and the annuity contract.

You then walk Peter through a claim of undue influence and what you'll need to prove to prevail on the claim.

II. Undue Influence

Almost all will contests assert a claim for undue influence as an alternative to lack of testamentary capacity, in large part because a lack of capacity by definition renders a testator vulnerable to undue influence.[13] Peter, of course, knows generally what undue influence is, but he asks you to walk him through the elements and the evidence you'll need to establish each.

The definition of undue influence, you tell him, is the type of influence that occurs when one person substitutes his intentions for those of the person making the will, such that the will expresses the "purpose and intent of the person exercising the influence, not those of the maker

---

10. This may vary from state to state. In Iowa, for instance, the standard to show lack of mental competence (at least in the context of probate proceedings) is that a person's "decision-making capacity is so impaired that [she] is unable to make, communicate, or carry out important decisions concerning [her] financial affairs." IOWA CODE § 633.553(2). Iowa courts are clear that the standard for testamentary capacity is less demanding than the standard to establish mental competence. *See, e.g.*, Ward v. Sears, 78 N.W.2d 545, 550–51 (Iowa 1956); *In re* Guardianship of Driesen, No. 18-1311, 2009 WL 1491871, at *3 (Iowa Ct. App. May 29, 2009).

11. *Algoe*, 2010 WL 2598326, at *6.

12. Daughton v. Parson, 423 N.W.2d 894, 897 (Iowa Ct. App. 1988).

13. "There are many cases of will contests where the issues of undue influence and mental incompetence are so interrelated in the evidence as not to be separable." 13 IA. PRAC., *Probate* § 10:39 (citing Matter of Estate of Olson, 451 N.W.2d 33 (Iowa Ct. App. 1989)).

of the will."[14] It is sometimes referred to as "the equivalent of moral coercion."[15] This is because not all influence is undue, and the law generally presumes that influence is proper.[16] To establish that Bennie's influence over Tessa was undue, you need to prove that (1) when Tessa made the second will, she was susceptible to undue influence, (2) Bennie had the opportunity to exercise undue influence for the purpose of getting an improper favor, (3) Bennie was inclined to influence Tessa unduly for the purpose of getting an improper favor, and (4) the result—Tessa changing the provisions of the earlier will—was clearly the result of Bennie's undue influence.[17]

In addition to these factors, you'll also have to establish that the undue influence was present at the "very time" the will was made and must be the "controlling" factor for Tessa's changes to the will.[18] Peter nods slowly, then asks, "What about Ivan? Couldn't he be the one influencing Tessa?"

Yes, he could, and proving that Ivan unduly influenced Tessa probably will be easier than proving that Bennie did. A primary consideration in determining the existence of undue influence is whether disposition of the testator's property is "unnatural." Courts tend to presume that the "natural" object of a testator's bounty is a spouse or blood relation.[19] Thus, courts more readily conclude that a bequest to a nonrelative is the product of undue influence than a bequest to relative.[20]

"Okay," Peter says. "Let's go through what we have to prove and then we can talk about whether to name Bennie or Ivan or both. Start with susceptibility. How do we go about proving that?"

---

14. Burkhalter v. Burkhalter, 841 N.W.2d 93, 96 (Iowa 2013) (quoting Iowa State Bar Ass'n, *Iowa Civil Jury Instructions* 2700.5 (2011).

15. 13 IA. PRAC., *Probate* § 10:38.

16. *Id.* ("The law presumes a person is free from undue influence."); *see also, e.g.*, Ray D. Madoff, *Unmasking Undue Influence*, 81 MINN. L. REV. 571, 575 (1997) ("All wills are the result of influence. The law recognizes this by drawing a distinction between influence and undue influence.") (internal citations omitted) (hereinafter "Madoff").

17. *Id.* Again, this test may vary depending on your state.

18. *Id.*

19. *See, e.g.*, Madoff at 590 (citing *In re* Estate of Maheras, 897 P.2d 268, 273 (Okla. 1995) ("[T]he natural object of a will maker's bounty is one related to him/her by consanguinity.")).

20. *Id.* at 591 (noting that "courts have generally relied on the intestacy statutes as a model for naturalness").

A. Susceptibility

Like the other factors tending to show undue influence, susceptibility is established almost exclusively by circumstantial evidence, because direct evidence is rarely available. And, like the other elements of undue influence, the result is often held up as proof of the act itself. Certainly, Tessa's dementia is strong circumstantial evidence of susceptibility.[21] Whether the fact that Tessa suffered from dementia is enough will depend on the degree to which she had declined. Based on Carrie's description, it seems that Tessa was pretty far gone when she changed the will, sold the farm ground, and put the money in the annuity. If her doctor and medical records confirm Carrie's description, you will have a very good chance of showing susceptibility based on the dementia alone. Other possibly relevant factors include that the testator suffers from a serious illness, recently suffered a stroke, recently suffered a tragedy, has some other type of diminished capacity, or relies heavily or exclusively on another person to manage her finances and/or get her basic needs met.[22] Tessa clearly relied on Bennie to manage her finances.

You digress a bit to give Peter a sense of the range of conduct that can support susceptibility to undue influence. In one case, a testator in his late 70s moved to a new state, lived in "filthy and unsanitary conditions" for several years, and then met a woman who became his caretaker for the next 16 years.[23] The court there had no problem finding that the testator, who was completely house-bound and relied on the caretaker for all of his physical needs, thus giving the caretaker much more power over him than she would otherwise have had, was susceptible to undue influence.[24] Other courts have found that dependence on another for access to money, medicine, and food generally renders a person susceptible to undue influence.[25] However, merely being susceptible to flattery and attention is not enough to prove susceptibility to undue influence.[26]

---

21. *See* Mendenhall v. Judy, 671 N.W.2d 452, 460 (Iowa 2003).

22. *See* In the Matter of the Estate of Schoppe, No. 05-0147, 2005 WL 3115916, at *3 (Iowa Ct. App. Nov. 23, 2005).

23. *In re* Estate of Masterhan, No. 00-2064, 2002 WL 31640607, at *2 (Iowa Ct. App. Nov. 25, 2002).

24. *Id.*

25. *See, e.g.*, Algoe v. Johnson, No. 09-1678, 20100 WL 2598326, at *4–*5 (Iowa Ct. App. June 30, 2010).

26. *See* Matter of Estate of Bayer, 574 N.W.2d 667, 672 (Iowa 1998) ("although Mrs. Bayer may have been susceptible to flattery and attention, and often consulted with defendants when making important decisions, the record does not show that she was so timid or weak-minded that her motives in executing her will were not her own").

You also explain that establishing Tessa's susceptibility will be easier with regard to Ivan than Bennie because it is common for children to care for their aging parents. It is less common for a person like Ivan—much younger than Tessa and unknown to her until a few years ago—to provide such care unless the person has an ulterior motive. The fact that Tessa bequeathed her house to Ivan is a strong evidence of her susceptibility to his undue influence.[27]

B. Opportunity

Peter then asks, "How is opportunity different from susceptibility? It seems that everything you've said supports a conclusion that Tessa's dementia afforded Bennie and Ivan more than ample opportunity to take advantage of her."

You agree. Where a testator suffers from dementia or a serious illness or has any of the other vulnerabilities you identified, there is ample opportunity for a person to unduly influence her. Thus, you continue, where courts find that the "opportunity" prong of the test is met, they usually rely on testimony that the wrongdoer spent a lot of time with the testator, or presented the testator with one or more documents to sign, or consulted an attorney on the testator's behalf, or even took the testator to an attorney to rewrite the testator's will.[28] Where the testator is unduly influenced by a caretaker or other third party, the length of time the caretaker has been caring for the testator may be a factor.[29] Finally, keeping changes to the will secret can also show undue influence.[30] This last factor is certainly an issue here.

C. Disposition

Showing a defendant's disposition to unduly influence a testator is similarly self-referential: If there is undue influence, a defendant clearly has a disposition to exert such influence. Behavior that courts have relied on includes a wrongdoer arranging for an attorney to revise a will and hiding the fact that a new will was executed from the testator's family.[31]

27. *Madoff* at 589 ("A will that shows the effects of undue influence through an 'unnatural bequest' or gifts during life to a beneficiary suspected of exerting undue influence can also serve as proof of . . . susceptibility to undue influence.") (internal citations omitted).

28. *See, e.g., In re* Estate of Bradshaw, No. 01-0728, 2002 WL 31114076, at *1 (Iowa Ct. App. Sept. 25, 2002).

29. *See* Estate of Masterhan, 2002 WL 31640607, at *2.

30. Estate of Bradshaw, 2002 WL 31114076, at *1.

31. *Id.*

The fact that Bennie never informed Cleo or their other sibling, Esther, that Tessa had changed her will is strong evidence of Bennie's disposition toward undue influence, with Ivan's participation or alone.

D. Result of Undue Influence

In your opinion, you tell Peter, this final factor is the most significant. In your state, you have to show that the outcome was "clearly" the result of undue influence.[32] Your state's courts are clear that this requirement does not change the standard of proof for undue influence, which remains a preponderance of the evidence,[33] but this is not the case in all states.[34] The qualification of the result as "clear" is meant to eliminate findings of undue influence where there is merely a suggestion that a beneficiary may have influenced the testator.[35] Although it's irrelevant to your client's claim, you comment that not every state requires the outcome be shown to be "clearly" the result of undue influence.[36]

But, Peter wonders, does Cleo bear the burden of proving undue influence, as she does lack of testamentary capacity? It depends. Regarding Tessa's changes to her will, yes, the client bears the burden of proving undue influence. However, if Bennie indeed made the multiple withdrawals of cash and used them for his own benefit, because he was Tessa's attorney-in-fact, and thus in a fiduciary relationship with Tessa when the withdrawals were made, the burden would shift to Bennie to prove an absence of undue influence.[37] Bennie also would be subject to

---

32. *Burkhalter*, 841 N.W.2d at 100–01.

33. *See id.* at 100 (noting "that because will contests in Iowa [are] actions at law where the preponderance-of-the-evidence standard ordinarily" applies, court would follow majority rule).

34. While the majority of states apply a preponderance of the evidence standard, some states impose a higher standard of proof. *Id.*; *see also* Matter of Estate of Todd, 585 N.W.2d 273, 275–76 (Iowa 1998); Estate of Langley, 586 A.2d 1270, 1271 (Me. 1991) (requiring proof by clear, satisfactory and convincing evidence); *In re* Estate of Perssion, 123 N.W.2d 465, 466 (Wisc. 1963) (same); *In re* Davis' Will, 101 A.2d 521, 522 (N.J. 1953) (same).

35. *See, e.g.*, Matter of Estate of Davenport, 346 N.W.2d 530, 532–33 (Iowa 1984) ("motive and opportunity alone [are] insufficient to support an inference of undue influence"); *see also* Smith v. First Nat'l Bank Iowa, No. 00-0534, 2001 WL 726079, at *3 (Iowa Ct. App. June 29, 2001) ("[m]ere suspicion, surmise, conjecture, or speculation is not enough to warrant a finding of undue influence").

36. *See, e.g.*, Dinan v. Marchand, 903 A.2d 201, 204 n.1 (Conn. 2006); Gmeiner v. Yacte, 592 P.2d 57, 63 (Idaho 1979); *In re* Will of Campbell, 573 S.E.2d 550, 560 (N.C. Ct. App. 2002); *In re* Estate of Dion, 623 N.W.2d 720, 728 (N.D. 2001).

37. *Mendenhall*, 671 N.W.2d at 455; In the Matter of the Estate of Todd, 585 N.W.2d 273, 277 (Iowa 1998).

a higher standard of proof: His evidence of freedom from undue influence must be "clear and convincing."[38]

You also explain that both Ivan and Bennie were in a confidential relationship with Tessa. A confidential relationship overlaps in many respects with a fiduciary relationship but they are not the same. Unlike a fiduciary relationship, a confidential relationship is created not by a legal relationship but by the parties' stances with regard to one another. It arises whenever one person puts her trust in the skill and integrity of another.[39]

Wouldn't that also apply to the money transferred to the annuity? Probably not. You explain: The burden of proof in cases alleging undue influence only shifts where there is a fiduciary or confidential relationship *and* the victim of the undue influence made an *inter vivos* gift to the influencer.[40] The former is satisfied here, but the latter is not. An annuity is not considered an *inter vivos* gift because Bennie could not receive the funds until after Tessa died. Theoretically, at least, Tessa maintained control over and possession of the funds in the annuity until she died and could have changed the beneficiary, had she so desired.

Pondering, Peter stares at the annuity paperwork. A puzzled look comes over his face. "What if Tessa didn't sign this? What if this signature is actually Bennie signing Tessa's name? Or Ivan? Would that change things?" Again, you say, it depends.

If Bennie or Ivan signed the paperwork opening the annuity but did so at Tessa's direction and while Tessa was present, under the doctrine of amanuensis, the court likely will consider the signature to be Tessa's.[41] "An 'amanuensis' is defined as 'one who copies or writes from the dictation of another.'"[42] Under the doctrine of amanuensis, "where the signing of a grantor's name to a [document] is done with the grantor's express authority, the person signing the grantor's name is not deemed an agent but is instead regarded as a mere instrument or amanuensis of the grantor, and the signature is deemed to be that of the grantor."[43]

The agent who wrote the annuity wasn't able to give you a lot of information about the transaction. Unfortunately, she couldn't remember it that well. She didn't recall whether Ivan was there. She didn't have any recollection of Bennie being overbearing, but she admitted that she

38. *Todd*, 585 N.W.2d at 275 (citing 25 Am. Jr. 2d *Duress and Undue Influence* § 42, at 555–56 (1996)).

39. *Id.*

40. Jackson v. Shrader, 767 N.W.2d 599, 607 (Iowa 2003).

41. Matter of Estate of Moore, 390 P.3d 551, 554 (Kan. Ct. App. 2017).

42. *Id.*

43. *Id.* at 559.

had never met either Bennie or Tessa before the meeting where she wrote the annuity. Because Tessa was frail, Bennie was guiding her. The agent didn't know whether Bennie's tone of voice might have meant something to Tessa that was apparent to other people or if Bennie had put any pressure on Tessa before the meeting that could have affected her at the meeting. This issue, you think, will hinge largely on whether Bennie and Ivan are credible witnesses.

III. Tortious Interference with Inheritance or Gift

Peter asks what you learned about whether Cleo can also assert a claim that Bennie and/or Ivan tortiously interfered with the client's inheritance by transferring the $400,000 to the annuity, influencing Tessa to remove the promissory notes from the will, and influencing Tessa to give the house to Ivan.

A claim for tortious interference with bequest is available to Cleo but she must raise it in the will contest proceeding.[44] If she doesn't, it will be lost.[45] To prevail on the claim, you will need to prove that Cleo had a reasonable expectation of receiving an inheritance that included the house, the money transferred to the annuity, and repayment of the promissory notes; that Bennie and/or Ivan committed an intentional and independent legal wrong, such as putting Tessa under fraud or duress; that the purpose of the independent legal wrong was to interfere with Cleo's expectancy, causing it to fail; and that Cleo suffered economic loss as a result.[46] Importantly, you note, Cleo will need to bring the claim for tortious interference with bequest in her individual capacity rather than on behalf of the estate because the alleged injury is personal to her.

Peter asks what you will be required to show to establish fraud or duress. Fraud, you explain, requires a showing that Bennie or Ivan made willfully false statements to Tessa; the statements were made in bad faith or with intent to deceive; Tessa was in fact deceived; and she changed the provisions of her will or entered into the other transactions

---

44. Youngblut v. Youngblut, 945 N.W.2d 25, 39 (Iowa 2020).

45. *Id.* (citing Restatement (Third) of Torts: Liab. for Econ. Harm § 19) (tort of intentional interference with bequest "not available to a plaintiff who has the right to seek a remedy for the same claim in a probate court").

46. Restatement (Third) of Torts: Liab. for Econ. Harm § 19 (2020). Not all state law follows the Restatement.

as a result of the deception.[47] At this point, nothing you've learned suggests that Bennie or Ivan made willfully false statements to Tessa. However, your state does not require that fraud be pleaded with particularity, as do some other states and the federal rules.[48] The same notice pleading requirements apply to fraud as to any other claim.[49] Depositions will be particularly useful to explore whether a fraud claim can be supported here.

You have not found any helpful cases in which a plaintiff alleges duress in a will contest (it is mentioned but rarely discussed). In general, though, you tell Peter that to prevail on a claim of duress, you will need to prove that Tessa involuntarily accepted terms made by Bennie and/or Ivan, under circumstances that permitted Tessa no other alternative, and the circumstances were the result of Bennie's and/or Ivan's coercion.[50] Again, nothing you've learned to date suggests that Bennie or Ivan placed Tessa under duress, but discovery will offer you the opportunity to explore Bennie's and Ivan's conduct in more depth. You suggest that it could be useful to take Bernie's and Ivan's depositions before serving any document requests. That way, you'll have a better sense of what documents you might need (that Cleo has not provided) to support the claims asserted. When you and Peter meet with Cleo to discuss the will contest, you should present this option to her.

IV. Other Issues

You wrap up by noting that you won't know whether there will be any creditor claims against the estate until the second publishing of notice and the period for asserting claims runs. In your state, that period is the later of four months after the second publication or one month after service of notice at the claimant's last known address.[51] Cleo was not aware of Tessa having any debts when she died but you have no way of knowing yet whether Bennie, as attorney-in-fact, incurred debt in Tessa's name.

---

47. *Id.*; *In re* Hollis' Estate, 12 N.W.2d 576 (1944).

48. *See* Matter of Estate of Glaser, No. 19-0008, 2020 WL 4200830, at **2 (Iowa Ct. App. July 22, 2020).

49. *Id.*

50. City of Asbury v. Iowa City Dev. Bd., 723 N.W.2d 188, 200 (Iowa 2006); *In re* Marriage of Shanks, 758 N.W.2d 506, 512 (Iowa 2008) (claim that contract was entered under duress requires showing that one party issued wrongful or unlawful threat and other party had no reasonable alternative to entering contract).

51. Iowa Code § 633.410 (2020).

"What about attorneys' fees?" Peter asks. Can the estate recover fees from Bennie, if the claims are successful? Possibly. Although there is no specific statutory provision entitling your client to attorneys' fees, you have a strong argument that, as a matter of public policy, if Bennie and/or Ivan took property from Tessa or her estate, the court should require them to pay the fees incurred to recover the property he improperly took from Tessa. This argument has been successful in family law cases involving custody but you aren't aware of any cases in your state in which it has been successful in a probate proceeding. However, you strongly believe this would be a good test case for the request in the estate context. If the wrongdoers are not required to pay attorneys' fees for making the estate whole, the fees would come out of the estate itself, unfairly diminishing Cleo's and Esther's shares of the estate.

V. Conclusion

Under the facts you have, you believe Cleo, on behalf of the estate, has grounds to contest the will as invalid due to Tessa's lack of testamentary capacity and Bernie's or Ivan's undue influence. You also believe the estate has grounds to undo the sale of the farm ground to Bennie and claw back his improper withdrawals or other transfers from Tessa's bank account. Because Bennie was in a fiduciary relationship with Tessa when the transfer was made, he will bear the burden to prove freedom from undue influence. The same likely applies to Ivan, if you can establish that he was in a confidential relationship with Tessa. The lawsuit should include a claim that Bennie and Ivan unduly influenced Tessa to purchase the annuity and name them as beneficiaries. Although you will carry the burden on this claim, it could create sufficient leverage with Bennie and Ivan and avoid having to go to trial.

You spend some time drafting the petition to contest the will. When you look up from your desk, the sun has gone down. It's your first day working after daylight since you left your Big Law job. Peter taps on your door to say goodnight. "Great job on this," he says. "Very happy to have you here."

Chapter 10

The Strange Case of Government as Fiduciary

By Alicia Hickok

I. Background

In *Leviathan*, Part II, Thomas Hobbes spoke of a commonwealth, but he envisioned it in contract terms. The United States became a nation founded primarily upon contracts and compacts. Contracting parties are generally held, however, to deal with one another at arm's length, and the contract is measured by its terms and the parties' intent alone. That changes when either the relationship between persons or the property that is the subject of the contract is in the nature of a trust. In such cases, the trustee has "a special and peculiar obligation to deal with the other person towards whom he stands so related, with a candor, a fairness, and a refusal to avail himself of superior information, or other favorable circumstance, not required by courts of justice in the usual business transactions of life."[1] Moreover, when a fiduciary undertakes a transaction that is challenged, the burden generally rests upon the fiduciary to demonstrate the fairness of the transaction—a significant shift from the burden on the challenger in an ordinary contract dispute.

On the one hand, there is an instinctive reaction that fiduciary duties cannot apply to government entities who are, after all, protected by sovereign immunity and the majoritarian process from *any* liability as to broad areas of decision making. Nonetheless, there are a handful of circumstances in which state governments (and in some cases their subdivisions) serve as "trustees" with "fiduciary duties" toward property or people. In perhaps no other area of the law has history and principles of

1. Brooks v. Martin, 69 U.S. 70 (1864).

constitutional and statutory construction intersected with trust law—and with contract and torts, property and government accountability—in such interesting and still-developing ways. This chapter is too brief to develop these themes in full, but it provides a taste of the complexity by (1) discussing the two primary means of creating such duties, (2) looking briefly at some of the ways such duties have been defined and developed, and (3) identifying a few of the current and ongoing challenges in litigating such claims as either a plaintiff or defendant.

II. The Creation of Governmental Trusts

A. Trusts Created by Federal Grants to States

1. Public Lands Associated with Navigable Waters (and Beyond)

Even when the land was British territory for the king to distribute as he wished, there were certain resources—and in particular, navigable waters—that were public at common law and "held by the king for the public benefit."[2] From the outset—and continuing as each state joined the union—that role passed to the individual states, placing each on "equal footing" in that regard.[3] The federal courts have held firm against any attempts to plead a "trust" and a "fiduciary duty" against federal agencies or under federal law for the administration of resources. Instead, subject only to federal regulation, the administration of resources held for the public is recognized as a question of state law. In general, of course, federal courts are highly sensitive about creating and defining state obligations. As a result, states have varied in whether the acquisition of title on an "equal footing" basis informs, dictates, or simply overlaps with the public trust doctrine.

The federal government makes an exception to the general rule, however, when the question is not the public nature of the resources but whether a special interest in the resources can be claimed by a specific group of people. The first example dates back to the 1800s, as the Supreme Court was struggling to determine whether the Cherokee Nation was a "foreign" nation for purposes of the Constitution, given that its lands are within the boundaries of the United States; the U.S. Supreme Court concluded that the relationship was in the nature of a

2. Martin v. Waddell's Lessee, 41 U.S. 367, 383 (1842).
3. *See* PPL Montana, LLC v. Montana, 566 U.S. 576, 590–91 (2012).

trust, a conclusion that was later expressly incorporated into various statutes, which the Supreme Court recognized gave rise to tribal claims for damages.[4]

In Hawaii, perhaps more than in any other state, a complex and unique body of law has arisen that combines all of the preceding elements—resources for the common good, resources for the good of native Hawaiians, constitutional provisions, statutory provisions, and administrative regulations and practices. This chapter barely touches the rich jurisprudence that the Hawaiian Supreme Court in particular has to offer in this regard. Even in that context, federal courts are reluctant to define the fiduciary duty involved, although they will enforce a state-defined duty.[5] This reflects the general sense of federal courts that such questions present "a most serious issue of federal-state relationships" that require careful handling in federal court.[6]

In the context of the more generic public trusts, the word "trust" was applied to the concept that resources are held by state governments for the common good, perhaps in order to give the government added rights vis-à-vis would-be private owners, but the government's role has been subject to the corresponding heightened duties associated with a trustee acting for a beneficiary. The U.S. Supreme Court provided the most commonly identified articulation in *Illinois Cent. R. Co. v. State of Illinois*,[7] which explained that the common law rationale for declaring navigable waters to be public was that they are "natural highways, and any obstruction to the common right, or exclusive appropriation of their use, is injurious to commerce, and, if permitted at the will of the sovereign, would be very likely to end in materially crippling, if not destroying it."[8] From this, the Supreme Court concluded that the ownership of the lands under Lake Michigan belonged to the state of Illinois, which had the power to repeal the grant of those lands to the railroad.[9] The consequence—that the state is a trustee who cannot abdicate its role to another—may be framed in fiduciary duty terms, but it really is a benefit that inheres to the state. The accompanying obligation—to ensure public access to public resources—is not onerous.

4. *See* United States v. White Mtn. Apache Tribe, 537 U.S. 465, 478–79 (2003).

5. *See, e.g.*, Price v. Hawaii, 921 F.2d 950, 956 (9th Cir. 1990) ("Whether the trust administration paradigm or some other paradigm informs the management method selected is a matter for the State's determination.").

6. *Id.* at 954.

7. Illinois Cent. R. Co. v. State of Illinois, 146 U.S. 387 (1892).

8. *Id.* at 458.

9. *Id.* at 463.

In the 1970s, however, that centuries-old concept began to change. In New Jersey, the Department of Environmental Protection sought to use its "role" as "trustee" affirmatively, arguing that tidal resources were being destroyed by pollution, and it had the right and fiduciary duty to seek damages to—as the trial court found—remedy "any diminution in that trust corpus."[10] The New Jersey Supreme Court reversed on other grounds, finding proximate causation lacking and the claim preempted, observing in conclusion that whether the State as *parens patriae* or as "public trustee" could assert damages claims in strict liability or is limited to injunctive relief were questions for another day.[11] In Washington, however, the Court of Appeals soon applied the reasoning of the New Jersey Appellate Division in *Jersey Central Power* to hold that the Department of Fisheries not only could recover from a landowner whose reconstruction of a stream bank, in violation of a state statute, damaged the state's salmon fishery, but held that it was "the fiduciary obligation of any trustee to seek damages for injury to the object of its trust"—and that here, the Department was the only one who could sue.[12]

In these transitional cases, trust principles were asserted *by states* as litigation swords. When plaintiffs sought to turn the tables and employ trust principles *against states*, some courts were receptive, but other courts were much more wary. California was an early embracer of a duty to use the good of the public as the measure of a project; indeed, the California Supreme Court traced its recognition of heightened duty to 1854. In *National Audubon Society v. Superior Court*,[13] the attorney general argued that the state's power permitted it to choose among whichever public uses it wished. The court rejected that view, defining the duty of the state as the protection of "the people's common heritage of streams, lakes, marshlands and tidelands, surrendering that right of protections only in rare cases when the abandonment of that right is consistent with the purposes of the trust."[14] As a result, the state "has an affirmative duty to take the public trust into account in the planning and allocation of water resources, and to protect public trust uses whenever feasible"—even if that means reconsidering prior decision making.[15] California continues to hold that perspective and recently found

10. State, Dep't of Env'l Protection v. Jersey Central Power & Light Co., 336 A.2d 750, 759 (N.J. Super. App. Div. 1975).
11. 351 A.2d 337, 344–45 (N.J. 1976).
12. State Dep't of Fisheries v. Gillette, 621 P.2d 764, 767 (Wash. Ct. Ap. 1980).
13. National Audobon Soc'y v. Superior Court, 658 P.2d 709, 717–18 (Cal. 1983).
14. *Id.* at 724.
15. *Id.* at 728–29.

that counties, as subdivisions of the state, "share[] responsibility for administering the public trust."[16]

Illinois and Minnesota are among the wary states. In *City of Elgin v. County of Cook*,[17] for example, a plaintiff argued that activities, including cutting trees and drilling wells, did not implicate a "fiduciary duty," while still recognizing that land to be used for a balefill was held in a public trust. The Illinois Supreme Court observed that "a legally prohibited purpose" would be "inconsistent with" the nature of a public trust; because the challenged acts were lawful, the court found the complaint failed to state a claim.[18] Similarly, the Minnesota Supreme Court read the "core rationale" of Minnesota's waterway public trust doctrine as protection of public use from "private interruption and encroachment."[19] The court refused to extend the doctrine to impute a fiduciary duty, and observed that caution is required "when a subject is extensively regulated by statutes and rules"—as public water use clearly is.[20]

2. Public School Land Grants

A second category of land held in trust by the various states has arisen from public school land grants that have been part of each state added since 1802. Those grants could be present or future interests. They initially were in the nature of contract—even including substitution and indemnity provisions. Over time, however, the language of the grants changed, and some courts adapted their view of the measure of obligations under the grants accordingly.[21] The evolution of the language in the grants has led courts to group school land grants into an interpretive continuum, from the grants in the early to mid-1800s (such as Alabama and Michigan), which are merely "honorary obligations" and "solemn agreements," to those at the turn of the century, such as New Mexico and Arizona, where Congress's language was held clearly to create a trust. Those in between (including Colorado and Utah) have

16. Envt'l Law Found. v. State Water Resources Control Bd., 26 Cal. App. 5th 844, 867–68 (Aug. 29, 2018).

17. City of Elgin v. Cnty. of Cook, 660 N.E.2d 875 (Ill. 1995).

18. *Id.* at 890.

19. White Bear Lake Restoration Ass'n, *ex rel.* State of Minnesota v. Minnesota Dep't of Natural Resources, 946 N.W.2d 373, 386 (Minn. 2020).

20. *Id.*

21. *See, e.g.*, Keys v. Carter, 318 So. 2d 862 (Miss. 1975) ("This Court is committed to the proposition that these lands constitute property held in trust for the public schools and must be dealt with by boards of supervisors as such and thus the rules applicable to trusts and trust property generally are to be applied.").

been analyzed to determine whether Congress enumerated duties in such a way that intent to create a trust could be inferred. In that analysis, Colorado was held to create a trust, and Utah was not.[22]

Although a governmental fiduciary duty over school lands most often stems from the terms of the federal land grant, there is nothing that stops a state from creating a *statutory* trust.[23] Accordingly, even if the state is not under a federally created trust obligation, it makes sense to consider the following points as well.

B. Trusts Created by Election and Adoption

In some states—particularly when it comes to natural resources—there is an overlap between the inherited construct of "public trust" and state constitutions or statutes. Though these cases are in some ways a subset of those just discussed, they have unique characteristics in that they are read according to standard rules of constitutional and statutory construction, and if the language chosen is informed by trusts, that language is given its trust meaning.

A primary example is the Environmental Rights Amendment that Pennsylvania adopted to its constitution during a 1971 referendum. Article I of the Pennsylvania Constitution has been held to "delineate[] the terms of the social contract between government and the people that are of such 'general, great and essential' quality to be ensconced as 'inviolate.'"[24] Within that context, Pennsylvania's Environmental Rights Amendment states:

> The people have a right to clean air, pure water, and to the preservation of the natural, scenic, historic and esthetic values of the environment. Pennsylvania's public natural resources are the common property of all the people, including generation yet to come. As trustees of these resources, the Commonwealth shall conserve and maintain them for the benefit of all the people.[25]

A plurality of the Pennsylvania Supreme Court construed this provision as setting forth two rights, the first to the listed resources and their protection, which the court defined as both keeping from harm and

22. *Compare* Branson Sch. Dist. RE-82 v. Romer, 161 F.3d 619 (10th Cir. 1998) *with* District 22 United Mine Workers of America v. Utah, 229 F.3d 982 (10th Cir. 2000).

23. *See, e.g.*, Director of Office of State Lands and Investments v. Merbanco, Inc., 70 P.3d 241 (Wyo. 2003) (school lands subject to a statutory trust, not a constitutionally created or Act of Admission-created trust).

24. Robinson Township v. Washington Cnty., 83 A.3d 901, 962 (Pa. 2013).

25. Pa. Const., Art. I, § 27, set forth in *Robinson Township*, 83 A.3d at 948–49.

damage and ensuring "maintenance and perpetuation of an environment of quality for the benefit of future generations."[26] That right imposes on the government—state and local—a duty to "refrain from unduly infringing upon or violating the right, including by legislative enactment or executive action."[27] The second right is a right of common ownership, in present and future generations. The provision sets forth both affirmative and negative duties of the government in its fiduciary role. Accordingly, the Commonwealth must "prevent and remedy the degradation, diminution, or depletion" of natural resources, employing "prudence, loyalty, and impartiality," and those duties can be enforced by "citizen beneficiaries."[28]

Pennsylvania's citizen-created trust over its natural resources rises to the level of an inherent and fundamental right. As the Pennsylvania Supreme Court recognized, only Rhode Island and Montana have incorporated similar protections into their Declaration or Bill of Rights, although other states have provisions with different terms.[29] But the distinctiveness of Pennsylvania's approach has not stopped plaintiffs from arguing that the way Pennsylvania has interpreted its trust principles should inform other states' analyses.[30]

Florida's constitutional provision regarding sovereign submerged lands, adopted in 1970, has been held to codify the public trust doctrine, but it stops short of creating an inherent right:

> The title to lands under navigable waters, within the boundaries of the state, which have not been alienated, including beaches below mean high water lines, is held by the state, by virtue of its sovereignty, in trust for all the people. Sale of such lands may be authorized by law, but only when in the public interest. Private use of portions of such lands may be authorized by law, but only when not contrary to the public interest.[31]

The primary body charged with implementing this provision is the board of trustees of the Internal Improvement Trust Fund. Far from a

26. *Robinson Township*, 83 A.3d at 951.
27. *Id.* at 952.
28. *Id.* at 957.
29. *Id.* at 963.
30. City of Longmont v. Colorado Oil & Gas Ass'n, 369 P.3d 573, 585 (Colo. 2016) (dismissing argument because Colorado's Constitution "does not include a similar provision"); Syngenta Seeds, Inc. v. Cnty. of Kauai, 842 F.3d 669, 676 (9th Cir. 2016) (Hawaiian law is different because its conservation clause may "obligate counties to use their authority to conserve public-trust resources, but it does not permit counties to exercise power that the State has not granted them.").
31. Article X, Section 11.

heightened duty, the decision making of that body is, under Florida law, entitled to significant deference and a presumption that they have acted as they should; "[t]he exercise of their judgment should not be subjected to adverse judicial scrutiny absent a clear showing of abuse of discretion or violation of law."[32]

In yet another variation, rather than set forth a generalized constitutional right that a beneficiary may enforce, Connecticut's Environmental Protection Act creates a cause of action for declaratory or equitable relief "for the protection of the public trust in the air, water, and other natural resources of the state from unreasonable pollution, impairment, or destruction," which can be asserted by the "Attorney General, any political subdivision of the state, any instrumentality or agency of the state or of a political subdivision thereof, any person, partnership, corporation, association, organization or other legal entity."[33] Once the plaintiff has made a prima facie showing, the burden shifts to the defendant to "rebut the prima facie showing by the submission of evidence to the contrary."[34] The evidence to the contrary is, at the least, expert testimony.[35]

C. In Trust for Hawaiians and in Trust for Hawaii

As mentioned earlier, the federal government has entered into various forms of legislation, which by their terms connote a trust, concerning the peoples of various tribes and those indigenous to Hawaii and Alaska.[36] For tribes, that obligation continues as a federal trust, but although there are continued federal aspects to Alaska and Hawaii, when they became states much of the responsibility passed to the state itself. Thus, in its constitution, Hawaii agreed to accept the responsibility to administer Hawaiian home lands "as a compact with the United States, or as conditions or trust provisions imposed by the United States." Hawaii further agreed to carry out those responsibilities faithfully.[37]

---

32. Trustees of Internal Imp. Trust Fund v. Levy, 656 So. 2d 1359 (Fla. App. 1995).

33. C.G.S.A. § 22a-16.

34. *Id.* § 22a-17.

35. Crouzet v. First Baptist Church of Stonington, 239 A.3d 321, 335 n.8 (Ct. App. Aug. 18, 2020). The Connecticut Supreme Court has granted review of one question in the case. 241 A.3d 703.

36. *See, e.g.*, Seminole Nation v. United States, 316 U.S. 286, 296–97 (1942) (describing "moral obligations of the highest responsibility and trust," giving rise to an assessment of such conduct by "the most exacting fiduciary standards").

37. *See* Hawaii Const. Art. XII, Section 2 (current).

Construing Article XII of the Hawaiian Constitution, the Hawaiian Supreme Court has held that government acts in furtherance of these obligations must satisfy strict scrutiny as the equivalent to the "most exacting fiduciary standards."[38] The court also determined that the government has two express fiduciary duties: "to administer the trust solely in the interest of the beneficiary"; and "to use reasonable skill and care to make trust property productive."[39] *Ahuna* itself involved a challenge to a decision to apportion less than ten acres to an individual, retaining the balance to reserve for a potential road. The Hawaiian Supreme Court concluded that the commissioners had breached their fiduciary duties, both in giving too little weight to the beneficiaries' interests and in prioritizing a speculative future project over the prospect of facilitating agriculturally productive land.

The Hawaiian Constitution was amended in 1978. Article XI governs the conservation, control, and development of resources, and it contains explicit trust provisions. Section 1, for example, expressly states that "all public resources are held in trust by the State for the benefit of the people." Section 7 places in the state "an obligation to protect, control and regulate the use of Hawaii's water resources for the benefit of its people." Section 9 gives each person a right to a "clean and healthful environment," and any person may enforce that right.[40]

Article XII of the Hawaiian Constitution was amended by enacting Section 4, which specifies that certain lands are to be "held by the State as a public trust for native Hawaiians and the general public." Similarly, Sections 5 and 6 specify that the Office of Hawaiian Affairs holds land in trust "for native Hawaiians and Hawaiians" and requires the land to be administered by the trustees of the Office of Hawaiian Affairs. Sections 5 and 6 establish and set forth the powers of those trustees.

In 2013, a plaintiff argued that the fiduciary duties set forth in Article XII require the Office of Hawaiian Affairs to expend trust funds "in the sole interest" of native Hawaiians under common law trust

---

38. Ahuna v. Dep't of Hawaiian Home Lands, 640 P.2d 1161, 1169 (Haw. 1982).

39. *Id.*

40. The Commission on Water Resource Management issues water permits as an agency governed by Hawaii's Administrative Procedure Act, which accords an agency's decision a presumption of validity. *In re* Waiola O Malokai, Inc., 83 P.3d 664, 683 (Haw. 2004) (other discussions of the administrative standard were clarified as an abuse of discretion in Paul's Electrical Service, Inc. v. Befitel, 91 P.3d 494, 499 (Haw. 2004)). Nonetheless, for public trust resources, the state has "duties of a trustee and not simply the duties of good manager" toward both present and future generations as beneficiaries. *Id.* at 684–85. Those duties include both protection and a duty to "promote the reasonable and beneficial use of water resources in order to maximize their social and economic benefits" to the public. *Id.* at 693. Toward that end, all water uses, public or private, must benefit the public.

principles. But the Hawaiian Supreme Court disagreed, explaining that the trustee's decisions can be to the benefit of nonbeneficiaries, so long as the trustee's decisions are within the trustee's discretion, advance the purposes of the trust, and do not benefit a nonbeneficiary instead of the trust.[41]

III. Issues in Litigating Government Trust Duties

Because of the contexts in which public trusts arose, the diverse development of such trusts, and the layers of common law, constitutional law, and statutory law that have created highly individualized definitions of duties and standards of review, litigating public trusts—whether as a plaintiff or a defendant—is extraordinarily textually and historically specific. What another jurisdiction has done is more often useful as a point of contrast than as a point of comparison. Nonetheless, as certain doctrines ebb and flow in general, they present special challenges to litigating claims and defenses in the public trust context.

A. Standing

In some instances, a statute can create a cause of action—both a right and a remedy. A right is not enough in itself to establish Article III standing in federal court—although sometimes courts will recognize 42 U.S.C. § 1983 as an independent basis for standing. Nonetheless, as the Supreme Court has recently reinforced, Article III requires individual and demonstrable injury, even where there is a statutory right to sue.[42] One of the first cases to apply this requirement was *Pierce v. Ducey*,[43] in which an Arizona resident claimed that recent amendments to Arizona's Constitution were contrary to Congress's intent in granting public school lands. The Court of Appeals for the Ninth Circuit rejected both the argument that his interest in seeing that the law was complied with gave him standing and that his status as a trust beneficiary gave him standing.

41. Kealoha v. Machado, 3115 P.3d 213, 228 (Haw. 2013).
42. *See* Thole v. U.S. Bank, N.A., 140 S. Ct. 1615 (U.S. 2020).
43. Pierce v. Ducey, 965 F.3d 1085 (9th Cir. 2020).

In order to invoke trust beneficiary standing, a litigant may have standing only in state courts.[44] Even in state courts, however, the reaction toward standing is mixed. In New Mexico, for example, there was no taxpayer right to challenge the administration of grazing (the fees of which funded public schools) on lands subject to a public trust because the public importance was not sufficiently great. Indeed, the court suggested that the parties should have asked the attorney general to bring suit on their behalf instead. The court held that only a "clear threat[] to the essential nature of state government guaranteed to New Mexico citizens under their Constitution" would have been important enough to warrant taxpayer standing.[45] Wyoming courts, however, have used a different rationale to reach the same conclusion, namely that the amount of funding that came from revenues from school lands was a relatively small portion of school funds.

B. Justiciability and Remedies

As discussed at the outset of the chapter, courts are reluctant to hold the government liable for the performance of a discretionary duty, and in particular, to hold it to the higher standard of a fiduciary. The instinctive reaction of a political body (and a court) is to invoke sovereign immunity, as well as the other defenses discussed here.

As noted earlier, federal courts are particularly reluctant to define state standards. That same reluctance can be seen in state courts, which often refuse to adjudicate "non-justiciable political questions"—those which either require assessing nonascertainable facts or deciding among alternatives committed to the discretion of the executive. Framing is critical, however, and states will not hesitate to apply their own precedent—including their own precedent in the generalized trust context—to determine whether executive action or legislation breaches a constitutional fiduciary duty.[46]

In the context of the statutory overlays on federal fiduciary duties toward tribes, the U.S. Supreme Court has recognized that where a trustee has a duty to preserve "it naturally follows that the Government

---

44. *E.g.*, Protect Our Parks, Inc. v. Chicago Park District, 971 F.3d 722 (7th Cir. 2020), *reh'g denied* (finding that the Illinois courts have found standing to enforce the trust over public lands, but that standing does not satisfy the requirements of Article III standing).

45. Forest Guardians v. Powell, 24 P.3d 803 (N.M. Ct. App. 2001).

46. *See* Ching v. Case, 449 P.3d 1146, 1174 (Haw. 2019) (drawing the distinction as to agencies); *Robinson Township*, 83 A.3d at 527–28 (drawing the distinction as to legislation).

should be liable in damages for the breach of fiduciary duty."[47] The right to damages can be found by "fair inference" from the duty, and does not need to be express.[48] It is simple to characterize any breach of fiduciary duty as a tort, for which damages are recoverable.[49] A state as trustee can, of course, always seek either restitution or damages, or both, if a third party damages the trust corpus. It may have additional rights (and remedies) if it proceeds in a *parens patriae* capacity as well.

But damage awards to private parties proceeding against the government are in the greatest tension with the principles of sovereign immunity and governmental discretion protected by the political question doctrine. Accordingly, some states have expressly provided private rights of action while simultaneously limiting private remedies to declaratory and injunctive relief. Connecticut's section 22a-16, for example, has a broad right of who can sue "for the protection of the public trust in the air, water and other natural resources of the state," but the suit is only for declaratory and equitable relief.[50]

The Alaska Supreme Court reached the same result, but by a different analysis. It expressly differentiates between claims for damages (or an accounting) premised on negligence in policy setting—which would be barred by sovereign immunity—and claims for declaratory and equitable relief for breach of fiduciary duties arising under the public trust doctrine and Article VIII of Alaska's Constitution—which are not.[51] The clear import of the court's analysis is that a breach of fiduciary duty when there is a public trust does not sound in tort, unless a "tort recovery" is sought.

In *Kanuk*, the plaintiff could not convince the court to compel prospective action. The court observed that it has applied public trust principles to restrain the state from limiting public access, not—as requested in *Kanuk*—to compel regulation of resources.[52] The court then took the unusual step of following up with the statement that "[a]llegations that the State has breached its duties with regard to the management of these resources do not depend on a declaratory judgment about the atmosphere."[53] This is similar to one of the principles the Pennsylvania Commonwealth

47. United States v. White Mountain Apache Tribe, 537 U.S. 465, 476 (2003).

48. *Id.* at 477.

49. *See, e.g.*, City of Oakland v. SSA Terminals, LLC, 12-cv-01446-YGR, 2012 WL 2501101, at *6 (N.D. Cal. June 27, 2012) ("Here, the statute at issue creates a public trust. As such, claims against the trustee for actions harmful to the trust sound in tort.").

50. *See* C.G.S.A. § 22a-16.

51. *See* Kanuk *ex rel.* Kanuk v. State Dep't of Natural Resources, 335 P.3d 1088, 1095–96 (Alaska 2014).

52. *Id.* at 1102.

53. *Id.* at 1103.

Court has pulled from *Robinson Township*, namely, that there is no affirmative duty for a municipality "to enact specific affirmative measures to promote clean air, pure water and the preservation of different values of our environment."[54]

On the other hand, an Oregon appellate court, based on its construction of that state's Declaratory Judgment Act, reached a very different conclusion from the Alaskan court in *Kanuk*, namely, that the plaintiffs there were entitled to a declaration whether the atmosphere is "a trust resource" and whether Oregon "as a trustee, has a fiduciary obligation" to protect it from climate change.[55] In weighing justiciability against the requirements of Oregon's Declaratory Judgments Act, Oregon has determined that "present facts" and "meaningful relief" are enough for a claim to be justiciable, and "meaningful relief" can be predicated on a declaration of the scope of a state's duties, coupled with the presumption that when the courts announce the duties a state has, the state will act in accordance with those duties.[56]

As noted earlier, courts typically permit only injunctive and declaratory relief for public trust violations. There are exceptions, however. For example, in *White Mountain Apache Tribe v. United States*,[57] the Court of Appeals for the Federal Circuit reasoned that the federal government had a fiduciary duty to preserve trust property, and that duty obligated the government to maintain and repair for the current and future beneficiaries, and the "waste" occasioned by a breach of that trust is remediable in damages.

IV. Conclusion

There may be no other area of law that is so individualized and at once so dependent upon context and yet so open-ended. Whether as a government plaintiff or government defendant, individual plaintiff or individual defendant, all the wealth of history and text can still be brought to bear to meld trust law principles into the amalgam of other principles that bear on how governmental entities are responsible for stewardship within and across generations.

54. Protect PT v. Penn Township Zoning Hearing Bd., 220 A.3d 1174, 1198 (Pa. Commw. 2019).

55. Chernaik v. Kitzhaber, 328 P.3d 799, 808 (Or. App. 2014).

56. *Id.* at 806–07.

57. White Mountain Apache Tribe v. United States, 249 F.3d 1364 (Fed. Cir. 2001).

Chapter 11
Lender Fiduciary Duties

By Mitchell Edwards and Katherine B. Savage

I. Introduction and General Principles

Generally speaking, lender-borrower relationships are arm's-length transactions that, by definition, do not create any special duties between the parties.[1] It is well-established that a borrower cannot unilaterally enter into a fiduciary relationship with its lender.[2] A borrower's unilateral belief that a lender is or should be acting in a fiduciary capacity, or a borrower's reliance on that belief in her decision making, does not create a fiduciary relationship.[3] For a lender to be held to a fiduciary

1. *See, e.g.*, Continental Bank N.A. v. Everett, 760 F. Supp. 713, 717, 15 U.C.C. Rep. Serv. 2d 253 (N.D. Ill. 1991), *aff'd*, 964 F.2d 701 (7th Cir. 1992) (lender does not stand in fiduciary relationship with guarantor); Berger v. Nationstar Mortg. LLC, 118 F. Supp. 3d 1121, 1126 (D. Minn. 2015) ("lenders bear no fiduciary duty to borrowers"); Abdel-Karim v. Egyptair Airlines, 116 F. Supp. 3d 389, 410 (S.D.N.Y. 2015) ("customers relationships are generally not fiduciary. . . ."); Wilson v. Everbank, N.A., 77 F. Supp. 3d 1202, 1223 (S.D. Fla. 2015) (lender-borrower, banker-borrower, creditor-debtor, and mortgagor-mortgagee relationships are not fiduciary); Dugan v. First Nat'l Bank in Wichita, 606 P.2d 1009 (Kan. 1980) ("The relationship between a bank and its depositor is ordinarily that of creditor-debtor and not of a fiduciary nature.").

2. Robley v. Blue Cross/Blue Shield of Mississippi, 935 So. 2d 990, 995 (Miss. 2006) ("Although one does not typically enter into a contract with another person unless he or she has a degree of trust or confidence in that person, without more, such a transaction amounts to merely a business relationship and not a fiduciary relationship."); *see also* Barry A. Cappello, Lender Liability 282 (5th ed. 2014) ("The majority rule is that if no more than an arm's-length debtor-creditor relationship is present, a fiduciary relationship will not be found."); Gerald L. Blanchard, Lender Liability: Law, Practice and Prevention § 5:2 (5th ed. 2014) ("A fiduciary duty cannot be imposed unilaterally. The trust and confidence which a party rests on the other party must be accompanied by some type of action on the second party showing that the relationship is recognized.").

3. Travel Servs. Network, Inc. v. Presidential Fin. Corp. of Massachusetts, 959 F. Supp. 135, 144 (D. Conn. 1997) (applying Massachusetts law and holding that "one party cannot

standard, either the contract must specifically impose that duty, or the lender must undertake some action, above and beyond that which is typical in a creditor-debtor relationship, that merits finding a fiduciary relationship between the parties.[4]

Fiduciary duties generally arise in two contexts: (1) those that arise as a matter of law, or contract—such as attorney-client relationships, guardian-ward relationships, or trustee-beneficiary relationships; and (2) those that arise as a matter of fact, often referred to as "confidential relationships"[5]—that is, relationships in which one party has reposed special trust or confidence in the other and has relied on that special confidence to his detriment.[6] A fiduciary duty in the lender-borrower context arises only when the contract specifically provides for it or

---

unilaterally transform a business relationship into a fiduciary relationship by reposing trust and confidence in another"); *In re* Greenberg, 212 B.R. 422, 428–29 (Bankr. D. Mass. 1997), *aff'd*, 229 B.R. 544 (B.A.P. 1st Cir. 1999) ("The Debtor's allegations that she was relying on the Bank to accurately advise her will simply not suffice to create a fiduciary duty to her by the Bank.").

4. *See, e.g.*, Ha-Lo Indus., Inc. v. Credit Suisse First Bos., Corp., No. 04 C 3163, 2005 WL 2592495, at *5 (N.D. Ill. Oct. 12, 2005) ("[A] fiduciary duty may be created by the express provisions of a contract, or by factors such as the length of the relationship of the parties, their financial interdependence, and their sharing of confidential and proprietary information. . . . However, not every commercial contract or relationship creates a fiduciary duty.") (quoting ADT Operations v. Chase Manhattan Bank, N.A., 662 N.Y.S.2d 190, 192 (Sup. Ct. 1997)); *In re* Sallee, 286 F.2d 878, 893, 2002 FED App. 0128P (6th Cir. 2002) (applying Kentucky law and finding that "[f]iduciary relationships arise when circumstances and the relationship of the parties show the parties understood and agree that confidence is reposed by one party and trust accepted by the other. Fiduciary relationships can be informal, but they must evidence circumstances showing both parties agreed that one party would be acting in the interest of the other."); *In re* Greenberg, 212 B.R. 422, 428–29 (Bankr. D. Mass. 1997), *aff'd*, 229 B.R. 544 (B.A.P. 1st Cir. 1999) ("Massachusetts law is clear that one party cannot unilaterally transform a business relationship into a fiduciary relationship. . . . Rather, to create such a relationship, the fiduciary, in this case the Bank, would have to know of and accept the plaintiff's trust.").

5. *See* D. Gordon Smith, *The Critical Resource Theory of Fiduciary Duty*, 55 VAND. L. REV. 1399, 1412–13 (2002) ("Formal fiduciary relationships are those well-settled cases—such as trustee-beneficiary, guardian-ward, partner-partner, director-shareholder, and attorney-client—where fiduciary duties apply as a matter of course. Informal fiduciary relationships—often referred to as "confidential relationships"—are those in which the court imposes fiduciary duties based on a qualitative evaluation of the relationship.") (footnotes omitted); *see also id.* at 1412, n.53 ("'Confidential relationships' and 'fiduciary relationships' are not congruent, but the overlap between the two concepts is substantial.").

6. Robley v. Blue Cross/Blue Shield of Mississippi, 935 So. 2d 990, 994 (Miss. 2006) ("Traditional fiduciary relationships are found in cases of trustee and beneficiary, partners, principal and agents, guardian and ward, managing directors and corporation. . . . However, our law applies a broad brush to this doctrine and does not preclude a jury's finding of a fiduciary relationship in other situations.") (citations omitted); Carter Equip. Co. v. John Deere Indus. Equip. Co., 681 F.2d 386, 390 (5th Cir. 1982).

when there exists a confidential relationship between the parties.[7] Similarly, parties can contractually waive their fiduciary duties.[8]

When a fiduciary relationship exists, the traditional fiduciary duties follow, that is, the duty of loyalty, duty of care, duty not to take unfair advantage, and duty of full disclosure.[9] In short, the fiduciary lender has a duty to place the borrower's interests ahead of its own.[10]

There are a few specific circumstances in which courts have imposed fiduciary duties on a lender, including:

1. Lender acts as financial adviser;
2. Lender acts as borrower's agent;
3. Lender exerts control over borrower;
4. Lender acts on its powers of foreclosure;
5. Lender induces, aids, or abets a breach of fiduciary duty; and
6. Special circumstances giving rise to a fiduciary relationship.

Each of these circumstances is examined next.

---

7. Denison State Bank v. Madeira, 640 P.2d 1235, 1241 (Kan. 1982) ("A fiduciary is in a position to have and exercise, and does have an exercise influence over another. A fiduciary relationship implies a condition of superiority of one of the parties over the other."); *see also* Hensler v. Busey Bank, 596 N.E.2d 1269, 1274 (Ill. 4th Dist. 1992) ("A fiduciary relationship exists when there is a special confidence reposed in one, who, in equity and good conscience, is bound to act in good faith and with due regard to the interest of the one reposing the confidence."); *see also* BLANCHARD, *supra* note 2 (citing *Denison*, 640 P.2d at 1241); CAPPELLO, *supra* note 2, at 287.

8. *In re* CMR Mortg. Fund, LLC, 416 B.R. 720 (Bankr. N.D. Cal. 2009) (contract stated that one party "owe[d] no fiduciary duty" to the other and "agree[d] not to assert any such claim"); *see also* BLANCHARD, *supra* note 2, § 5:3 ("Parties may also contractually waive any fiduciary duty that may exist between them.").

9. Capital Bank v. MVB, Inc., 644 So. 2d 515, 520 (Fla. 3d DCA 1994) ("A fiduciary owes to its beneficiary the duty to refrain from self-dealing, the duty of loyalty, the overall duty not to take unfair advantage and to act in the best interest of the other party, and the duty to disclose material facts."); Matter of Cooperman, 83 N.Y.2d 465, 611 N.Y.S.2d 465, 633 N.E.2d 1069, 1071 (1994) (fiduciary duties include honesty, good faith, fair dealing, loyalty, confidentiality, and competency in safeguarding beneficiary interests); *see also* Avary v. Bank of Am., N.A., 72 S.W.3d 779, 791 (Tex. App. 2002) ("As independent executor of the estate, the Bank had a fiduciary relationship with Brett and Timothy and, therefore, owed them a fiduciary duty of full disclosure of all material facts known to [it] that might affect [the beneficiaries'] rights.") (quotations omitted); CAPPELLO, *supra* note 2, at 295 (noting that the "standard fiduciary duties . . . include the duty of loyalty, the duty to refrain from insider transactions and overreaching, the duty to not take unfair advantage, and the duty of full disclosure").

10. *See, e.g.*, Zastrow v. Journal Commc'ns, Inc., 718 N.W.2d 51, 59 (W.I. 2006) ("A consistent facet of a fiduciary duty is the constraint on the fiduciary's discretion to act in his own self-interest because by accepting the obligation of a fiduciary he consciously sets another's interests before his own.").

II. Circumstances in Which Courts Have Imposed Fiduciary Duties on Lenders

A. Lender Acts as Financial Adviser

When a lender provides investment advice, holds itself out as a financial adviser, or negotiates on a borrower's behalf in a financial transaction, a fiduciary duty may arise.[11] The mere rendering of advice, however, even if given to help the borrower prosper and succeed, does not transform a business relationship into a fiduciary one.[12] Rather, courts look to the nature of the relationship between the lender and its customer to determine whether a fiduciary duty exists based on the lender's provision of financial advice.[13]

In the context of investment advice, one court has explained the different possible duties a lender may owe as follows:

> There are three types of securities accounts typically employed by banks and brokerage firms: a custodian account, a discretionary account and a custodian management account. The duty to the customer and the degree of management responsibility assumed vary with the type of account. In a custodian account, the responsibility to the customer is minimal, because the custodian merely holds, buys or sells, transfers or receives securities as directed by the customer. Maximum responsibility is assumed in a discretionary account.[14]

Thus, whether the bank will be held to a fiduciary standard depends on the type of account and the role the bank agrees to play in the customer's management of that account. While a bank that serves as custodian for an IRA account may not have a fiduciary obligation to the

---

11. UBS Bank USA v. Ibby, LLC, No. 2:09-CV-372 TS, 2009 WL 4884383 (D. Utah Dec. 10, 2009); *see also* CAPPELLO, *supra* note 2, at 288–91.

12. Union State Bank v. Woell, 434 N.W.2d 712, 721 (N.D. 1989) ("In a commercial context, the mere rendering of advice by the lender to the borrower, even if given in a sincere effort to help the borrower prosper, does not transform a business relationship into a fiduciary relationship.").

13. Farm Credit Servs. of N. Dakota PCA v. A & C Soaring Eagle Trucking, No. CV 17-117-BLG-DWM, 2020 WL 3832665, at *8 (D. Mont. July 8, 2020) ("[A] fiduciary relationship may arise under circumstances, which reflect a borrower's reposing of faith, confidence and trust in a bank with a resulting domination, control or influence exercised by the bank over the borrower's affairs.").

14. Erlich v. First Nat'l Bank of Princeton, 505 A.2d 220, 233, 232 (N.J. Super. Law. Div. 1984).

customer, a bank that gives investment strategy advice likely will be held to a fiduciary standard of care.[15]

In *Frydman & Co v. Credit Suisse First Boston Corp.*, the court held the bank to a fiduciary standard based on its role as financial adviser and negotiator for the plaintiff.[16] In that case, the plaintiff sought to acquire an entity, Starrett Corp., and entered into a financing agreement with the defendant-bank. In the acquisition process, the bank offered the plaintiff significant investment advice and negotiated with Starrett on the plaintiff's behalf. Less than a week after the plaintiff's deal fell through, the bank executed a financing commitment letter that enabled a different entity to acquire Starrett. The plaintiff sued for breach of fiduciary duty, arguing that the timing of the bank's commitment letter indicated that the bank had been working on the third party's behalf when it was supposed to be negotiating the same deal for the plaintiff. The trial court dismissed the action, finding that the contract language "provid[ed] that legal obligations would not arise by virtue of th[e] agreement except as specifically agreed to therein."[17] The appellate court reversed, finding that the contract terms did "not preclude the finding of a fiduciary duty arising from CSFB's alleged provision of investment banking services," because that duty would not exist "by virtue of" the contract.[18] Specifically, the appellate court held that the complaint adequately alleged that the bank provided the plaintiff "with investment banking advice and other services, including conducting negotiations with Starrett on [the plaintiff's] behalf, in connection with the attempted acquisition."[19] In sum, the bank's actions, as alleged, were enough to create a fiduciary duty that obligated the bank to place the plaintiff's interests ahead of its own.

In *Capital Bank v. MVB, Inc.*,[20] the bank had two customers engaged in the business of selling hair care products. The bank advised

---

15. Estate of Pauli v. Wachovia Bank, N.A., No. A-4851-12T2, 2014 WL 8765427, at *10 (N.J. Super. Ct. App. Div. May 5, 2015) ("Plaintiffs incorrectly assert that the term "custodian" used in the IRA Agreement established a fiduciary obligation. . . . We find neither evidence nor legal authority that would support plaintiffs' argument that upon opening an IRA CD, a special relationship of trust and confidence arose between Mr. Pauli and Wachovia, or that opening an IRA CD was an 'intrinsically fiduciary' transaction.") (quoting *Erlich*, 505 A.2d at 232).

16. Frydman & Co v. Credit Suisse First Boston Corp., 708 N.Y.S.2d 77 (N.Y. App. Div. 2000).

17. *Id.* at 79.

18. *Id.*

19. *Id.*

20. Capital Bank v. MVB, Inc., 644 So. 2d 515 (Fla. Ct. App. 1994).

and encouraged one of those customers, MVB, to purchase some defective manufacturing equipment from the other, without informing MVB of the defects or the fact that the other entity was on the verge of bankruptcy. Despite knowing that MVB's business was in a weak financial position, heavily indebted and with little capital, the bank encouraged MVB to take on additional debt to acquire the defective assets and ultimately financed the transaction.[21] Predictably, after MVB bought the equipment, it continuously broke down, causing MVB to miss production deadlines and fall behind on its sales targets. MVB sued the bank for fraud and breach of fiduciary duty.[22] Finding that the bank knew or had reason to know that MVB had placed its trust and confidence in the bank and was relying on the bank's advice, the court held that a fiduciary relationship existed between MVB and the bank.[23] Specifically, the court found that the bank's representatives had expressly invited and fostered MVB's reliance on the bank's advice, with statements such as "You are part of [the] Capital Bank Family. You help the bank, we are going to help you."[24] The bank also commissioned an appraisal of the equipment and presented it to MVB as supporting evidence that the purchase was a good business decision, despite knowing that the appraisal was fundamentally flawed.[25] Additionally, the court found that special circumstances militated in favor of finding a fiduciary relationship existed, namely, the fact that the bank received a greater economic benefit from MVB's acquisition than it would have received from a typical transaction.[26] The bank stood to benefit from the sale of defective assets because, "[w]ithout the sale, [the other customer] would have been unable to pay its debts to the bank. Having lured its customer into a borrowing transaction . . . the bank dealt with [MVB] as a tool with which to alleviate the result of its own prior poor loan judgment."[27]

In sum, courts may hold lenders liable as fiduciaries based on their roles as financial or investment advisers if the facts and circumstances militate in favor of such a finding. A lender that does not plan on providing financial or investment advice should consider requiring its

21. *Id.* at 519.
22. *Id.* at 518.
23. *Id.* at 520.
24. *Id.* at 519.
25. *Id.* at 520.
26. *Id.*
27. *Id.*

customers to sign disclaimers, as part of a loan application process, that will absolve the lender from any responsibility for their investment decisions.[28]

B. Lender Acts as Borrower's Agent

The general rule in agency law is that an agent owes a fiduciary duty to its principal.[29] In the lender-borrower context, the agent-principal relationship arises only when the parties expressly agree to it, though the agreement need not be formalized.[30] Thus, where a bank agrees to forbear its rights to foreclose in exchange for a percentage of the profits from the sale of the property securing the loan, the lender may have entered into a joint venture relationship that gives rise to a fiduciary duty.[31] Similarly, where a bank agrees to act as a closing agent for a transaction, it has a fiduciary duty to the beneficiaries of that transaction to close the sale in accordance with the terms of the underlying contract.[32] Likewise, where a lender acts as an escrow agent by holding investors' funds, it assumes a fiduciary duty to disclose known fraud to

28. *See, e.g.*, Cogan v. Triad Am. Energy, 944 F. Supp. 1325 (S.D. Tex. 1996) ("The effect of the disclaimers is clear. Each plaintiff agreed, as a condition to borrowing money from Atlantic, that it had not received representations from the lender and was not relying on what the lender had said or done in making his investment decision.").

29. Restatement (Third) of Agency § 8.01 (2006) ("An agent has a fiduciary duty to act loyally for the principal's benefit in all matters connected with the agency relationship."); *see also* PowerPath Transp., LLC v. Pflumm, No. 18CV6444, 2020 WL 4630444, at *6 (Kan. Dist. Ct. Aug. 11, 2020) ("An agent owes a fiduciary duty to its principal—one that demand[s] trust and confidence and imposes an obligation of individual service and loyalty.") (quotations omitted); MDM Grp. Assocs., Inc. v. CX Reinsurance Co., 165 P.3d 882, 889 (Colo. App. 2007) ("In the principal-agent context, it is the *agent* who owes a fiduciary duty to the principal as a matter of law."); Arst v. Stifel, Nicolaus & Co., 86 F.3d 973, 978 (10th Cir. 1996) (observing that an agent is "a fiduciary with respect to matters within the scope of [the] agency").

30. *See, e.g.*, First Nat'l Bank v. Wernhart, 555 N.W.2d 819, 820 (Wis. Ct. App. 1996); *see generally* Cappello, *supra* note 2, at 291–92.

31. RFF Family P'ship, LP v. Link Dev., LLC, 907 F. Supp. 2d 155, 162 (D. Mass. 2012) ("[P]artners in a joint venture owe one another the same fiduciary duties imposed upon members of a partnership.") (citing Shain Inv. Co. v. Cohen, 443 N.E.2d 126, 131 (Mass. App. Ct. 1982)); *see also In re* Fordham, 130 B.R. 632, 648–49, 15 U.C.C. Rep. Serv. 2d 400 (Bankr. D. Mass. 1991) (lender was not joint venturer with developer merely because lender was entitled to partial release fee of $1,500 as each condominium unit sold and was released from lender's construction mortgage).

32. Reebles, Inc. v. Bank of Am., N.A., 29 Kan. App. 2d 205, 209, 25 P.3d 871, 874 (2001).

the investors.[33] In sum, when a lender agrees to undertake a particular action on the borrower's behalf, which is above and beyond those actions intrinsic to the lender-borrower relationship, it may have entered into an agency relationship that gives rise to a fiduciary duty.

In *First National Bank v. Wernhart*, the Wernharts executed a mortgage to finance construction of their new home with First National Bank, and also deposited some personal funds with the bank to cover unforeseen expenses.[34] The construction contract called for installment payments based on work completed, and the bank told the Wernharts that it would make payouts directly to the general contractor, rather than using a title company, despite the fact that the loan documents included no provision for the bank to inspect the project to determine the progress of construction.[35] Once construction was underway, the bank disbursed the Wernharts' loan funds whenever the general contractor presented an invoice and depleted the Wernharts' entire loan, plus all of their personal funds, within three months. When the Wernharts learned of the last payment, they instructed the bank not to make additional payments without permission, and expressed their concern that the general contractor had not made sufficient progress to justify the amount of money he had received. The general contractor filed for bankruptcy and the Wernharts recovered only $3,500 of the $125,000 they paid. Shortly thereafter, the bank initiated foreclosure proceedings against the Wernharts and the Wernharts counterclaimed for negligent distribution of loan proceeds. The trial court held that the bank owed a duty to the Wernharts to inspect prior to payout and that it breached that duty. The appellate court affirmed, finding that, under principals of agency law, "when a mortgagee undertakes to disburse loan funds for a mortgagor under a construction contract, a fiduciary relationship between the parties arises." Specifically, the court held that "a mortgage lender who consents to disburse the loan proceeds and personal funds of the borrower, without further participation by the borrower, is an

---

33. Powell v. H.E.F. P'ship, 793 F. Supp. 91, 94–95 (D. Vt. 1992). The Powell court also found that a lender's duty to disclose in this situation was not necessarily tied to its role as escrow agent:

> Indeed, even outside its role as escrow, as a lender and participant in the sales of units [the bank] may have had a duty to disclose to the plaintiffs information that it obtained without substantial investment, much as a seller is required to "disclose that the house he is trying to sell is infested with termites."

Id. at 95 (quoting Federal Deposit Ins. Corp. v. W.R. Grace & Co., 877 F.2d 614, 619 (7th Cir. 1989)).

34. First Nat'l Bank v. Wernhart, 555 N.W.2d 819, 820 (Wis. Ct. App. 1996).

35. *Id.*

agent of the borrower and therefore owes a duty of due care to assure the funds are paid for work actually done."[36]

C. Lender Exerts Control over Borrower

If a lender actively participates in or exercises control over the business of a borrower, a fiduciary relationship can arise.[37] Creditor control involves more than just the normal leverage a creditor has with a debtor, however; it requires actual dominance and control over the debtor's decision-making process.[38] As with all aspects of the lender's fiduciary duties, the question of control is fact-intensive and "necessarily depends on the cumulative impact of the facts and circumstances of the particular case."[39] Generally, however, control does not arise unless the debtor can show that the creditor had the power to direct the debtor's day-to-day management.[40]

A lender has the power to impact a borrower's daily affairs when it places bank officers on the board of directors, hires or fires employees, or otherwise weighs in on the granular details of day-to-day business operations.[41] A creditor does not assume "control" sufficient to justify imposing a fiduciary duty simply by relying on its contractually guaranteed position of leverage to procure a more favorable outcome for itself.

---

36. *Id.*; *see also* M & I Bank of S. Wisconsin v. Poehling, 690 N.W.2d 885 (Wis. App. 2005).

37. FAMM Steel, Inc. v. Sovereign Bank, 571 F.3d 93, 103 (1st Cir. 2009); *see also* Cappello, *supra* note 2, at 292–93.

38. Blanchard, *supra* note 2, §§ 9:7, 9:8.

39. *Id.* at § 5:8 (quotations omitted).

40. FAMM Steel, Inc. v. Sovereign Bank, 571 F.3d 93, 103 (1st Cir. 2009). This question frequently arises in the context of bankruptcy, wherein the court considers whether to equitably subordinate certain creditors based on an "alter ego" or "instrumentality" theory. *See, e.g.*, *In re* Aluminum Mills Corp., 132 B.R. 869 (Bankr. N.D. Ill. 1991) ("The fundamental aim of equitable subordination is to undo or offset any inequity in the claim position of a creditor that will produce injustice or unfairness to the creditor in terms of Bankruptcy results.") (quotations omitted). However, equitable subordination and its related doctrines are beyond the scope of this chapter. For more information, *see* Blanchard, *supra* note 2, §§ 5:4, 9.

41. *In re* T. E. Mercer Trucking Co., 16 B.R. 176 (Bankr. N.D. Tex. 1981) (holding that a creditor from a nonfinancial institution was in control when loan agreement provided creditor with right to place its designee on the board of directors and required that all corporate bylaws, stock books, and certificates be delivered to the creditor's counsel); *In re* Am. Lumber Co., 5 B.R. 470 (D. Minn. 1980) (holding that "the bank's control over ALC operations and its inequitable exercise of that control [was] overwhelming" based, in part, on the bank's "forc[ing] the termination of all employees allowing only those necessary for liquidation to be rehired," and "cut[ting] the corporate officers' salaries to one-sixth of their original amount").

As a general matter, there is no prohibition against a creditor using his superior bargaining position to improve the status of his existing claim, including calling the loan, foreclosing on collateral, or refusing to make further advances.[42] Thus, "[a] creditor is under no fiduciary obligation to its debtor or to other creditors of the debtor in the collection of its claim."[43] Furthermore, a lender may offer advice and use the leverage of its position without being deemed to have "control" over the debtor that would impose a fiduciary duty, so long as the debtor continues to operate and make its own business decisions.[44]

In *In re W.T. Grant Co.*, the junior creditors in a bankruptcy case argued that

> [t]he bank claimants used their position of control over [the debtor's] management to prevent [the debtor] from promptly seeking relief under the Bankruptcy Act, feeding it just enough money to keep its head above water while strengthening their security position, allowing the passage of the four months period for avoiding preferences . . . and hoping to allow the passage of the one year provision of . . . for the avoidance of liens and fraudulent transfers.[45]

The bankruptcy judge rejected these creditors' argument that the bank exercised such control and dominion over the debtor as to give rise to a special relationship of trust or confidence to the debtor and other creditors leading up to the bankruptcy. Specifically, it found,

---

42. *In re* Fordham, 130 B.R. 632, 648–49, 15 U.C.C. Rep. Serv. 2d 400 (Bankr. D. Mass. 1991) (lender was not joint venture with, or in control of, developer merely because lender was entitled to partial release fee of $1,500 as each condominium unit sold, and was released from lender's construction mortgage); *In re* Sleepy Valley, Inc., 93 B.R. 925, 933 (Bankr. W.D. Tex. 1988) ("Although Leisure Valley achieved a leveraged bargaining position by placing a lien on the real property subject to the contracts for deeds, the defendant in no way attained the heightened degree of control which is necessary to be considered an alter ego."); *In re* W.T. Grant Co., 699 F.2d 599 (2d Cir. 1983).

43. *In re* W. T. Grant Co., 699 F.2d 599, 609 (2d Cir. 1983); *see also In re* E. End Dev., LLC, No. 8-12-76181-REG, 2017 WL 1277443, at *3 (Bankr. E.D.N.Y. Apr. 4, 2017) (citing *W. T. Grant* and considering whether plaintiff adequately alleged breach of fiduciary duty based on lender's control).

44. Blanchard, *supra* note 2, § 5:7 (citing *In re W. T. Grant*, 699 F.2d 599 (2d Cir. 1983)); Ed Shory & Sons, Inc. v. Soc. Nat'l Bank, 662 N.E.2d 1074, 1082 (Ohio 1996) ("[A]dvice given by a creditor to a debtor in a commercial context in which the parties deal at arm's length, each protecting his or her respective interests, insufficient to create a fiduciary relationship.").

45. *In re* W. T. Grant, 699 F.2d 599, 605 (2d Cir. 1983).

> The permissible parameters of a creditor's efforts to seek collection from a debtor are generally those with respect to voidable preferences and fraudulent conveyances proscribed by the Bankruptcy Act; apart from these there is generally no objection to a creditor's using his bargaining position, including his ability to refuse to make further loans needed by the debtor, to improve the status of his existing claims.[46]

Because the bank claimants had acted within the "permissible parameters" of their role as a creditor in an arm's-length transaction, the court held that there was no special relationship creating a fiduciary duty and refused to equitably subordinate the bank's claims.[47]

In contrast, in *Johnson v. First Nat'l Bank of Shreveport*, the borrower alleged that the bank breached its fiduciary duties by engaging in self-dealing transactions and exercising inappropriate managerial control over the borrower's cattle operations.[48] In that case, the bank's vice president was also its agricultural loan officer.[49] On advice from the bank's vice president, the borrower changed his cattle operation from cow/calf to rye grass, mortgaged his land within one week of acquiring it by inheritance, and sold valuable mineral interests.[50] The bank's vice president represented that he was an excellent cattleman and cattle broker, that his demands regarding management of debtor's cattle operations were the institution's demands rather than his personal preferences, and that the bank would not finance cow/calf operations but would finance rye grass operations.[51] Additionally, the vice president comingled his personal cattle with the borrower's cattle and forced the borrower to engage in unprofitable hedging transactions, from which the bank collected interests and fees.[52] The court found that the bank's vice president purposefully created relationships of trust in order to control customers' businesses, thereby causing them to become deeply indebted to the bank; and "[o]nce heavily indebted, his customers did not have the option of changing banks."[53] As indicia of control with this borrower, the court noted that the vice president made decisions about when to

46. *Id.* at 610.

47. *Id.*

48. Johnson v. First Nat'l Bank of Shreveport, 792 So. 2d 33, 44 (La. App. Ct. 3 Cir. 6/20/01), *writ denied*, 805 So. 2d 212 (La. 01/04/02).

49. *Id.* at 43.

50. *Id.* at 45–46.

51. *Id.* at 49.

52. *Id.*

53. *Id.* at 41.

buy and sell cattle, as well as managerial decisions about feedlots and hedging.[54] Finally, the court found it was more likely than not that the failure of the cattle farm business was related to the bank vice president's imprudent actions, rather than prevailing poor market conditions.[55] Accordingly, the court concluded that the bank owed a fiduciary duty to the borrower based on the amount of control it exercised over him, and that it was vicariously liable for the vice president's breach of those duties.

In *Credit Managers Assn. v. Superior Court*,[56] the court found that the plaintiff adequately alleged a breach of fiduciary duty based on the outsized control the bank's consultant exercised over the corporation's operations, which caused the corporation to become insolvent. Specifically, the complaint alleged that the bank, through its consultant, took over the management of the business when it instituted strict and oppressive credit policies, sales procedures, and inventory policies toward the distributors of the products of said corporation "*without heed or regard to the wishes or votes of the directors or shareholders of said corporation* and acting in complete disregard of the officers of the corporation."[57] The court held that the plaintiff adequately alleged a fiduciary duty because "the complaint, in effect, alleges that [the consultant] was placed in such complete management control of the corporation that it was able to, and did, overrule and supplant the board of directors and the shareholders."[58]

D. Lender Acts on Its Powers of Foreclosure

As a general rule, there is no fiduciary relationship between a mortgagor and mortgagee.[59] Once a loan is in default and the mortgagee assumes the role of a seller of mortgaged property, the mortgagee may owe a fiduciary duty to the mortgagor, and possibly the guarantors, to obtain

54. *Id.* at 47.

55. *Id.* at 45.

56. Credit Managers Ass'n v. Superior Court, 51 Cal. App. 3d 352, 124 Cal. Rptr. 242 (Ct. App. 1975).

57. *Id.* at 359 (emphasis original) (quotations omitted).

58. *Id.*

59. LaBauve v. JP Morgan Chase Bank, N.A., 2018 WL 1125660 (M.D. La. 2018) (noting that existence of a mortgage is insufficient in and of itself to create the special relationship needed to establish a fiduciary relationship); Marketic v. U.S. Bank Nat'l Ass'n, 436 F. Supp. 2d 842 (N.D. Tex. 2006) (finding no fiduciary duty between mortgagor and mortgagee); *see also* BLANCHARD, *supra* note 2, § 5:3.

a commercially reasonable foreclosure sale price.[60] In the context of a loan modification agreement, the potential for a fiduciary duty arises only out of the lender's role as an "active advis[or]"[61] when its actions move "beyond its conventional role as a loan servicer"[62] and induce the borrower to take actions that it otherwise would not have taken.

In *First NH Mortgage Corp. v. Greene*, the bank foreclosed on a promissory note for $691,000, which was secured by a mortgage on a 267-acre tract of land and the joint and several guaranty of each of the defendants.[63] At the auction, the lender was the only attendee and he purchased the property for $500,000, despite having an appraisal that estimated the property's market value to be approximately $935,000.[64] When the lender sought deficiency judgments, the guarantors raised the affirmative defense that the foreclosure sale was commercially unreasonable. The trial court agreed, finding that the lender failed to properly market the property, failed to adjourn the foreclosure, failed to set an upset price, and accepted a sale price that was "clearly inadequate."[65] Finding that the lender had assumed a fiduciary duty of good faith and

---

60. *See, e.g.*, Royal Park Investments SA/NV v. HSBC Bank USA, Nat'l Ass'n, 2015 WL 3466121, at *12 (S.D.N.Y. 2015) (noting that, upon the occurrence of an event of default, an indenture trustee takes on a special fiduciary duty to exercise its power in order to secure the trust); Pearson v. United States, 831 F. Supp. 2d 514, 519–20 (D. Mass. 2011) (deciding that, although a lender generally does not owe a fiduciary duty to a borrower, "one such instance in which a fiduciary duty arises between a lender and a borrower is in the context of a foreclosure sale . . . to refrain from committing fraud, bad faith or failing to use reasonable diligence in the sales process"); Solfanelli v. Corestates Bank, N.A., 203 F.3d 197, 200, 35 Bankr. Ct. Dec. (CRR) 163, 40 U.C.C. Rep. Serv. 2d 914 (3d Cir. 2000) (applying Pennsylvania law and finding that "the creditor acts as the debtor's fiduciary and has a corresponding good faith duty to maximize the proceeds of the collateral's sale"); First NH Mortgage Corp. v. Greene, 653 A.2d 1076 (N.H. 1995) ("In his role as a seller, the mortgagee's duty of good faith and due diligence is essentially that of a fiduciary. . . . This fiduciary duty is owed not only to mortgagors, but also to guarantors.") (quotations omitted); *but see* Oceanic Inn, Inc. v. Sloan's Cove, LLC, 133 A.3d 1021, 1028 (Me. 2016) (rejecting the majority rule and holding that "[i]n the absence of specific facts sufficient to support the elements of a fiduciary relationship, a mortgagee foreclosing by power of sale does not owe a fiduciary duty to the mortgagor"); *but see* Bellard v. JP Morgan Chase Bank, N.A., No. CIV.A. G-10-124, 2010 WL 1960079, at *2 (S.D. Tex. May 14, 2010) (noting that "the long-standing principal that there is no fiduciary duty between a lender and a borrower has been applied in the context of foreclosure").

61. Morrow v. Bank of America, N.A., 324 P.3d 1167, 1178 (Mont. 2014).

62. Crilley v. Bank of America, N.A., 2012 WL 1492413, at *10 (D. Haw. 2012) ("Defendant went beyond its conventional role as a loan servicer by soliciting Plaintiffs to apply for a loan modification and by engaging with them for several months.").

63. First NH Mortg. Corp. v. Greene, 653 A.2d 1076 (N.H. 1995).

64. *Id.* at 1077.

65. *Id.* at 1079.

due diligence in its role as a seller of the mortgaged property, the court held that the lender violated its fiduciary duty to the mortgagor and the guarantors. The court further held that the guaranty agreement's exculpatory clause—purporting to waive the defense of commercial unreasonableness—was unenforceable because the breach of fiduciary duty at issue was the result of affirmative negligence, namely, misrepresenting the property's location and discouraging other buyers from attending the foreclosure sale.[66]

In *Morrow v. Bank of America, N.A.*, the mortgagors claimed that the loan servicer advised them to deliberately miss a payment and default on their loan so that they could qualify for a loan modification.[67] The loan servicer's pattern of active advising in this regard continued for over a year with regular and frequent contact between the parties in which the servicer continually instructed the borrowers to pay a reduced amount each month and ignore notices of default.[68] The court found that the borrowers had stood at arm's length to the lender in the original loan negotiations, but once the loan was in default, "they had little choice but to continue placing their trust in the bank" and it would be "unrealistic to say [the bank] and [the borrowers] continued to hold equal footing throughout the negotiations."[69] Because "instructing a borrower not to repay a loan, to pay less than the amount required by the loan documents, or to ignore notices of impending foreclosure and avoid curing a default is not the type of advice common in the usual arms-length debtor/creditor relationship," the court held that the bank "owed a duty to manage the modification process in a manner that would not cause the [borrowers] to suffer loss or injury by reason of its negligence."[70] The court was clear, however, that the bank did not have any duty to avoid foreclosure or grant a loan modification; rather, it merely owed a fiduciary duty in the processing of the application for loan modification.[71]

In *Bank of Am., N.A. v. Narula*, the borrower entered into a loan modification agreement extending the deadline for repayment of a construction loan; the borrowers obtained the loan on the belief that it would eventually ripen into a permanent loan.[72] The bank allowed the borrowers to sign the Second Modification and Extension Agreement

66. *Id.* at 1078.
67. Morrow v. Bank of America, N.A., 324 P.3d 1167, 1178 (Mont. 2014).
68. *Id.* at 1178.
69. *Id.*
70. *Id.*
71. *Id.* at 1178–79.
72. Bank of Am., N.A. v. Narula, 261 P.3d 898 (Kan. App. 2011).

despite knowing that the borrowers were entering into the loan modification under a mistake about an early termination fee on a previously signed swap interest rate agreement. The bank sued when the borrowers were unable to repay the loan and the borrowers counterclaimed for breach of fiduciary duty and fraud. The court found that the bank owed a fiduciary duty to the borrowers in the loan modification process because the bank described itself as borrowers' "trusted financial adviser," cultivated that trust in a wide range of financial dealings, was integrally involved in borrowers' estate planning, and encouraged and invited the borrowers to place their trust and confidence in that bank's agents to guide them through an unfamiliar loan process.[73]

E. Lender Induces, Aids, or Abets Breach of Fiduciary Duty

If a lender induces, aids, abets, or otherwise participates in a breach of fiduciary duty to a third party, it may be held liable for the damages caused by that breach.[74] To establish a claim for inducing a breach of fiduciary duty, the borrower or claimant must prove "(1) a breach by a fiduciary of obligations to another, (2) that the defendant knowingly induced or participated in the breach, and (3) that the plaintiff suffered damages as a result of the breach."[75] Courts have held that the lender must have actual knowledge that it is facilitating a transaction in which its customer is breaching a fiduciary duty; the fact that the bank *should* have known of the illegal activity is not generally sufficient.[76] Thus,

73. *Id.* at 918.

74. *See* BCE Emergis Corp. v. Cmty. Health Sols. of Am., Inc., 148 F. App'x 204, 213 (5th Cir. 2005) ("Kentucky law holds aiders and abetters of fiduciary violators of their corporate duties jointly and severally liable for any profits that accrue from such a breach."); Garot Anderson Agencies, Inc. v. Blue Cross & Blue Shield United of Wisconsin, No. 88 C 20265, 1993 WL 78756, at *23 (N.D. Ill. Feb. 26, 1993) ("[O]ne who knowingly joins with or aids a fiduciary in an enterprise constituting a breach of the fiduciary relationship becomes jointly and severally liable with the fiduciary."); Steelvest, Inc. v. Scansteel Service Center, Inc., 807 S.W.2d 476 (Ky. 1991) (holding that a bank that knowingly joins with or aids and abets fiduciary in enterprise constituting breach of fiduciary relationship becomes jointly and severally liable with fiduciary for any profits that may accrue); Whitney v. Citibank, N.A., 782 F.2d 1106, 1115 (2d Cir. 1986) ("[O]ne who knowingly participates with a fiduciary in a breach of trust is liable to the beneficiary for any damage caused thereby.") (quotations omitted).

75. Whitney v. Citibank, N.A., 782 F.2d 1106, 1115 (2d Cir. 1986).

76. *See, e.g.*, Baron v. Galasso, 921 N.Y.S.2d 100, 104 (2d Dep't 2011) (rejecting the borrower's argument that bank "knew or should have known" of attorney's alleged breach of fiduciary duty and finding that the bank had no duty to monitor the account because there was no evidence that bank had actual knowledge of the allegedly improper diversions from the escrow account.); Gibson v. Ameris Bank, 420 S.C. 536, 546, 804 S.E.2d 276, 281

"[i]f an illegal scheme exists and a bank's loan assists in that scheme, the bank's knowledge of the scheme is the crucial element that prevents it from suffering automatic liability for the conduct of insiders to whom it loaned the money."[77]

The standard of proof for a claim of aiding and abetting a breach of fiduciary duty is somewhat more onerous, in that it requires actual knowledge plus "substantial assistance":

> For harm resulting to a third person from the tortious conduct of another, a person is liable if he
> (a) orders or induces such conduct, knowing of the conditions under which the act is done or intending the consequences which ensue, or
> (b) knows that the other's conduct constitutes a breach of duty and gives substantial assistance or encouragement to the other so to conduct himself, or
> (c) gives substantial assistance to the other in accomplishing a tortious result and his own conduct, separately considered, constitutes a breach of duty to the third person.[78]

The "substantial assistance" threshold requires an analysis of the lender's scienter, the nature of the act, and how much assistance it actually provided.[79] Mere inaction usually does not satisfy the "substantial assistance" threshold[80] because, as a general matter, lenders owe no affirmative duty to protect their borrowers from a breach of fiduciary duty by

(Ct. App. 2017) ("Because the evidence does not show that Ameris had actual knowledge of Villavicencio's breach of fiduciary duty while Villavicencio was committing his breach, we hold the master erred in finding Ameris knowingly participated in Villavicencio's breach.").

77. K & S P'ship v. Cont'l Bank, N.A., 952 F.2d 971, 977 (8th Cir. 1991) (citing Woodward v. Metro Bank of Dallas, 522 F.2d 84, 96 (5th Cir. 1975)).

78. Restatement (First) Torts § 876 (1939).

79. *Id.* (in determining whether the defendant offered substantial assistance, "the nature of the act encouraged, the amount of assistance given by the defendant, his presence or absence at the time of the tort, his relation to the other and his state of mind are all considered"); *see In re* Sharp Int'l Corp., 281 B.R. 506 (Bankr. E.D.N.Y. 2002), *aff'd*, 302 B.R. 760 (E.D.N.Y. 2003), *aff'd*, 403 F.3d 43 (2d Cir. 2005) (holding that mere inaction—such as by "dodging" phone calls—does not satisfy the "substantial assistance" threshold because "inaction can create aider and abettor liability only where there is a conscious or reckless violation of an independent duty to act").

80. Lerner v. Fleet Bank, N.A., 459 F.3d 273, 295 (2d Cir. 2006) ("[M]ere inaction of an alleged aider and abettor constitutes substantial assistance only if the defendant owes a fiduciary duty directly to the plaintiff.").

their agents, management, or other persons.[81] However, inaction in the context of egregious facts, or inaction that creates a patently inequitable result, might rise to the level of substantial assistance.[82] Additionally, it is worth noting that not all states recognize a cause of action for inducing, aiding, or abetting a breach of fiduciary duty.[83]

In *Aetna Cas. & Sur. Co. v. Leahey Constr. Co.*, a construction company's principal obtained a $275,000 loan from the bank and informed the bank that he required the loan as a condition to secure certain surety bonds for his construction projects.[84] The principal explained to the loan officer that he had to show the surety company he had the loan proceeds in his account at the end of the month and that he intended to repay the loan two days after that; thus the entire loan term was only four days long.[85] The court held that the loan officer knew enough about the bonding business to realize that adding significant funds to a construction company's bank account for a four-day period would not serve to meet the surety's capitalization requirements and, therefore, providing the loan constituted "substantial assistance" in aiding and abetting the construction company's fraudulent activities.[86]

In *Whitney v. Citibank, N.A*, a partnership financed the purchase of some land with a loan from the bank.[87] When the partnership defaulted, the bank began foreclosure proceedings and requested a deed in lieu of foreclosure.[88] During these negotiations, the bank gave one of the partners false information about the status of the deed in lieu of foreclosure, and backdated documents to support the false information; the other

81. *In re* Sharp Int'l Corp., 281 B.R. 506 (Bankr. E.D.N.Y. 2002), *aff'd*, 302 B.R. 760 (E.D.N.Y. 2003), *aff'd*, 403 F.3d 43 (2d Cir. 2005) (holding that bank had no duty to protect borrower from breach of fiduciary duty by its management); *but see* Liu Yao-Yi v. Wilmington Trust Co., 301 F. Supp. 3d 403, 427 (W.D.N.Y. 2017) (applying Delaware law and holding that inaction may form the basis of aiding and abetting liability if it rises to the level of providing substantial assistance or encouragement).

82. 301 F. Supp. 3d 403, 427.

83. Cohen v. Dulay, 94 N.E.3d 1167, 1176 (Ohio Ct. App. 2017) (claim of aiding, abetting, inducing, or participating in breaches of fiduciary duties is not cognizable under state law).

84. Aetna Cas. & Sur. Co. v. Leahey Constr. Co., 219 F.3d 519 (6th Cir. 2000).

85. *Id.*

86. *Id.* at 537 ("By securing the $275,000 loan, [the principal] was able to 'verify' to [the surety company] that he had complied with its first funding request, thereby establishing a vital and initial level of credibility. Because this credibility served as the foundation for increased trust between the parties, we conclude that the extension of the loan was of substantial assistance to [the principal].")

87. Whitney v. Citibank, N.A., 782 F.2d 1106, 1108 (2d Cir. 1986).

88. *Id.* at 1108–09.

two partners were fully informed about the actual status of the negations. The partner sued, alleging that the bank induced the other partners to breach their fiduciary duties to him.[89] The trial court awarded actual and punitive damages, finding that the bank had knowingly induced and participated in a breach of fiduciary duty. The Second Circuit affirmed, noting that the bank and other partners engaged in a "conspiracy of silence and misinformation," that the bank "was fully aware that the transaction violated [the partner's] rights," and that it "deliberately kept [the partner] unaware of material facts."[90]

In *Liu Yao-Yi v. Wilmington Trust Co.*, the court found a bank was liable for aiding and abetting a breach of fiduciary duty when it was aware that its investors' funds were being "chronically sapped from fiduciary accounts and placed into other accounts for purposes," which the bank knew were not what the investors intended, and when it failed to take any action to prevent the diversion.[91] The court observed that, in some circumstances, "'inaction' and 'action' may be substantive equivalents, different only in form."[92] Accordingly, the court held that, under Delaware law, the bank's "failure to act upon this duty represents inaction that rises to the level of 'substantial assistance' in the primary violator's fiduciary breach to the beneficiaries of the fiduciary accounts."[93]

F. Other Special Circumstances Giving Rise to a Lender's Fiduciary Duty

The other fact patterns where courts have held lenders to a fiduciary standard combine various elements from the preceding categories. Usually, these cases involve a less sophisticated borrower who reposed a unique level of trust and confidence in the lender, and a lender who took advantage of that trusting relationship to obtain some benefit at the borrower's expense.[94]

---

89. *Id.* at 1115.

90. *Id.* at 1117.

91. Liu Yao-Yi v. Wilmington Trust Co., 301 F. Supp. 3d 403, 427 (W.D.N.Y. 2017).

92. *Id.* (quoting Hubbard v. Hollywood Park Realty Enters., Inc., No. CIV. A. 11779, 1991 WL 3151, at *10 (Del. Ch. Jan. 14, 1991)).

93. *Id.*

94. Anderson v. ReconTrust Co., N.A., 407 P.3d 692, 697 (Mont. 2017) ("an otherwise arms-length relationship between a lender and borrower or applicant may ripen into a fiduciary relationship of trust and confidence, with attendant fiduciary duties, if the lender gives advice beyond that customary in arms-length lending and loan servicing transactions.") (quotations omitted); Ikeri v. Sallie Mae, Inc., No. CV 13-1943 (DSD/JSM), 2014 WL 12599634, at *16 (D. Minn. Feb. 5, 2014) ("[A]bsent facts to establish that lenders know that a customer is placing trust in them, there is a confidential relationship,

In *Smith v. Saginaw Savings and Loan Association*, an elderly couple took out a $25,000 construction loan to build a retirement home, and deposited an additional $1,500 of their own funds into the bank's loan account, from which mortgage draws could be made in order to periodically pay the builder.[95] The bank's branch manager personally approved the builder and the construction contract, charged a $250 fee that was intended to cover the bank's expenses in sending an employee to inspect the progress of the construction prior to the release of any payments, and assured the borrowers that no payments would be made without proof of adequate progress in the project.[96] The bank knew that the borrowers lived 250 miles away from the construction site and were in poor health, and that, as a result of these circumstances, they placed their trust in the branch manager's judgment regarding the builder, the construction contract, and the quality of the progress of the construction.[97] Unbeknownst to the borrowers, the builder was also constructing a house for the branch manager and, when the builder encountered serious financial difficulties, the branch manager took steps to protect his own interests, without in any way doing the same for the plaintiffs.[98] The court also found that the branch manager permitted the builder to fall behind in construction and allowed the release of funds for work not fully completed. Accordingly, the court held that "[t]hese facts plainly established the existence of a fiduciary obligation and the breach thereof."[99]

In *Deist v. Wachholz*, a bank's vice president had a long-standing relationship with a rancher, both as his banker and his family friend.[100] When the rancher passed away, the vice president contacted the rancher's widow and informed her that she needed to take some action on her $200,000 mortgage on the ranch, and advised her to completely liquidate the ranch.[101] Having virtually no real estate experience and relying on the long-standing relationship with the lender, the widow agreed and asked him to help her find a buyer. The vice president introduced her to a real estate investor, whom he represented as a reputable buyer, and

---

or the lender invites a borrower to place his confidence in the lender, the general rule is that lenders owe no fiduciary duty to borrowers."); *see also* CAPPELLO, *supra* note 2, at 293–94.

95. Smith v. Saginaw Savings & Loan Ass'n, 288 N.W.2d 613, 618 (Mich. App. Ct. 1979).

96. *Id.*

97. *Id.*

98. *Id.*

99. *Id.*

100. Deist v. Wachholz, 678 P.2d 188 (Mont. 1984).

101. *Id.*

informed her that a contract with him would be a "good deal."[102] The day she signed the contract for the sale, however, she learned that the vice president was, in fact, partners with the buyer in the transaction for her ranch, as well as in other transactions. She sued to rescind the contract, alleging breach of fiduciary duty and constructive fraud based on the contention that the sale price, interest rate, and annual payments were all lower than market value and, therefore, the vice president had negotiated terms more favorable to the purchasers—including himself—than to the widow as seller. The trial court found for the widow, and the Montana Supreme Court affirmed, finding that the vice president "had an obligation to inform [the widow] fully as to his involvement in the ranch purchase and to do nothing which would place [her] at a disadvantage."[103] The court observed that the vice president would not have breached any duty had he only made "a reasonable legitimate profit from his dealing . . . so long as he disclosed fairly and honestly all the information which might be presumed to have influenced her in the transaction."[104] Accordingly, the totality of circumstances, including the vice president's conspicuous silence about facts material to the transaction, militated in favor of finding a fiduciary relationship.

In *Boatmen's Nat'l Bank of Hillsboro v. Ward*, a relatively unsophisticated farmer encountered serious financial difficulties and sought advice and guidance from his bank.[105] He had used the same bank for decades, his father had previously served on the board of directors, and had been friendly with the bankers on a personal level for years. When the bank recommended he take out additional loans, he signed the loan documents without reading them, as was his custom. When the bank ultimately cut off his credit, the farmer became desperate and suicidal. He considered bankruptcy but did not understand how to file or who to consult, and the bank neither recommended bankruptcy nor suggested that the farmer should seek independent professional advice.[106] Eventually, the bank executed an elaborate workout agreement under which the farmer mortgaged all of his property in favor of the bank and assumed an additional debt, which he was unable to service.[107] When the bank sued to foreclose, the farmer argued that the bank should be estopped by its misconduct from collecting the debt owed based,

102. *Id.* at 196.
103. *Id.* at 195.
104. *Id.*
105. Boatmen's Nat'l Bank of Hillsboro v. Ward, 595 N.E.2d 622 (Ill. App. Ct. 1992).
106. *Id.* at 626.
107. *Id.*

essentially, on a breach of fiduciary duty.[108] At trial, experts agreed that the workout agreement was not compatible with the farmer's business and was destined to fail, that an independent adviser would have told the farmer to file for bankruptcy, and that filing for bankruptcy would have saved the farmer half a million dollars.[109] Based on these facts, the jury found that a fiduciary relationship existed and that the bank breached that duty. On appeal, the court found ample evidence indicating that the farmer was older, with declining mental health, had long-standing personal ties to the bank and many of its key employees, increasingly relied on the bank to manage his financial affairs, and was willing to accept whatever requirements the bank imposed so long as he was able to continue his farming operations.[110] Finding that "[t]he only real beneficiary under the plan was the Bank," the appellate court sustained the verdict and damages awards.[111]

In contrast, in *Dugan v. First National Bank in Wichita*, the court held there was no fiduciary relationship between the bank and the elderly widow-lessor, despite the long-standing relationship between the two, because there was no evidence that the bank offered financial advice, made false representations, induced the borrower to enter into subordination agreements, or failed to disclose material information.[112] In short, the only indicia of a special relationship of trust was the length of the borrower's relationship with the bank and his advanced age, but since borrowers cannot establish a fiduciary relationship unilaterally, these indicia were insufficient to prove that any fiduciary duties existed.[113]

---

108. *Id.* at 623.

109. *Id.* at 627 ("Although the Bank did permit Ward to continue his farming operations for several more years, his farming operations were basically doomed at the time the new plan was implemented. The only real beneficiary under the plan was the Bank.").

110. *Id.* at 626.

111. *Id.*

112. Dugan v. First Nat'l Bank in Wichita, 227 Kan. 201, 606 P.2d 1009 (1980).

113. Robley v. Blue Cross/Blue Shield of Mississippi, 935 So. 2d 990, 995 (Miss. 2006) ("Although one does not typically enter into a contract with another person unless he or she has a degree of trust or confidence in that person, without more, such a transaction amounts to merely a business relationship and not a fiduciary relationship."); *In re* Greenberg, 212 B.R. 422, 428–29 (Bankr. D. Mass. 1997), *aff'd*, 229 B.R. 544 (B.A.P. 1st Cir. 1999) ("Massachusetts law is clear that one party cannot unilaterally transform a business relationship into a fiduciary relationship."); *see also* Blanchard, *supra* note 2 ("A fiduciary duty cannot be imposed unilaterally. The trust and confidence which a party rests on the other party must be accompanied by some type of action on the second party showing that the relationship is recognized.").

III. Conclusion

As a general matter, there is a presumption that lender-borrower relationships are arm's-length transactions in which no fiduciary duty arises. However, when a lender undertakes some action, above and beyond that which is typical in a creditor-debtor relationship, it may create a fiduciary relationship. This may happen when, for example, the lender acts as financial adviser, the lender acts as borrower's agent; the lender exerts control over borrower; the lender acts on its powers of foreclosure; the lender induces, aids, or abets a breach of fiduciary duty; or where other special circumstances give rise to a fiduciary relationship. Alternatively, the contract between the parties may create a fiduciary relationship between the parties, or may waive any fiduciary duties that would otherwise arise. Although a borrower cannot unilaterally create a fiduciary relationship simply by relying on a lender's advice, a lender may find itself subject to fiduciary duties where the borrower is particularly unsophisticated, reposes a unique and heightened level of trust in the lender, the lender knows of this reliance and trust, and the lender thereafter uses that trust to obtain some sort of advantage for itself.

Chapter 12

Litigating Breach of Fiduciary Duties in the Zone of Insolvency

By Aaron Krauss

Dave Director wakes up in the middle of the night in a cold sweat. Although he wishes it were just a dream, he knows it isn't. The Acme Widget Company, on whose board he sits, has entered the dreaded Zone of Insolvency. Perhaps not as bad as entering the Twilight Zone,[1] but with almost as many plot twists. And with all of the horror, at least for those on the Acme Widget Company's board. Because, thanks to Chancellor Allen,[2] now that the Acme Widget Company has entered into the zone of insolvency, everyone can sue Dave.

I. What Is All the Fuss About?

Do you remember all that stuff you read in Chapters 2 through 4 about how a board of directors owes its fiduciary duty to the stockholders? In *Credit Lyonnais Bank Nederland, N.V. v. Pathe Communications Corp.*, Chancellor Allen said

> At least where a corporation is operating in the vicinity of insolvency, a board of directors is not merely the agent of the

1. Apologies to Rod Sterling and everyone at CBS who worked on the *Twilight Zone*.

2. *See* Credit Lyonnais Bank Nederland, N.V. v. Pathe Commc'ns Corp., 1991 WL 277613 at *34 and n.55 (Del. Ch. Dec. 30, 1991).

> residue risk bearers [i.e. the stockholders], but owes its duty to the corporate enterprise.[3]

Many judges (and lawyers) interpreted Chancellor Allen's statement as meaning that, if a company[4] is operating "in the zone of insolvency," the company's board owes a duty to the company's creditors, in addition to its stockholders.[5] Owing a duty to creditors seemingly puts the company's directors in a "catch-22"[6] because

> especially when a corporation is in financial distress, the interests of the shareholders and the corporation itself may inherently collide with those of the creditors, making any respective duties owed by directors to each constituency potentially in conflict and making the scope of each respective duty elusive and difficult to ascertain.[7]

As Chancellor Allen put it

> The possibility of insolvency can do curious things to incentives, exposing creditors to risks of opportunistic behavior and creating complexities for directors. Consider, for example, a solvent corporation having a single asset, a judgment for $51 million against

---

3. *See* Credit Lyonnais, 1991 WL 277613, at *34. *See also* Berg & Berg Enterprises, LLC v. Boyle, 178 Cal. App. 4th 1020, 1038 (2010) (labeling Credit Lyonnais as the "genesis" of "the modern common law notion that the individual directors of a financially distressed corporation operating in the zone of insolvency or even upon insolvency owe a duty of care to its creditors").

4. Generally speaking, the duties owed by a corporation's officers and directors and a limited partner's general partner and managers are the same. Limited partnerships can, however, eliminate fiduciary duties by using the right language in their partnership agreements. *See, e.g.*, Bandera Master Fund LP v. Boardwalk Pipeline Partners, LP, 2019 WL 4927053, at *7 (Del. Ch. Oct. 7, 2019). If a limited partnership choses to eliminate fiduciary duties, the limited partners are protected by whatever contractual obligations the limited partnership agreement imposes on the general partner(s) and the manager(s). *See, e.g.*, *Bandera Master Fund*, 2019 WL 4927053, at *8. Although the (deleted) fiduciary duties and the (imposed) contractual duties may be substantively similar (or even identical), a creditor is not a party to the limited partnership agreement and will therefore be unable to assert contractual claims. The creditor will, however, be able to assert claims for the breach of whatever contract created the credit relationship. *See, e.g.*, *Bandera Master Fund*, 2019 WL 4927053, at *21–22); Berg & Berg Enterprises, LLC v. Boyle, 178 Cal. App. 4th 1020, 1038 (2010).

5. Other courts got to a similar place by employing the "trust fund doctrine," which holds that when a company is in the "zone of insolvency," the directors must treat the company's assets as a "trust fund" to pay creditors, and must avoid diverting, dissipating, or unduly risking those assets. *See, e.g.*, *Berg & Berg*, 178 Cal. App. 4th, at 1032.

6. Apologies to Joseph Heller.

7. *See, e.g.*, *Berg & Berg*, 178 Cal. App. 4th, at 1037–38.

a solvent debtor. The judgment is on appeal and thus subject to modification or reversal. Assume that the only liabilities of the company are to bondholders in the amount of $12 million. Assume that the array of probable outcomes of the appeal is as follows

	Expected Value of Judgment on Appeal	**Expected Value**
25% chance of affirmance	$51mm	$12.75
70% chance of modification	$4mm	$2.8
5% chance of reversal	$0	$0

Thus, the best evaluation is that the current value of the equity is $3.55 million ($15.55 million expected value of judgment on appeal – $12 million liability to bondholders). Now assume an offer to settle at $12.5 million (also consider one at $17.5 million). By what standard do the directors of the company evaluate the fairness of these offers? The creditors of this solvent company would be in favor of accepting either a $12.5 million offer or a $17.5 million offer. In either event they will avoid the 75% risk of insolvency and default. The stockholders, however, will plainly be opposed to acceptance of a $12.5 million settlement (under which they get practically nothing). More importantly, they very well may be opposed to acceptance of the $17.5 million offer under which the residual value of the corporation would increase from $3.5 to $5.5 million. This is so because the litigation alternative, with its 25% probability of a $39 million outcome to them ($51 million – $12 million = $39 million) has an expected value to the residual risk bearer of $9.75 million ($39 million × 25% chance of affirmance), substantially greater than the $5.5 million available to them in the settlement. While in fact the stockholders' preference would reflect their appetite for risk, it is possible (and with diversified shareholders likely) that shareholders would prefer rejection of both settlement offers.

But if we consider the community of interests that the corporation represents it seems apparent that one should in this hypothetical accept the best settlement offer available providing it is greater than $15.55 million, and one below that amount should be rejected. But that result will not be reached by a director who thinks he owes duties directly to shareholders only. It will be reached by directors who are capable of conceiving of the corporation as a legal and economic entity. Such directors will recognize that in managing the business affairs of

> a solvent corporation in the vicinity of insolvency, circumstances may arise when the right (both the efficient and the fair) course to follow for the corporation may diverge from the choice that the stockholders (or the creditors, or the employees, or any single group interested in the corporation) would make if given the opportunity to act.[8]

So, does Dave Director have a way out of this catch-22? Actually, he might, because some judges, especially the Delaware Supreme Court in *North American Catholic Educational Programming Foundation, Inc. v. Gheewalla*,[9] have reinterpreted (some might even say "walked back" or overruled) Chancellor Allen's holding.

Gheewalla involved a dispute over licenses to the wireless spectrum. The plaintiffs sued the directors of Clearwire (a company that had promised to pay them to acquire their licenses), claiming that Clearwire's directors had impermissibly favored Clearwire's stockholders over Clearwire's creditors such as the plaintiffs.[10] The plaintiff in *Gheewalla* was not a stockholder of Clearwire.[11] Instead, it was a putative creditor.[12] Additionally, the plaintiff alleged "direct, not derivative, fiduciary duty claims against the Defendants, who served as directors of Clearwire while it was either insolvent or in the 'zone of insolvency.'"[13] Specifically, the plaintiffs alleged that when Clearwire entered the zone of insolvency, its directors should have liquidated Clearwire's assets to benefit Clearwire's creditors, and that its directors breached their fiduciary duty to Clearwire's creditors by allowing Clearwire to remain in business (which caused Clearwire to "burn through" assets that would otherwise have been available to pay creditors).[14] After considering Chancellor Allen's comments, the Delaware Supreme Court "h[e]ld that the creditors of a Delaware corporation that is either insolvent or in the zone of insolvency have no right, as a matter of law, to assert direct

8. *See Credit Lyonnais*, 1991 WL 277613, at *34 n.55.

9. N. Am. Catholic Educ. Programming Found., Inc. v. Gheewalla, 930 A.2d 92 (Del. 2007).

10. *See id.* at 93–94. The plaintiffs claimed that, when prices of the wireless spectrum dropped following the WorldCom bankruptcy (which "dumped" huge "amounts" of the wireless spectrum on the market), Clearwire's directors—who all worked for Goldman Sachs, which was Clearwire's sole "backer"—worked with Goldman Sachs to dry up liquidity for Clearwire so that Clearwire could not (and would not have to) pay plaintiffs for their portion of the spectrum as it has promised. *Id.* at 94–96.

11. *Id.* at 93.

12. *Id.* at 93–94.

13. *Id.* at 94.

14. *Id.* at 95.

claims for breach of fiduciary duty against the corporation's directors."[15] The Delaware Supreme Court reached this conclusion[16] because

> It is well established that the directors owe their fiduciary obligations to the corporation and its shareholders. While shareholders rely on directors acting as fiduciaries to protect their interests, creditors are afforded protection through contractual agreements, fraud and fraudulent conveyance law, implied covenants of good faith and fair dealing, bankruptcy law, general commercial law and other sources of creditor rights. Delaware courts have traditionally been reluctant to expand existing fiduciary duties. Accordingly, "the general rule is that directors do not owe creditors duties beyond the relevant contractual terms."[17]

15. *Id.* at 94. *See also In Re* Tribune Co. Fraudulent Conveyance Litig., 2018 WL 6329139, at *7 (S.D.N.Y. Nov. 20, 2018).

16. "Trust fund" courts have reached similar conclusions using different reasoning. *See, e.g., Berg & Berg*, 178 Cal. App. 4th, at 1041 ("While no California cases 'expressly limit the fiduciary duty under the trust fund doctrine to the prohibition of self-dealing or the preferential treatment of creditors, the scope of the trust fund doctrine in California is reasonably limited to cases where directors or officers have diverted, dissipated, or unduly risked the insolvent corporation's assets.' In other words, the doctrine is not applied to create a duty owed by directors to creditors solely due to a state of corporate insolvency. Application of the doctrine requires, in addition, that directors have engaged in conduct that diverted, dissipated, or unduly risked corporate assets that might otherwise have been used to satisfy creditors' claims. Accordingly, based on this established doctrine, we conclude that under the current state of California law, there is no broad, paramount fiduciary duty of due care or loyalty that directors of an insolvent corporation owe the corporation's creditors solely because of a state of insolvency, whether derived from Credit Lyonnais or otherwise. And we decline to create any such duty, which would conflict with and dilute the statutory and common law duties that directors already owe to shareholders and the corporation. We also perceive practical problems with creating such a duty, among them a director's ability to objectively and concretely determine when a state of insolvency actually exists such that his or her duties to creditors have been triggered. We accordingly hold that the scope of any extra-contractual duty owed by corporate directors to the insolvent corporation's creditors is limited in California, consistently with the trust-fund doctrine, to the avoidance of actions that divert, dissipate, or unduly risk corporate assets that might otherwise be used to pay creditors claims. This would include acts that involve self-dealing or the preferential treatment of creditors. Further, because all the California cases applying the trust-fund doctrine appear to have dealt with actually insolvent entities, and because the existence of a zone or vicinity of insolvency is even less objectively determinable than actual insolvency, we hold that there is no fiduciary duty prescribed under California law that is owed to creditors by directors of a corporation solely by virtue of its operating in the 'zone' or 'vicinity' of insolvency.") (citations and footnotes omitted). *See also In re* AWTR Liquidation, Inc., 548 B.R. 300, 324–25 (Bankr. C.D. Cal. 2016).

17. *Gheewalla*, 930 A.2d at 99 (citations omitted).

In fact, the Delaware Supreme Court went further, and noted that "an otherwise solvent corporation operating in the zone of insolvency is one in most need of effective and proactive leadership—as well as the ability to negotiate in good faith with its creditors—goals which would likely be significantly undermined by the prospect of individual liability arising from the pursuit of direct claims by creditors."[18]

> In this case, the need for providing directors with definitive guidance compels us to hold that no direct claim for breach of fiduciary duties may be asserted by the creditors of a solvent corporation that is operating in the zone of insolvency. When a solvent corporation is navigating in the zone of insolvency, the focus for Delaware directors does not change: directors must continue to discharge their fiduciary duties to the corporation and its shareholders by exercising their business judgment in the best interests of the corporation for the benefit of its shareholder owners.[19]

As much as Dave Director will no doubt be pleased with this "definitive guidance" from the Delaware Supreme Court, that guidance did not come without a price. Indeed, the Delaware Supreme Court gave that guidance because it knew that directors of a corporation operating in the zone of insolvency faced the herculean task of trying to save the company.[20] The Delaware Supreme Court explicitly acknowledged that creating a new fiduciary duty owed to creditors would make that task next to impossible—even for Hercules.

> Recognizing that directors of an insolvent corporation owe direct fiduciary duties to creditors, would create uncertainty for directors who have a fiduciary duty to exercise their business judgment in the best interest of the insolvent corporation. To recognize a new right for creditors to bring direct fiduciary claims against those directors would create a conflict between those directors' duty to maximize the value of the insolvent corporation for the benefit of all those having an interest in it,

18. *Id.* at 100–01 (citations omitted).

19. *Id.* at 103 (citations omitted). *See also* Bandera Master Fund, 2019 WL 4927053, at *15 n.9.

20. As a bankruptcy court put it: "As a practical matter, the alternative to such essentially unchanging duties would be for directors' and officers' duties to change substantially once the corporation crossed some invisible line that is later determined to constitute insolvency. Such a rule would be unfair to directors and officers, and it would harm all constituent groups by creating conflicting incentives and unclear directions for risk management." *See AWTR*, 548 B.R. at 306.

> and the newly recognized direct fiduciary duty to individual creditors. Directors of insolvent corporations must retain the freedom to engage in vigorous, good faith negotiations with individual creditors for the benefit of the corporation.[21]

So what is the status of the law following this "spat" between the Delaware Court of Chancery and the Delaware Supreme Court?[22] As one judge summarized,

> Before *Gheewalla* and its forerunners, the following principles were frequently asserted as true:
>
> - The fiduciary duties owed by directors extended to creditors when the corporation entered the vicinity of insolvency.
> - Creditors could enforce the fiduciary duties that directors owed them through a direct action for breach of fiduciary duty.
> - Under the trust fund doctrine, the directors' fiduciary duties to creditors included an obligation to manage the corporation conservatively as a trust fund for the creditors' benefit.
> - Because directors owed fiduciary duties both to creditors and stockholders, directors faced an inherent conflict of interest and would bear the burden of demonstrating that their decisions were entirely fair.
> - Directors could be held liable for continuing to operate an insolvent entity and incurring greater losses for creditors under a theory known as "deepening insolvency."
>
> * * *
>
> After *Gheewalla* and the decisions by Chief Justice Strine, at least as I read them, none of these assertions remain true. In their place is a different regime in which the following principles are true:
>
> - There is no legally recognized "zone of insolvency" with implications for fiduciary duty claims. The only transition point that affects fiduciary duty analysis is insolvency itself.
> - Regardless of whether a corporation is solvent or insolvent, creditors cannot bring direct claims for breach of fiduciary duty. After a corporation becomes insolvent, creditors gain

21. *Gheewalla*, 930 A.2d at 101 (citations omitted).

22. It should be noted that, even post-*Gheewalla*, some courts continue to hold that "when a corporation is insolvent, corporate directors and officers owe a fiduciary duty to the creditors of the corporation." *See, e.g.*, Eddystone Rail Co. v. Bridger Logistics, LLC, 2020 WL 1233557, at *3 (E.D. Pa. Mar. 12, 2020).

standing to assert claims derivatively for breach of fiduciary duty.

- The directors of an insolvent firm do not owe any particular duties to creditors. They continue to owe fiduciary duties to the corporation for the benefit of all of its residual claimants, a category which now includes creditors. They do not have a duty to shut down the insolvent firm and marshal its assets for distribution to creditors, although they may make a business judgment that this is indeed the best route to maximize the firm's value.
- Directors can, as a matter of business judgment, favor certain non-insider creditors over others of similar priority without breaching their fiduciary duties.
- Delaware does not recognize the theory of "deepening insolvency." Directors cannot be held liable for continuing to operate an insolvent entity in the good faith belief that they may achieve profitability, even if their decisions ultimately lead to greater losses for creditors.
- When directors of an insolvent corporation make decisions that increase or decrease the value of the firm as a whole and affect providers of capital differently only due to their relative priority in the capital stack, directors do not face a conflict of interest simply because they own common stock or owe duties to large common stockholders. Just as in a solvent corporation, common stock ownership standing alone does not give rise to a conflict of interest. The business judgment rule protects decisions that affect participants in the capital structure in accordance with the priority of their claims.[23]

Needless to say, Dave Director will almost assuredly spend may (billable) hours with Lisa Lawyer trying to understand this guidance. His questions are likely to fall into the following categories: What is the zone of insolvency (and how do I know when I get there)? Does the director of an insolvent company owe any duties directly to the company's creditors? If a director doesn't owe a direct fiduciary duty to an insolvent company's creditors (as *Gheewalla* and *Quadrant Structured Products* suggest) what—if any—duties does a director owe to the creditors of an insolvent company? And what defenses are available when creditors start filing lawsuits?

23. *See, e.g.*, Quadrant Structured Products Co. v. Vertin, 115 A.3d 535, 544–49 (Del. Ch. 2015) (citations omitted).

II. What Is the Zone of Insolvency?

Actually, no one knows.[24] It turns out that the zone of insolvency is like the penumbra of a constitutional right.[25] You "know it when you see it."[26] Fortunately, this indefiniteness has led some—but not all—judges to hold that there is no legal significance to a company's entering the zone of insolvency.[27] Instead, according to these judges, all that matters is whether the company is, or is not, insolvent. Because most judges agree with Dave Director (and directors everywhere) that a "bright line rule" is necessary.[28]

So what does it mean to be insolvent? Generally, there are two tests for insolvency: the balance sheet test and the ability to pay debts test.[29] The balance sheet test focuses on whether the company's total assets exceed its total liabilities. The ability to pay debts test focuses on whether the company has sufficient cash to pay its creditors as its debts come due, regardless of whether its total assets (which may be illiquid or difficult to value) exceed its total liabilities.[30]

It should be noted that the solvency test is applied at the time suit is filed.[31] There is no need for a company to be "irretrievably insolvent."[32] On the contrary, judges have recognized that it is possible for a company to go "back and forth" over the "line of insolvency" many times during the course of a lawsuit.[33] It would be counterproductive (some would say unworkable, or at best an invitation to gamesmanship) for a

---

24. "There is no generally accepted meaning for the term 'zone of insolvency.'" *See In re* Jimenez, 608 B.R. 322, 328 n.1 (Bankr. M.D. Ga. 2019). *See also Gheewalla*, 930 A.2d at 98 n.20 ("In light of its ultimate ruling, the Court of Chancery did not attempt to set forth a precise definition of what constitutes the 'zone of insolvency.' Our holding in this opinion also makes it unnecessary to precisely define a 'zone of insolvency.'") (citations omitted).

25. *See, e.g.*, Griswold v. Connecticut, 381 U.S. 479, 482 (1965) (Douglas, J.).

26. *See, e.g.*, Jacobellis v. Ohio, 378 U.S. 184, 197 (1964) (Stewart, J.).

27. *See, e.g.*, *Quadrant*, 115 A.3d at 546; *Berg & Berg*, 178 Cal. App. 4th at 1041.

28. *See, e.g.*, *Quadrant*, 115 A.3d at 553.

29. *See, e.g.*, *Gheewalla*, 930 A.2d at 98; *Quadrant*, 115 A.3d at 561. Some courts have rejected an "unreasonably small capital" test as being inconsistent with the Delaware Supreme Court's rejection of the "zone of insolvency" theory, reasoning that "unreasonably small capital" is subjective and appears to be another way of stating that the company is operating in the "zone of insolvency." *See, e.g.*, *In re* Tribune Company Fraudulent Conveyance Litigation, 2018 WL 6329139, at *8 (S.D.N.Y. Nov. 20, 2018).

30. This is the classic "cash flow problem" that sinks many companies with illiquid or unsaleable assets. It is also the most common reason for a Chapter 11 restructuring, and proof that "cash is king."

31. *See, e.g.*, *Quadrant*, 115 A.3d at 548.

32. *Id.*

33. *Id.* at 553.

plaintiff to gain and lose standing many times during the course of a lawsuit.[34] This is especially true because whether a company is insolvent is often subject to dispute, and is usually determined in hindsight.[35]

III. Does the Director of an Insolvent Company Owe a Duty Directly to the Company's Creditors?

Although Dave Director can take some comfort from the fact that courts usually find that nothing changes when a company enters the zone of insolvency,[36] actual insolvency is another story. This is because courts have held that "the creditors of an insolvent corporation have standing to maintain derivative claims against directors on behalf of the corporation for breaches of fiduciary duties."[37]

> Specifically, the most relevant duty of directors and officers remains the same regardless of insolvency: the duty to exercise their business judgment in an informed, good faith effort to preserve and grow the corporation's value. That duty must be exercised for the benefit of the whole corporate enterprise, encompassing all of its constituent groups, without undue preference to any. What principally changes upon insolvency is who can sue. For acts or omissions occurring outside of insolvency, the creditors cannot sue because they have no cognizable harm. But when the corporation is insolvent or is rendered insolvent by any standard measure—balance sheet, cash flow, or inadequate capitalization—then creditors join stockholders in being able to sue derivatively for breaches of fiduciary duties

34. *Id.* at 553.

35. *Id.* at 552.

36. Dave Director is likely to pepper Lisa Lawyer with questions about whether the particular judge picked to hear the case against him is likely to be one of the minority who still thinks that duties change when a company enters the zone of insolvency. Unless the judge has already written an opinion on the issue (which is a long shot if the case is not pending in Delaware), Lisa Lawyer is likely to be left attempting to reassure Dave with platitudes about what usually happens. She is also likely to remind Dave of the advantages of both incorporating in Delaware and inserting Delaware choice of forum clauses into articles of incorporation, bylaws, and contracts.

37. *See Gheewalla*, 930 A.2d at 101.

> to the corporation that divert, dissipate, or unduly risk corporate assets.[38]

Why should creditors of an insolvent company be allowed to bring derivative claims in addition to the insolvent company's stockholders? Because

> The corporation's insolvency "makes the creditors the principal constituency injured by any fiduciary breaches that diminish the firm's value." Therefore, equitable considerations give creditors standing to pursue derivative claims against the directors of an insolvent corporation. Individual creditors of an insolvent corporation have the same incentive to pursue valid derivative claims on its behalf that shareholders have when the corporation is solvent."[39]

So, if creditors can bring derivative claims, what is the nature of a Dave Director's duty to the Acme Widget Company's creditors? Like so many other things, people disagree. One Judge explained that a creditor's claim against a director could be either

> (i) an easily invoked theory that a creditor can assert directly as the firm approaches insolvency, (ii) a powerful cause of action that defendant directors will struggle to defeat because of an inherent conflict between their duties to creditors and their duties to stockholders, and (iii) a vehicle for obtaining a judicial remedy that would involve a forced liquidation of a firm that otherwise might continue to operate and return to solvency
>
> [or] (i) something creditors only can file derivatively once the corporation actually has become insolvent, (ii) subject by default to the business judgment rule and not facilitated by any inherent conflict between duties to creditors and duties to stockholders, and (iii) only a vehicle for restoring to the firm self-dealing payments and other disloyal wealth transfers.[40]

Again, unless the particular judge assigned to the case has written on these issues, Lisa Lawyer will be left explaining to Dave Director that there are two schools of thought, one of which is much more favorable to him.

---

38. *See AWTR*, 548 B.R. at 305–06.

39. *See Gheewalla*, 930 A.2d at 101 (citations omitted).

40. *See, e.g.*, *Quadrant*, 115 A.3d at 544. Vice Chancellor Laster ultimately held the latter view.

Regardless of whether the judge views a creditor's claim as powerful or routine, a creditor (like a stockholder) must usually bring a derivative, rather than a direct, claim.[41] Creditors, rather than stockholders, are allowed to bring derivative claims after a company becomes insolvent because they, and not the stockholders, are the "residual claim holders" post insolvency.[42] They, and not the stockholders, will benefit from any increase in the company's value, and are therefore entitled to sue to make sure that the directors live up to their obligation to attempt to increase the company's value.[43]

The ability of creditors to bring derivative claims against Dave Director for breaching his fiduciary duty does more than "just" increase the number of potential plaintiffs who might want to sue Dave. It also increases the likelihood of someone filing suit because the two pools of potential plaintiffs (i.e., stockholders and creditors) prefer radically different strategies.

> Stockholders and creditors are likely to have different approaches to risk, especially upon insolvency. Creditors, "holding fixed claims, generally prefer corporate decisions that minimize the risk of failure," whereas stockholders "generally prefer risky strategies because they profit from the success of [those] decisions but share the losses with creditors if the decisions fail."[44]

Indeed, "the closer to the line of insolvency, the more likely it is that stockholders will have nothing to lose and everything to gain by taking excessively large risks, and conversely the more likely that creditors will have the opposite incentive to take minimal if any risks."[45] As a result, to the extent Dave Director pursues a riskier strategy (to appease the stockholders and to try and pay everyone off), the creditors are likely to be aggrieved. To the extent Dave Director pursues a more conservative strategy (to appease the creditors and make sure they get at least something), the stockholders are likely to be aggrieved. As a result, at the end of the day, someone is going to be aggrieved. And that someone is going to go looking for a lawyer.

41. *See, e.g.*, *Quadrant*, 115 A.3d at 546. It should be noted, however, that some courts have allowed creditors to bring direct, rather than derivative, claims. *See, e.g.*, Eddystone Rail Co. v. Bridger Logistics, LLC, 2020 WL 1233557, at *4 (E.D. Pa. Mar. 12, 2020).

42. *See, e.g.*, Quadrant, 115 A.3d at 551.

43. *Id.*

44. *See* AWTR, 548 B.R. at 327 (citations omitted).

45. *Id.* at 329–30.

IV. If Dave Director Doesn't Owe Creditors a Direct Fiduciary Duty, What Duties Does He Owe the Acme Widget Company's Creditors?

As set forth in Chapters 1 through 4, Dave Director owes the Acme Widget Company a duty of care and a duty of loyalty.[46] When the Acme Widget Company becomes insolvent, the company's creditors can sue (usually derivatively) to enforce those duties.[47] The duty of care requires Dave Director to act with skill and diligence. A creditor of an insolvent company is likely to claim either that Dave Director mismanaged the company by permitting (or, heaven forbid, causing) the company to engage in pursuits that were not likely to be profitable, or that Dave Director permitted (or, heaven forbid, orchestrated) fraudulent transfers.[48] The easiest way for Dave Director to breach the duty of care is through nonfeasance. It is amazing how many directors abdicate their responsibilities, especially when things are not going well. Simply put, the ostrich defense doesn't work.[49] Not even for an ostrich.

A breach of the duty of loyalty is equally easy for Dave Director to avoid if he follows Lisa Lawyer's good advice. Although Dave Director is entitled to take a salary (or stock),[50] he can't self-deal, and he certainly can't loot the company. Courts have recognized that creditors can bring claims against anyone who (allegedly) looted the company.[51] Creditors can even do so after a bankruptcy trustee is appointed, assuming the bankruptcy trustee declines to pursue the claim, because the claim against the "corporate looter" originally belonged to the

---

46. *See, e.g.*, *Quadrant*, 115 A.3d at 549.

47. *See, e.g.*, *AWTR*, 548 B.R. at 322.

48. A fraudulent transfer occurs when a debtor transfers an asset without receiving fair value in return for that asset at a time when the debtor is (or when the transfer makes the debtor) insolvent. *See, e.g.*, 12 Pa. Const. Stat. Ann. §§ 5104(a) and 5105. A transfer is also fraudulent if it is made with the intent to hinder, delay, or defraud a creditor. *See, e.g.*, 12 Pa. Const. Stat. Ann. § 5104(a).

49. *See, e.g.*, *AWTR*, 548 B.R. at 314 ("a director cannot close his eyes to what is going on about him in the conduct of the business of the corporation and have it said that he is exercising business judgment") (citations omitted).

50. *See, e.g.*, *Quadrant*, 115 A.3d at 547.

51. *See, e.g.*, *In re* Wilton Armetale, ___ F.3d ___, 2020 WL 4460000, at *1 (3d Cir. Aug. 4, 2020).

company's creditors, and it reverts to the creditors if it is explicitly or implicitly abandoned by the bankruptcy trustee.[52]

Although Dave Director will almost certainly focus on the creditors to whom the Acme Widget Company owes the most money (under the completely understandable belief that the Acme Widget Company will need to appease—or at least deal with—its major creditors if it is to survive), there are two classes of creditors who deserve particular attention when operating in the zone of insolvency: employees and the government.

Many states have enacted statutes that give employees the right to sue officers and directors in their personal capacity for unpaid wages.[53] These wage payment and collection laws arise out of legislature's (correct) belief that, if the people who are making the decision to pay or not pay employees' wages know that they will be personally liable for any unpaid wages, they will (somehow) arrange the company's affairs so that employees are paid. And, lest Dave Director think that employees might be too busy or too poor to hire lawyers to sue him, Lisa Lawyer will be quick to point out that not only do most wage payment and collection laws include fee-shifting provisions,[54] many are enforceable by state agencies,[55] and some include criminal provisions.[56] In addition to requiring that wages be paid, these statutes require that wages to be paid in a timely manner (usually no more than 15 days after the end of a pay period),[57] and often include hefty fines and penalties for late payment.[58] Wage payment and collection laws also require that wages be paid by cash or check (as opposed to credits, scrip, or "in kind").[59]

As for the government, "under the Internal Revenue Code, any individual responsible for the collection of, accounting for, and payment of trust-fund taxes who willfully fails to perform these obligations may be held personally liable for a penalty equal to the amount of the trust-fund taxes owed."[60] The government imposes this penalty because

52. *See, e.g.*, *Wilton Armetale*, 2020 WL 4460000, at *7.

53. *See, e.g.*, Pennsylvania's wage collection law, 43 P.S. §§ 260.1, *et seq*.

54. *See, e.g.*, 43 P.S. § 260.9a(f). Interestingly, Pennsylvania's wage payment and collection law explicitly provides that only the plaintiff (and not the defendant) can collect fees. *See* 43 P.S. § 260.9a(f).

55. *See, e.g., id.* § 260.9a(e).

56. *Id.* §§ 260.11a(b); 260.11a(c).

57. *Id.* § 260.3(a).

58. *Id.* § 260.10.

59. *Id.* § 260.6.

60. *See* Crisci v. United States, 407 Fed. App'x 573, 574 (3d Cir. 2010). *See also* United States v. Gregg, 2013 WL 6498249, at *5 (W.D. Pa. Dec. 11, 2013); 26 U.S.C. § 6672.

"withheld monies can be a tempting source of ready cash to a failing corporation beleaguered by its creditors."[61] As tempting as it may be, Lisa Lawyer will surely advise Dave Director that this is one temptation that should be resisted.

V. What Defenses Can Dave Director Employ?

Dave Director's most potent defense against creditors' claims is the business judgment rule. Numerous courts have held that directors can use the business judgment rule to defeat creditors' claims.[62] Under the business judgment rule, a director will not be held liable for the good faith exercise of reasonable business judgment—even if that business judgment turns out to be wrong—if the director is not engaged in self-dealing. A director can, for example, take the "long view" and approve actions that may cost the company money (or depress profits) in the short term, in the hopes that those actions will lead to long-term gains.[63] So, for example, if a creditor accuses Dave Director of breaching his fiduciary duty (and wasting corporate assets that could have been used to pay creditors) by approving expenses such as bonuses, above-market wages, advertising costs, or charitable contributions, Dave Director can defend by arguing that he approved those expenses because he believed they would lead to increased profits (and an increased ability to pay creditors) in the future. Ideally, if the reasonableness of Dave Director's belief is questioned, he will be able to point to the reports he received from experts showing that the expenditures were expected to lead to future profits, and to the board minutes stating that he relied on those experts when voting in favor of the expenditures.[64] Even courts holding that directors owe duties to creditors acknowledge that a director does not have to give creditors' interests priority, and the director's duty is "not a duty to liquidate and pay creditors when the corporation is near insolvency, provided that in the directors' informed, good faith judgement there is an alternative."[65]

61. *See Gregg*, 2013 WL 6498249, at *7 (citations omitted).

62. *See, e.g.*, *Quadrant*, 115 A.3d at 547.

63. *See, e.g.*, *Bandera Master Fund*, 2019 WL 4927053, at *14.

64. Certainly, if Lisa Lawyer had a hand in drafting the board minutes, those minutes would reflect such reliance. The lack of such a statement would enhance a creditor's claim.

65. *See Berg & Berg*, 178 Cal. App. 4th at 1032.

In addition to defending based on the business judgment rule, Dave Director can defend by arguing that his actions did not cause any damage to creditors.[66] Specifically, Dave Director can argue that nothing he did (or could have done) damaged the creditors. Instead, they were damaged by investing an a business that failed through no fault of Dave Director's. Although an argument—based on 20/20 hindsight, of course—that Dave Director should have done something different often has some appeal, 20 years of government statistics show that approximately half of all businesses fail in the first five years.[67] It would strain credulity to suggest that all of these businesses were mismanaged.

Relatedly, Dave Director may have to face claims of "deepening insolvency"—that is, that his actions (or inactions) turned a small loss into a large loss. While "deepening insolvency" may make sense under the "things can always get worse" theory, at least some states have rejected it (under the "if you are already dead you can't be further damaged" theory).[68]

Finally, Dave Director can defend against at least some claims by arguing that he was acting in his "individual," as opposed to "corporate," capacity when he took the action giving rise to the claim.[69] For example, Dave Director may have become a member of the Acme Widget Company's board because he was (or represented) a significant investor in (or creditor to) the company. Leaving aside the question of whether Dave Director owned (or controlled) enough stock to elect himself to the board, it is common for a startup company to offer a board seat to the investors who purchase a "round" or a "class" of stock (i.e., the owners of the "class B" or "B round" get to elect a director regardless of who the owners of the "class A" or "A round" stock wish to see on the board). As a company approaches insolvency, it is common for the company to ask existing investors (or debt holders) to put additional money into the company.[70] A company usually does so

66. Depending on the case, this defense can be a lack of causation, a lack of damages, or both.

67. *See, e.g.*, https://www.bls.gov/bdm/us_age_naics_00_table7.txt.

68. *See, e.g.*, Tow v. Bulmahn, 2016 WL 1722246, at *5 (E.D. La. Apr. 29, 2016); *Quadrant*, 115 A.3d at 547.

69. *See, e.g.*, *Bandera Master Fund*, 2019 WL 4927053, at *10.

70. This "new money" can come in as either debt or equity. If it comes in as debt, it is likely to include collateral (assuming there is any that is unencumbered), priority, and "conversation rights" (i.e. the right to either convert the debt to equity at some future point, or to acquire equity as a "kicker"—often as a result of a warrant—in the future). If it comes in as equity, it is likely to "cram down" the existing equity holders (i.e., dilute their ownership

for two reasons. First, the "old money" already knows the status of the company and its likely prospects. As a result, "old money" does not need to perform nearly as much due diligence as "new money," and can therefore move faster, and at a lower cost and with less disruption to the company.[71] Second, "new money's" first question is inevitably going to be "why isn't old money coming to the table." If the company does not have a very good answer to this question, "new money" will assume that "old money" is not coming to the table because it believes doing so would be "throwing good money after bad." If Dave Director is "old money," he is entitled to make his own decision about whether he (or his principal) should put more money in. Specifically, he can decide not to invest more money even if he knows that the practical impact of his decision will be to "scare off" other potential investors. In making that decision, he is acting in his individual capacity (and exercising his individual rights) rather than acting in his capacity as a director of the Acme Widget Company.[72] Similarly, to the extent Dave Director accepts compensation from the Acme Widget Company, he is doing so in his individual capacity, and (absent any additional allegations of wrongdoing) not in breach of his fiduciary duty.[73]

VI. So What Is Dave Director to Do?

At the end of the day, Dave Director's duty to the Acme Widget Company is the same as it has always been. He has to keep himself informed, avoid conflicts and self-dealing, and make the best decisions he can to try and maximize the value of the Acme Widget Company as a whole. In doing so, he can take the interests—and desires—of both stockholders and creditors into account. Indeed, he can take many constituencies

percentage drastically). Existing equity holders often have anti-dilution rights. Anti-dilution rights allow existing equity holders to buy "their proportionate share" of any new equity on the same terms as the new equity holders. If they do so, they will continue to own the same proportion of the company as they owned before the "new money" came in.

71. The costs of gathering the information demanded during due diligence are not to be understated. Neither are the opportunity costs of having management take time and energy to respond to due diligence requests, especially when management has its hands full trying to save the company. Indeed, every hour management has to spend trying to raise money is an hour management cannot spend trying to solve whatever problems necessitated the fundraising in the first place.

72. *See, e.g.*, *Bandera Master Fund*, 2019 WL 4927053, at *10.

73. *See, e.g.*, Tow v. Bulmahn, 2016 WL 1722246, at *25 (E.D. La. Apr. 29, 2016).

into account, including employees, customers, and the environment.[74] But at the end of the day, he has to do what is best for the company as a whole, even if doing so will anger one or more constituencies. After all, he has Lisa Lawyer on retainer, and she can defend him against whatever claims may be brought against him. At least until the D&O policy runs out.[75]

74. "B corporations" notwithstanding, a director who wishes to take things like environmental impact into account is well advised to do so under the rubric of increasing the value of the company over the long run. The business judgment rule can be invoked to justify a decision to take environmental considerations into account—even though they may cost the corporation more money in the short run—because doing so reduces the long term risk of (losing) an environmental or "public nuisance" lawsuit, or because the positive press associated with benefiting the environment will (again in the long run) increase sales sufficiently to make the decision a net positive for the company.

75. Many directors and officers liability insurance policies have "eroding limits" (i.e., any money spent defending claims reduces the amount available to pay claims). Directors and officers liability insurance policies also usually include "insured versus insured" exclusions. Depending on the wording of the exclusion and the wording of the claim, these exclusions can come into play. Finally, if a company goes out of business (through bankruptcy or otherwise), it would be well advised to purchase tail coverage if it is available.

Chapter 13

What Fiduciaries Should Know (and Not Be Afraid to Ask) about D&O Insurance

By Sherilyn Pastor

Following disappointing earnings results, TALA Inc.'s stock price plummets. It soon finds itself the target of a suit alleging securities fraud. Even some of its employees sue, alleging TALA Inc., its board of directors, and certain officers breached their fiduciary duties causing damage, including the loss of the value of employee's stock and stock options. TALA Inc.'s risk manager calls you for advice regarding the scope of insurance coverage offered by TALA Inc.'s directors and officers liability policy. You now need to become familiar with the insurance issues and jargon surrounding directors and officers (D&O) liability coverage.

Many companies purchase D&O policies to protect against lawsuits arising from key decisions and management practices. D&O policies cover directors, officers, employees, and sometimes the company against allegations of wrongful conduct, such as breach of duties, neglect, error, misstatements, misleading statements, and other omissions or acts. Most D&O policies defend and indemnify against alleged wrongful acts that have taken place prior to or during the policy's period (although some policies may exclude certain past acts). D&O insurance coverage has become an increasingly hot topic as the number of claims against directors and officers increase.

I. Who Is Insured?

A. The "Sides" of a D&O Policy

D&O coverage typically protects directors and officers against claims alleging breach of their corporate duties. D&O coverage can be viewed as a variation on professional liability coverage. It is intended to safeguard directors and officers against liabilities associated with their corporate responsibilities.

D&O polices typically provide two, or in some cases three, types, or "sides," of coverage. Most policies provide direct "Side A" coverage to directors and officers, which provides coverage if the corporation is not legally obligated, or is obligated but unwilling or unable, to indemnify them. Sometimes a corporation's charter or bylaws will, for example, prohibit the corporation from providing indemnification.

D&O policies usually also provide "Side B" coverage. Side B coverage basically provides reimbursement to a company that has properly indemnified its directors and officers for an otherwise covered claim. It is an indirect form of D&O coverage.

Some, but not all, policies also provide "Side C" coverage. It is known as "entity coverage." It offers coverage for the direct liabilities of the corporation. Such coverage affords the company protection from judgments or settlements of covered claims, including the cost of hiring counsel to defend the claims (up to the policy limits, of course).

From the company's perspective, Side C coverage can be desirable, especially for publicly traded companies that might become the target of a securities lawsuit. Absent Side C coverage, if a lawsuit is brought against directors, officers, and the company, the insurer will pay for only the defense of, and indemnification arising from, the covered claims against the directors and officers. If it does not have coverage, the company itself will have to pay for the defense of the claims against the corporate entity, as well as for any ensuing settlement of or judgment on such claims.

B. Sharing Policy Limits

On learning that TALA Inc. has coverage for the corporate entity and its directors and officers, TALA Inc.'s CEO calls to ask you about the policy's limits. That is the total amount the insurer is obligated to pay in the event of a covered loss. Not surprisingly, she and other directors and officers want to know how much coverage is potentially available to meet the lawsuits against them. What should you tell her, beyond the dollar amount stated on the policy's declaration's page, are the policy's limits?

Directors and officers, and the entity when covered, often share D&O policy limits with each other. This means that each payment the insurer makes on behalf of one insured reduces the limits available to defend and indemnify the other insureds against the same or subsequent claims. A single lawsuit could potentially cost millions to defend. Claims against one "bad actor" can reduce the limits left for defense and indemnity of innocent insureds.

Many, but not all, D&O policies contain a Priority of Payments provision. It sets forth the order in which policy proceeds will be paid out to the policy's various insureds. The provision often provides that the policy's proceeds are the property of the insured directors and officers, rather than a bankruptcy trustee, in the event the insured company becomes insolvent.

C. Dedicated "Side A" Only Coverage

When policy limits are exhausted before a matter resolves fully, individual directors' and officers' personal assets are placed at risk. TALA Inc.'s CEO asks if there is dedicated coverage available to the directors and officers? You agree to look into it.

Some companies purchase another layer of protection for their directors and officers, referred to as Side A Difference in Conditions, or "Side A DIC," coverage. Dedicated Side A coverage protects directors and officers from nonindemnifiable claims. It is valuable where the company's underlying insurance is exhausted by the payment of claims on behalf of other insureds, including the company. It also provides additional protection if the company enters bankruptcy and a court freezes the policy as an asset of the bankruptcy estate.

Side A DIC coverage often is broader coverage than that under traditional D&O policies. It has no deductible, and is typically not rescindable. Side A DIC coverage provides an additional level of protection for directors and officers when the company is unable or unwilling to indemnify them.

D. Capacity Issues

A director or officer may wear many hats, including serving on the boards of other companies. D&O policies typically cover only the wrongful acts committed by an individual insured in their capacity as a director or officer of the insured company.[1] Some policies extend

1. *E.g.*, McAninch v. Wintermute, 491 F.3d 759, 769 (8th Cir. 2007). *See also* Feldman v. Fidelity & Deposit Co. of Maryland, 2016 WL 885041 (Md. Ct. Spec. App. Mar. 7, 2016)

coverage to those that serve on other companies' boards at the insured company's direction.

II. What Generally Is Covered?

D&O policy terms vary. All policies are subject to their own terms, conditions, and exclusions. Now that a suit has been filed against TALA Inc. and its management, you need to read the policy carefully, and consider the facts involved and the governing law.

A. Covered Claims

D&O policies provide coverage for losses arising from a "claim." The policy will define claim. A typical D&O policy may define claim broadly and as follows:

> "Claim" means:
> (1) a written demand for monetary relief, non-monetary or injunctive relief;
> (2) a civil, criminal, administrative, regulatory or arbitration proceeding for monetary, non-monetary or injunctive relief which is commenced by: (i) service of a complaint or similar pleading; (ii) return of an indictment, information or similar document (in the case of a criminal proceeding); or (iii) receipt or filing of a notice of charges; or
> (3) a civil, criminal, administrative or regulatory investigation of any Insured Person:
> (i) once such Insured Person is identified in writing by such investigating authority as a person against whom a proceeding described in Definition (b)(2) may be commenced; or
> (ii) in the case of an investigation by the SEC or a similar state or foreign government authority, after service of a subpoena upon such Insured Person.
>
> The term Claim shall include any Securities Claim . . .[2]

(claim did not allege a covered wrongful act because it was not made against a director "solely" in his capacity as a director of the insured bank; rather, the claim included allegations regarding director's misconduct as a member of an outside LLC).

2. AIG Executive and Organization Liability Insurance Policy [75011 (02/00)] issued by National Union Fire Insurance Company, Pittsburgh, PA.

Where claim is defined broadly, D&O policies may respond to a host of government investigations, subpoenas, and suits by stakeholders, customers, consumer groups, competitors, venders, suppliers, government enforcement agencies, and regulatory groups. Some courts, for example, have interpreted claim, when defined to include demands for nonmonetary relief and/or government investigations, to include responses to subpoenas.[3]

Some policies define claim to encompass only civil, administrative, and regulatory proceedings; meaning, the policy may not cover "investigations" or it may expressly exclude investigations conducted by the Securities and Exchange Commission (SEC). Some policies cover investigations, but only those "pending against an Insured Person"—that is, a natural person (not the covered corporate entity). Meaning, SEC investigations may not be covered if there is no individual target. Still other policies define claim broadly to include formal civil, criminal, administrative, or regulatory proceedings or investigations, including those commenced by the filing or issuance of a notice of charges, formal investigative order, or similar document identifying in writing an insured person or corporate entity. For such policies, the definition of claim extends to SEC investigations of corporate entities (even those without named targets).

B. Claims-Made Coverages and Notice Requirements

If sued, policyholders should determine when and how their policy requires they give notice of the claim to involved insurers. D&O policies

3. *E.g.*, Syracuse Univ. v. Nat'l Union Fire Ins. Co., 975 N.Y.S.2d 370 (N.Y. Sup. Ct. Mar. 7, 2013), *aff'd*, 112 A.D.3d 1379 (N.Y. App. Div. 2013) (grand jury subpoenas constituted a "written demand . . . for non-monetary relief"); Patriarch Partners, LLC v. AXIS Ins. Co., 16-CV-2277 (VEC), 2017 WL 4233078 (S.D.N.Y. Sept. 22, 2017) ("non-monetary relief" includes an SEC subpoena); Minuteman Int'l, Inc. v. Great Am. Ins. Co., No. 03 C 6067, 2004 WL 603482 (N.D. Ill. Mar. 22, 2004) ("the relief sought by the subpoena itself is the production of documents or testimony"); Gold Tip, LLC v. Carolina Cas. Ins. Co., Civil No. 2:11-CV-00765, 2012 WL 3638538, at *4 (D. Utah Aug. 23, 2012) (letters and requests for information sought "non-monetary relief"); Agilis Benefit Servs. LLC v. Travelers Cas. & Sur. Co., Civil Action No. 5:08-CV-213, 2010 WL 8573372, at *6 (E.D. Tex. Apr. 30, 2010) ("relief" includes a demand to produce documents or appear before a grand jury). *But see* Diamond Glass Cos., Inc. v. Twin City Fire Ins. Co., No. 06-CV-13105, 2008 WL 4613170, at *4 (S.D.N.Y. Aug. 18, 2008) (grand jury subpoenas not a "Claim" because they did not seek "non-monetary relief"); Employers' Fire Ins. Co. v. ProMedica Health Systems, Inc., 524 F. App'x 241 (6th Cir. 2013) (defining "relief'" as "a remedy provided by a court"); McCalla Corp. v. Certain Underwriters at Lloyd's, London, No. 13-1317-SAC, 2014 WL 1745647 (D. Kan. May 1, 2014) (neither a criminal information nor a search warrant seeks "damages" or "relief").

are almost always "claims made" policies, as opposed to "occurrence" policies. Meaning, to be covered, a claim must be first asserted or made against the policyholder during the policy period. So, for example, if TALA Inc. bought D&O insurance effective January 1, 2020, to January 1, 2021, and the suit is filed against it on December 28, 2020, relating to conduct that is not otherwise excluded, the claim may be covered. To access coverage, TALA Inc. will want to give its insurer timely notice of the claim.

Most D&O polices require that notice of the claim be given to the insurer "as soon as practicable" or "immediately," and often during the policy period or alternatively within some short time period after the policy expires—often referred to as the "discovery period." This extended reporting period may be 30 to 90 days. Most courts have interpreted the phrase "as soon as practicable" to mean "within a reasonable time" under the facts particular to the circumstances.[4]

Insurers assert that failure to adhere to a policy's notice requirements voids coverage, and some courts agree. That is because D&O insurance is usually written on a claims-made (not occurrence) basis. In most jurisdictions, insurers cannot refuse to provide occurrence-based coverage on grounds of late notice unless they can demonstrate they are prejudiced from the timing of the notice. A majority of jurisdictions, however, refuse to apply the notice-prejudice rule to claims-made policies. These courts find that claims-made policies are different in nature than occurrence-based policies, and that under them notice is a contractual condition to coverage. D&O insurers, therefore, in most instances, need not show prejudice to disclaim coverage based on late notice.

Complicating matters, there are two distinct types of claims-made policies, and knowing the difference can be critical. A claims-made-and-reported policy requires that not only must a covered claim be made against the insured during the policy period, it must also be reported to the insurer during the policy period (or any extended reporting period).

Under a pure claims-made policy, a claim must be made against the insured during the policy period. It need be reported to the insurer, however, only as the policy directs. This may allow the report of a claim to be regarded as timely when shared with the insurer "as soon as practicable," even after the policy's expiration, if that is what is required by the policy.

In either circumstance, coverage is available only when the involved claim is made against an insured during the policy period. If TALA Inc.

4. *See e.g.*, Argent Fin. Group Inc. v. Fid. & Deposit Co. of Md., No. 3:04CV02323, 2006 WL 1793609, at *3 (W.D. La. June 28, 2006).

has a pure claims-made form, it may be required to provide notice of the claim to the insurer only as soon as practicable. If TALA Inc. has a claims-made-and-reported policy, it may be required to provide notice to the insurer as soon as practicable and no later than the date its policy or any extended reporting period expires.

To ameliorate the harshness of these strict notice requirements, many D&O policies allow insureds to provide early notice of circumstances that may, in the future, result in a potential claim. These provisions, for practical purposes, provide extended coverage past the policy period "where 'facts and circumstances' that might give rise to a claim are known, but no 'claim' has been asserted against the insured."[5]

C. Covered Loss Arising from Wrongful Acts

To be covered, the claim must assert a "wrongful act," as defined by the policy. Under some policies, wrongful act means any breach of duty, neglect, error, misstatement, misleading statement, omission, or act by a company's officers and directors. Other policies limit coverage to "negligent" acts, error, omissions, and the like.

D&O policies also define what is and is not covered "loss." Some policies, for example, cover civil fines; others do not.

D&O policies cover defense costs, including attorneys' fees. Typically, an insured retains its own counsel, although sometimes the policy requires the insured to choose from a panel of insurer-approved counsel. The insured's reasonable and necessary defense costs are then regarded as covered loss, which is advanced or reimbursed by the insurer after the policy's deductible or self-insured retention is satisfied. A D&O policy will typically have provisions describing how the insurer will address claims involving both covered and uncovered claims, or insured and uninsured persons or entities.[6]

D&O policies also offer indemnity, meaning that they pay covered settlements or judgments. Under Side A (providing coverage for directors and officers), loss is often defined as any amount for which the insured is legally liable and that arises out of a claim made against them for wrongful acts. Under Side B, loss generally includes the amount for which the corporation indemnifies its directors and officers for covered wrongful acts. Under Side C entity coverage, loss is typically limited to losses a corporation incurs as a result of securities claims.

5. *In re* Ambassador Group, Inc. Litig., 830 F. Supp. 147, 157 (E.D.N.Y. 1993).
6. *See* Section IV.c., *infra*.

The definition of loss may become important in suits seeking disgorgement. If, for example, the stock drop suits against TALA Inc. assert claims relating to alleged misstatements in the public offering of securities, an insurer may claim that there is no loss. Some courts have held that disgorgement of profits gained at the expense of shareholders by virtue of misrepresentations or omissions that affect a security's price is not a loss.[7] Rather, it is an amount that was wrongfully taken by the insured, and therefore must be returned to investors.

Some policies exclude punitive and treble damages from the definition of loss. Other policies define loss to encompass damages, judgments, and settlements, including punitive or exemplary damages "where insurable by law." Policies permitting reimbursement of punitive damage awards are more likely to be enforced when the policy also includes a "favored jurisdiction" provision. Such a provision requires the law of the jurisdiction most favorable to the insurability of punitive damages be applied (as some states find this coverage void against public policy). Indeed, some policies provide that if, "based on the written opinion of counsel for the Insured," punitive damages are insurable under applicable law, the insurer "will not dispute the written opinion of counsel for the Insured."

III. What May Be Excluded from Coverage?

D&O policies have exclusions and limitations of which counsel must be mindful as they defend and seek to resolve a fiduciary claim. Most courts hold that exclusions and conditions in insurance policies should be read narrowly and against the insurer that drafted the policy.[8] The burden of proving the applicability of an exclusion is on the insurer.[9]

A. Dishonesty and Ill-Gotten Gain Exclusions

D&O policies usually exclude coverage for dishonest, criminal, and/or fraudulent acts. They also exclude coverage for obtaining of a gain or profit to which the insured is not legally entitled. Many policies also

7. Many D&O policies also contain an exclusion barring coverage for restitutionary awards or the return of so-called ill-gotten gains or illegal profits.

8. *E.g.*, Borough of Moosic v. Darwin Nat'l Assur. Co., 556 Fed. Appx. 92, 98 (3d Cir. 2014); Gastar Expl. Ltd. v. U.S. Specialty Ins. Co., 412 S.W.3d 577, 583–84 (Tex. Ct. App. 2013); Capital Bank & Trust Co. v. Equitable Life Assur. Soc. of U.S., 542 So. 2d 494, 496 (La. 1989).

9. *E.g.*, Reynolds v. Select Props, Ltd., 634 So. 2d 1180, 1183 (La. 1994).

exclude coverage for matters not insurable at law. These exclusions take on various forms, some broadly excluding dishonest acts, others also encompassing fraudulent and/or criminal acts. Some exclusions do not apply unless the involved conduct is deliberate and/or active. The intent of these exclusions is to limit coverage for certain misconduct that is intended to be dissuaded as a matter of public policy. This prevents a fiduciary from deciding, for example, that there is no financial downside to intentionally defrauding others because their insurer will reimburse the victims.

The standard for applying these exclusions varies among policies.[10] Less favorable exclusions apply when the insured "in fact" commits fraud or procures an illegal profit or gain. What establishes "in fact" that such conduct occurred is open to interpretation and insurers may seek to avoid coverage on the basis of facts they allege exist.

Many policies apply these exclusions only upon a "final adjudication" in the underlying suit that such conduct occurred, or a finding of guilt in a criminal matter. This is a higher threshold. Insurers cannot simply apply the exclusion based on their view of the facts. They can avoid coverage only when, and if, a final adjudication establishes the requisite facts in the lawsuit giving rise to the claim.[11] Most courts recognize that the settlement of a civil lawsuit does not constitute a "final adjudication" for purposes of a policy exclusion.[12] This higher standard can be quite significant where a policyholder is seeking its defense costs be reimbursed, and any "final adjudication" is years away.

B. The Insured versus Insured Exclusion

The breach of fiduciary duty and securities fraud suits against TALA Inc. and its board involve putative classes that would include officers, directors, and management and their stock and stock options. TALA Inc.'s Risk Manager and CEO want to know if this presents any issues in terms of coverage. You tell them it may, depending on the policy language and controlling law.

---

10. *See* Int'l Surplus Lines Ins. Co. v. Univ. of Wyo. Research Corp., 850 F. Supp. 1509, 1525 (D. Wyo. 1994); *accord* Cont'l Cas. Co. v. Tierney, No. 89-0679-CV-W-6, 1991 WL 207398 (W.D. Mo. July 2, 1991).

11. *E.g.*, *In re* Enron Corp. Secs. Derivative & "ERISA" Litig. (Newby v. Enron Corp.), 391 F. Supp. 2d 541, 570 (S.D. Tex. 2005) (requiring a judgment or "final adjudication" of fraud); Int'l Surplus Lines v. Univ. of Wyo. Research Corp., 850 F. Supp. at 1524 (same).

12. *E.g.*, Stein v. Axis Ins. Co., 10 Cal. App. 5th 673, 216 Cal. Rptr. 3d 804 (2017), *as modified* (Apr. 6, 2017); Arch Ins. Co. v. Murdock, 2016 WL 7414218 (Del. Super. Ct. Dec. 21, 2016).

An insured versus insured exclusion limits coverage for suits between the corporate policyholder and its directors and officers.[13] It was initially designed to exclude coverage for internal disputes between directors and officers, former management and/or the company, as well as to avoid potentially collusive suits by one insured against another insured. This exclusion can become problematic, however, when a third party, like a bankruptcy trustee, takes control of a company and pursues claims against directors and officers,[14] or a derivative suit is filed.[15]

Many insurers have narrowed the exclusionary language so that it does not apply to directors and officers who have not held their position for a set number of years, or to claims brought by a bankruptcy trustee. Some policies also make clear that it does not apply to shareholder derivative suits or cross-claims asserted in underlying litigation. A careful reading of the provision is required, as is the review of the mixed case law regarding the scope and application of the exclusion.[16]

IV. What Else May Come Up?

A. Severability

Like other contracts, an insurer can seek to void its policy if it was obtained by fraud or misstatement. Having a severability clause in the

---

13. Fid. & Deposit Co. of Md. v. Zandstra, 756 F. Supp. 429, 432 (N.D. Cal. 1990).

14. *See, e.g.*, Stratton v. Nat'l Union Fire Ins. Co., No. Civ. A. 03-CV-120180-RGS, 2004 WL 1950337 (D. Mass. Sept. 3, 2004) (insured versus insured exclusion applies to suit brought against insured directors and officers by a successor corporation formed pursuant to a plan of reorganization in bankruptcy). *But see* Pintlar Corp. v. Fidelity & Cas. Co. of N.Y., 205 B.R. 945 (Bankr. D. Idaho 1997), *aff'd*, Case No. CV 97-250-N-EJL (D. Idaho Sept. 11, 1997), *appeal docketed*, No. 98-35007 (9th Cir. Dec. 31, 1997) (holding exclusion did not apply to litigation trustee's claims because there was no collusion and trustee was acting on behalf of the creditors, not the company).

15. *See, e.g.*, Sphinx Int'l, Inc. v. Nat'l Union Fire Ins. Co. of Pittsburgh, Pa., 226 F. Supp. 2d 1326, 1337 (M.D. Fla. 2002); Level 3 Communication, Inc. v. Fed. Ins. Co., 168 F.2d 956 (7th Cir. 1999). Some courts have found the exclusion need be applied rationally, and consistent with a policyholder's reasonable expectations. *See* Miller v. St. Paul Mercury Ins. Co., 683 F.3d 871 (7th Cir. 2012) (an insured versus insured exclusion does not bar coverage when some plaintiffs in a lawsuit are insureds but other plaintiffs are non-insureds); Hardin v. Greenwich Ins. Co., No. SACV 11-1785-JST (ANx), 2012 WL 3217704 (C.D. Cal. Aug. 3, 2012) (insured versus insured exclusion applied solely to counts asserted by the insured company, but not those asserted by the corporate shareholder plaintiff).

16. *Compare* Sphinx Int'l, Inc. v. Nat'l Union Fire Ins. Co., 226 F. Supp. 2d 1326 (M.D. Fla. 2002) *and* Level 3 Commc'n. Inc. v. Fed. Ins. Co., 168 F.2d 956 (7th Cir. 1999) *with* Fidelity & Deposition of Maryland v. Zandstra, 756 F. Supp. 429 (N.D. Cal. 1990).

application and the policy may help limit an insurer's ability to impute one insured's knowledge of misstatements to others covered by the policy. In this regard, some policies provide that no statement in the application or knowledge possessed by one insured will be imputed to another insured; other policies permit the knowledge of those signing the application to be imputed only to the company.

Many policies also offer severability provisions relating to the policies' exclusions. Thus, the conduct of each insured will be viewed separately, such that where one "culpable" insured's conduct triggers an exclusion, that conduct will not be imputed to defeat all insureds' coverage rights.

B. Rescission

If TALA Inc.'s stock drop was caused by misstatement of its financial condition, its insurer might seek to deny coverage and for rescission of the policy based on alleged misrepresentations in the insurance application. The insurer might argue that it would not have issued the policy at the agreed upon premium had the financial information contained in the company's application been complete and accurate. Therefore, the argument goes, the insurer is justified in rescinding the entire policy from its inception.

Misstatements of a company's financial condition is not uncommon and not always indicative of prior misstatements or omissions. In fact, the misstatements likely are indicative of legitimate change in accounting practices or a revision based on unforeseen circumstances and events.[17] Policy language is often the key in determining the scope of an insurer's rescission rights.[18] Where an insurer can rescind based solely on a knowing misrepresentation by one that signs the application for insurance, only the knowledge of those involved in signing the application is dispositive.[19] Where they provided information that they believed was accurate, or provided it only to the best of their knowledge and belief, the insurer may not be able to rescind.[20]

---

17. *See* Josephine H. Hicks, *D&O Coverage in the Post-Enron World*, COVERAGE (Dec. 2002).

18. *See, e.g.*, Federal Ins. Co. v. Homestore, Inc., 144 Fed. Appx. 641 (9th Cir. 2005) (holding policy envisioned rescission of coverage to all insurers on a material misrepresentation known to the insured that signed the application for the policy).

19. Executive Risk Indem., Inc. v. AFC Enterprises, Inc., 510 F. Supp. 2d 1308 (N.D. Ga. 2007).

20. *Id.* at 1324–28.

Some D&O policies specifically define the term application very broadly to include a company's prior financial filings, such as earnings statements, submitted with the application and/or filed with a regulatory agency, such as the SEC. Generally, the CEO or CFO will be required to represent on the application that the company's financial filings are accurate and are not likely to give rise to a claim. If the filings are ultimately found to be incomplete or inaccurate, the insurer may attempt to rescind the policy, claiming that it relied on material misrepresentations or omissions in issuing the policy. A subsequent earnings misstatement, therefore, could lead to an insurer's denial of coverage for claims arising from an ensuing suit.

C. Allocation

D&O policies contain allocation provisions, allowing an insurer to deny coverage for whatever part of the cost of defending or settling a lawsuit is attributable to uninsured persons or entities, or to uninsured claims. D&O policies contain provisions aimed at allocating between covered and uncovered matters, and/or covered and uncovered parties. These provisions vary. Some policies call for allocation of judgments and settlements, but not defense costs. Under those policies, the insurer advances all defense expenses, but reserves its right to recoup amounts that are ultimately not covered. Other policies call for the parties to the contract to use their best efforts to determine a fair and appropriate allocation as between covered and uncovered amounts. Where the policyholder and insurer cannot agree, the insurer need only advance those defense expenses that it believes are covered or believes to be fair until a different allocation is negotiated, arbitrated, or judicially determined. Under these latter allocation terms, insurers often agree to pay only those amounts that reflect the insured parties relative legal and financial exposures. TALA, Inc. will want to be mindful of the insurer's defense obligations as it hires counsel to defend the suits against it.

Chapter 14
Briefing the Board

By Lori A. Goldman

If your client is a company of any kind (including a nonprofit), the company's board is sure to be intensely interested in any allegation of a breach of fiduciary duty, and often it will be incumbent upon the board of directors or a committee of the board to make a determination themselves about a breach of fiduciary duty. As a result, at some point (or points) you may have to stand up in front of the board and give a briefing. How bad could this be, you say? After all, you stand up in front of judges all the time. But just as you would never dream of standing up in front of a judge without proper preparation, you should never stand up in front of a board without proper preparation. After all, a judge can only rule against you in one particular case. A board can rule against you, fire you, and make it very difficult for you to work for other companies in the area.[1]

Why do you brief the board? The board is the ultimate body responsible for the company, and needs to be briefed as part of their oversight function. Additionally, they may be the decision maker as to whether a breach has occurred. That said, by definition, board members have limited time, and they want to make the most of it. Additionally, the one thing board members hate more than having their time wasted is being blindsided, especially by someone outside the company. So the timing of your brief is important.

How do you prepare to brief the board? The same way you prepare to argue before a judge: know why you are conducting the briefing, submit the proper materials in advance of the applicable deadlines, prepare yourself for likely questions, and follow up on any orders that result.

1. Not only do the same people often serve on, or have connections to, multiple boards but board members talk to each other, and share recommendations—both good and bad.

I. Why You Brief the Board

The board is the ultimate body responsible for the company. They need to have an understanding of potential threats or inappropriate conduct, such as allegations of breach of fiduciary duty by an officer or director, so that they can properly carry out their oversight function and guide the company in an appropriate manner.

Additionally, from a corporate governance perspective, the board, or one of its committees, will likely be the governing body that ultimately decides (from the company's perspective) whether a breach occurred. So, depending on the stage that you, as counsel, are brought into the matter, your briefing may have different functions. It could be a briefing because:

1. An event has occurred (e.g., facts have come to light suggesting a fiduciary breach may have occurred, and follow-up/investigation is required);
2. An investigation has been completed and the matter needs to be decided upon (e.g., the board instructed that you, as outside counsel, conduct an investigation into the allegations and now you have to report to the board on any findings/lack of findings so that the board can rule on the matter); or
3. Litigation is ongoing (e.g., a suit has been filed and you've been brought in to litigate and you need to brief the board regarding the status of the litigation).

II. Laying Your Foundation to Brief the Board

Breach of fiduciary duty claims can come to you as outside counsel at a variety of different stages. You may be the company's trusted adviser who management reaches out to because a claim has just been alleged. Or the company might seek your advice after the company has already gone through the preliminary stages of assessment of the claim, or even after the company is in, or preparing for, litigation. Regardless of which stage the matter is at, you will need to review the relevant corporate formation documents (i.e., corporate bylaws, limited liability company operating agreement, etc.), Code of Ethics, board committee charters, and any other company policies and procedures that deal with governance surrounding assessment of the fiduciary breach claim ("governing documents"). If you have been brought in at the early stages of the claim, the governing documents will help guide the process that the company, and possibly you, will need to undertake to assess the matter and bring it to the board. If you have been brought in at a later stage, once the board or appropriate board committee has already made its determination about whether a fiduciary breach occurred, you will need to review those documents to ensure that the appropriate process was undertaken in connection with their determination.

If the matter came up due to a whistleblower or third-party allegation, you will also want to review all material that has been submitted from that person/party. Depending on the nature of the alleged breach, you may need to also review additional internal policies and other documents (e.g., contracts, communications, etc.) that could be relevant.

Once you have gotten a baseline understanding of the governing documents and other materials, you should be able to formulate a basic strategy and move forward to briefing the board.

A. Briefing the Board: Different Stages

1. Early Stage Briefing

If you have been brought in at the early stages of a fiduciary breach allegation, great! This means that you are a trusted adviser and the company is looking for your guidance in how to handle the fiduciary breach allegation right from the start. The company and the board will likely be looking to you to provide direction about what to do. The first step will be to assess the situation—you want to get a handle on the facts of the matter that are being alleged, and review the governing documents (more on that later) and other policies or documents that may be applicable to the allegation. The severity and nature of the breach and the status of the alleged breaching party will inform how quickly the board needs to be briefed, the nature of the briefing, and whether independent or forensic resources should be brought in to aid in the investigation of the breach.

If the alleged breaching party is a lower-level officer, chances are that executive management will direct the investigation. This doesn't mean that they won't need your advice as counsel, rather it means that management may get further down the road on the investigation before the board is fully briefed on the matter. On the other hand, if the alleged breaching party is a member of executive management or a director, the matter should be brought to the board's attention as soon as possible.

In all events, however, it is important to have enough of an understanding of what occurred before going in to brief the board that you will be able to answer basic questions about the allegations, and provide guidance as to recommended next steps.

2. Mid-Stage Briefing

Mid-stage briefings are often the meatiest of board briefings in fiduciary breach situations. This is because an investigation has already been performed, or is at least underway, and you may be called upon to share the results and help the board/committee to work through the process toward a determination. If the results of the investigation are relatively straightforward, your preparation will likely be easier, as you'll be able to anticipate the questions and direction that the board/committee is likely to go in and tailor your presentation accordingly. On the other hand, if the results of the investigation are more subjective, part of your role will be to assist the board/committee in navigating their own duties in working toward a determination. When the board/committee is tasked with making a determination, it is important for you, as counsel, to remain neutral, guiding them through the process but allowing them the time and freedom to deliberate and come to their own conclusions.

3. Late Stage/Litigation Briefing

Late stage or litigation briefings can occur for a few reasons. These briefings can occur because litigation is threatened or has been filed—in which case the briefing may not only be to brief the board on the issues raised but also to outline and advise on legal strategy. For example, in a public company merger or acquisition, there is the possibility that a shareholder will allege breach of fiduciary duty of the entire board and possibly senior management in negotiating the deal terms. This is not an uncommon occurrence in the public company M&A space, and, regardless of the merits of what is being alleged, it is important for the allegations to be taken seriously and the board to be briefed both on the allegations, and on the legal strategy to move forward.

Late stage/litigation briefings can also occur because litigation is ongoing and time has passed—boards generally expect a regular briefing at board meetings regarding ongoing litigation matters. In these instances, the board will often rely on a written update brief from counsel that management presents, as opposed to an in-person briefing from counsel.

III. Materials

Once you have decided (or been invited) to brief the board or a board committee, what materials do you submit? Unlike a judge, who might read everything (and potentially be very annoyed if you go on too long), some board members will read almost nothing. Others will be both insulted and angry if they aren't given the "full picture." So how do you balance the two, especially when you aren't sure which board members fall into which camp? An effective strategy is to submit a short executive summary that is "keyed" (or footnoted) to the relevant source material. And, just as you would never think of missing a court deadline, or filing papers in an unapproved form or format, you never want to send materials to staff late, and you want to be sure to send them in the right format.

A. When to Submit the Materials

It is important for the board/committee to receive the materials with enough time to be able to digest the information and formulate appropriate questions. Often corporate secretaries will have deadlines for board material submissions a week or two prior to a scheduled meeting so that they have enough time to get the board book[2] out well in advance of the meeting. Timeframes may be condensed if a special meeting is called for a particular matter. Regardless, the important thing is to ensure that you confirm with the client when they want to receive the materials, and make sure you hit that deadline. Additionally, for materials that may need to be reviewed internally by management before submission to the board/committee, make sure you take into account at least a few days of cushion for internal review and potential comments. Clients hate getting material at the last minute and having no time to review, ask questions, or provide comments. Having open communication with your client about what their expectations are regarding timing and any internal review prior to board/committee submission will go a long way to building a trusted relationship.

B. How to Submit the Materials

How you submit materials to the board or committee will depend on the circumstances. Companies will have a system for board distribution. Many companies have board portals that provide the directors with the board materials electronically. Sometimes these require the materials to be in a specific format, for example, PDF. Smaller companies may not

---

2. A board book is an informational and governance tool used in connection with board and committee meetings. The board book generally consists of the meeting agenda; any formal resolutions being submitted for board approval; and a set of documents to brief the board on financial results, operations, risks, and important strategies of the company.

have adopted the technology for a board portal, so may use e-mail (hopefully secured/encrypted), or hard copy board books. Generally, the materials will be submitted to the corporate secretary (or their office) and distributed from there. However, in highly sensitive matters, management or the board may request that your briefing be handled separately. Here again, you will want to have open communication with the client about their preferred method of board material submission.

C. How Deep to Go versus How Much to Summarize

The depth of the materials that you submit in connection with your board briefing will largely depend on the stage of the matter.

1. Early Stage Briefing

If you are conducting an early stage briefing, you will likely submit a variety of materials, including a summary of the allegations, potentially a memo outlining the steps required by the governing documents, copies of the governing documents themselves, and any other policies or relevant material to give the board or committee a full picture of the alleged breach. All of these materials will give the board/committee the opportunity for an in-depth understanding of the matter, and will inform the decisions they may need to make regarding next steps (e.g., the type of investigation that should be undertaken and by whom). At the same time, you'll want to supplement these materials with an executive summary to help the board members synthesize and focus in on the material issues. You may also want to summarize the various potential options the board/committee will have in determining the course of investigation. Be cognizant of the dividing line, however, between advising and decision making. It is often best in the written brief to stick to facts—point out pros and cons of each of the options, and recite standard or industry practices. Be careful not to overlay your own preferences in a manner that unduly influences the board/committee. Remember, you are there to advise. They are there to make decisions on behalf of the company.

2. Mid-Stage Briefing

For a mid-stage briefing, an investigation regarding the alleged fiduciary breach has already been performed, or is at least underway, and you may be called upon to share the factual results of the investigation and/or help the board/committee to work through the process toward a determination. The materials should facilitate that process. However, the depth that you go into will depend on a number of factors, including whether the board will be interviewing individuals themselves regarding the matter (and therefore will ascertain the facts directly as opposed to through a report), and how much you want in the official record/board materials versus just providing a high level agenda and then verbally briefing the board or committee (with the minutes recording the nonprivileged[3] portion of the briefing). Bear in mind that board materials can be a powerful evidentiary tool in the event of litigation or regulatory investigation. Materials submitted to the board and minutes from the meeting can help to build a record that the board took the right steps, reviewed and considered all of the material facts, and exercised their duties appropriately.

If the investigation has been completed, and you are briefing the board/committee regarding the results, you will want to provide an overview of the process that was undertaken, the people who were interviewed, a brief description of the materials reviewed, and any factual information or documentation that would be important for the board or committee to know when deliberating on the matter. If the investigation is ongoing and the board/committee will be participating in the process (e.g., the board or a special committee are interviewing key players themselves), you will want to provide an overview of the process that the board/committee is undertaking, a description of any required governing procedures and documents, and key information and questions that should be pursued in the course of the investigation.

3. Late Stage/Litigation Briefing

When providing a late stage or litigation briefing, you may be requested to provide a written briefing/update memo, but not actually attend the board or committee meeting. This is typically because the board/committee has already been briefed on the matter, internal determinations have been made, and the matter is at a point where the board members are aware of the basics of the case and simply need to be kept abreast of developments and case status. If the matter did not go through an internal investigatory process, and instead came to the company's attention through threatened or filed litigation (such as in a mergers and acquisitions context), you as counsel should decide, based on the nature and context of the matter, whether to brief the board or committee in

3. *See* Section VI, "A Note Regarding Privilege," later in this chapter for additional discussion on privilege.

the manner of a typical litigation briefing (described later), or to go into more depth, taking on the characteristics of an early stage brief (with a memo outlining any steps required by the governing documents, copies of the governing documents themselves, and any other policies or relevant material to give the board a full picture of the alleged breach). Whichever route you choose, you will want to include an overlay of your recommended legal strategy.

With respect to fiduciary duty litigation briefings, these briefs will likely take the form of a standard litigation brief. Litigation briefs are generally provided at each board meeting, and can come in a variety of forms and sizes. Some attorneys like to provide a full overview of the case in each brief, and then include a section for recent developments or updates either at the front or back end of the brief. Other attorneys will choose to give a very short summary of the nature of the matter, and then an update as to recent developments. Additionally, some attorneys will include a high-level overview of case strategy within the briefing, while others will hold back and report solely on case history, developments and upcoming events that are scheduled. While any of these are fine, and largely dependent on the preference of the client, the brief that includes a more fulsome overview of the case on whole can be helpful to ensure that new directors coming onto the board, and likewise any new management, can quickly get up to speed on the matter.

IV. What Questions Are the Board Likely to Ask?

Although the questions board members ask are limited only by the board members' imaginations, as with judges, one can often predict likely areas of questioning. From a board's perspective, most questions center around risk: financial risk, operational risk, reputational risk, and personal risk.

A. Questions about Financial Risk

- What is the level of financial harm that could/did arise from this matter?
- Will the company be required to restate its financial statements?

- Does the company have a material weakness in its internal controls over financial reporting?
- Will the company need to make changes to its disclosure controls and procedures?
- What are the legal/audit/investigatory/etc. fees expected to be generated in connection with this matter?
- Do we have D&O or other insurance coverage for these claims?
- Will the company's stock value decrease?

B. Questions about Operational Risk

- Does the company have a material weakness in its internal controls over operations?
- What area was responsible for detecting the breach, and was it detected timely? If not, what is being done about it?
- Have we identified the scope of the breach and the individuals involved?
- How do we deal with the plaintiff (if internal) and/or the persons alleged to be involved in the wrongdoing in the meantime?

C. Questions about Reputational Risk

- What risk does this matter pose to the reputation of the company?
- Is there anything that can be done to mitigate the risk?
- How do we, as an organization, maintain appropriate confidentiality over the matter to mitigate reputational harm to the company?
- Should the company engage a public relations firm?

D. Questions about Personal Risk

- What are my duties and responsibilities for this matter?
- What is my personal liability if a suit is brought?
- Will the company provide a lawyer for me?
- Am I entitled to be indemnified for any personal liability?
- Am I covered by the company's D&O policy?
- Will I be named personally?

V. How Do You Follow the Board's Orders?

On the one hand, following the board's/committee's orders is easy. As Nike says, just do it. But there is the minor matter (well, maybe not so minor from the board's perspective) of documenting the orders, and then letting the board or committee know that its orders have been carried out.

When you are in front of the board/committee briefing them, you have an ideal opportunity to discuss with them how their orders should be documented, and how it should be reported back to them that their orders have been carried out. Documentation of the board's orders can take a few different forms, and while you may have an opinion as to what form it should take, discussing your anticipated documentation with the board members will accomplish a few things. It will help to manage their expectations, and give you the opportunity to remind them of the importance of maintaining confidentiality (and potentially privilege) over any documentation you provide. It will also provide the board members with an opportunity to voice any feedback or input about what they would like to see, both in documentation of their orders, and also in receiving back word that their orders have been carried out. Remember, board members like things succinct and to the point, and they are looking to you as counsel to advise how best to achieve the desired results. That being the case, the "discussion" regarding these materials should likely consist of you indicating the method that you feel is appropriate for both documentation and reporting back, and entertaining their reaction to your proposed methods.

Often, however, you will not have the opportunity to discuss your proposed method of documentation and reporting with the board or committee (either because you are providing only a written briefing or because there is not the time or opportunity to discuss it in the meeting). If that is the case, you should discuss it with your main point of contact at the company and they can act as a gauge.

A. Documenting the Board's Orders

If the briefing took place during the minuted portion of a board/committee meeting, the board's orders may be included in the minutes. If this is the case, you should request that the corporate secretary send you a draft copy of the minutes before they have been finalized and ratified by the board/committee to ensure that they appropriately reflect the orders that have been given. Note, however, that at times the briefing may take place in executive session with the board/committee, or the minutes may be high level and not reflect the full discussion and orders. That's okay since you will likely not rely on the minutes as the sole record of the board's orders.

In addition to any minuted record, you as counsel will likely also want to follow up with a written record documenting the board's orders. This may take the form of a memo, letter, or even e-mail, and could be addressed to the full board or committee, a representative of the board (e.g., chairperson), or the member(s) of management that have been your key point(s) of contact at the company. This record should document not only the board's orders as to how the matter should be handled, but also the next steps that are planned in order to carry out those orders.

As a reminder, it is important to be mindful of the attorney-client privilege and any concerns that could result in the privilege being lost. If your briefing is early or mid-stage (prelitigation), bear in mind that the matter may still be subject to litigation and all that discovery might entail. You want to be sure to preserve privilege where appropriate, and consider how materials may look when put up in front of a jury.

B. Letting the Board Know That Its Orders Have Been Carried Out

Once the board's orders have been carried out, you will want to let the board members know. Ultimately, having documentation evidencing that the board's orders were carried out is important. It is important not only so that the board or committee knows their orders were complied with, but also as potential evidence in litigation that the board carried out their duty of care in managing and/or overseeing the matter. This may be done in a few different ways. One way would be via letter to the board that can be included in the board materials in the next meeting, or can be sent to the board (likely through the corporate secretary) between meetings. Another way to report back would be if you are called back for another briefing at a board meeting to report on the results of carrying out the board's orders. In that instance, you may want to include written work product regarding the results that can be distributed to the board in advance of the meeting and will complement your verbal briefing with the board. Here too, if your briefing occurs during the minuted portion of a meeting, you should be sure to review a copy of the minutes before they are finalized to ensure they accurately reflect your briefing.

VI. A Note Regarding Privilege

It goes without saying that maintaining attorney-client and/or work-product privilege is critical in such highly sensitive matters as those discussed in this chapter. Many clients do not understand the guiderails of privilege, so it is important that you communicate what they are, and give clear instruction about staying within their bounds. The most common pitfalls relate to internal communications without lawyers involved for the purpose of providing legal advice, and communications with third parties.

With respect to internal communications, an important foundational element for the client to understand is that anything and everything that is "said" without a lawyer "present" is not privileged. This means that internal e-mails, texts, voicemails, notes, and so on, as well as conversations that do not include a lawyer will all be discoverable and required to be handed over in the event of litigation. That said, it's not enough to simply include an attorney on a communication. There is a common misconception, particularly where in-house counsel is involved, that including a lawyer on an e-mail automatically makes it privileged. A communication is not privileged simply because the lawyer is present, but instead because the lawyer is present in order to provide legal advice. For example, an e-mail exchange between two officers of a company where one officer is reporting to the other officer about a meeting that occurred is not privileged simply because a lawyer is cc'd. However, an e-mail exchange including the same two officers and lawyer, discussing the same meeting, but seeking legal advice as to the potential legal consequences of what is discussed, is privileged. You should make sure that the client is aware of this distinction and appropriately communicates it to all internal parties involved in or aware of the matter.

With respect to third parties, it is important to help the client navigate engagements and communications in a manner that maintains privilege. To the extent that third parties will be involved in an investigation, you will want to give thought to how best to engage those third parties. If you want the results of any investigation to remain under the cloak of privilege, you will need to facilitate engagement either by internal counsel (if applicable) or external counsel. It is important that the engagement letter/agreement expressly states that the services are being provided at the direction of, and in support of, counsel for the client in anticipation of litigation, and that the party will take all necessary steps to maintain confidentiality and applicable privilege.

Additionally, when you are meeting with the board or management, it is important that only those individuals who are employees or directors of the client, or third parties engaged by counsel under the cloak of privilege, be present. To the extent others are present, you should ask that they exit the meeting while privileged matters are discussed. Further note that, while meeting minutes can be very helpful in building a record for potential litigation, it is best to refrain from recording any privileged information or communications in the minutes. This is because it is not uncommon to share the minute books, or minutes of certain meetings, with third parties for other reasons (e.g., auditors), and the privilege over those communications can easily be blown.

VII. Conclusion

In conclusion, briefing the board is an important part of any fiduciary breach matter. You, as counsel, are in the unique position of being able to advise the company/board on how to navigate the matter and, in many ways, drive the discussions that are central to the case. Having a strong handle on the company's policies and procedures, as well as the rules and regulations surrounding fiduciary duty is a must. Additionally, having good lines of communication with the client, being cognizant of the company's process for board communications, and having open and candid conversations with your client are keys to success.

TABLE OF CASES

A

B

C

D

E

F

G

I

J

K

N

O

P

Q

R

S

T

U

V

W

Y

Z

INDEX

R

S

T

U